Alaska's Wolf Man

FRANK GLASER'S ALASKA

Alaska's Wolf Man

*The 1915–55 Wilderness Adventures
of Frank Glaser*

by JIM REARDEN

PICTORIAL HISTORIES PUBLISHING COMPANY, INC.
Missoula, Montana

Library of Congress
Catalog Card Number 98-66445

ISBN 1-57510-047-9

First Printing: April 1998
Second Printing: March 1999
Third Printing: September 1999
Fourth Printing: April 2000
Fifth Printing: August 2001
Sixth Printing: September 2002
Seventh Printing: November 2003
Eighth Printing: February 2005
Ninth Printing: December 2005
Tenth Printing: July 2006
Eleventh Printing: March 2007
Twelfth Printing: November 2007
Thirteenth Printing: March 2008

COVER GRAPHICS Mike Egeler
TYPOGRAPHY & BOOK DESIGN Arrow Graphics

Pictorial Histories Publishing Company, Inc.
713 South Third Street West, Missoula, MT 59801
PHONE (406) 549-8488, FAX (406) 728-9280
EMAIL phpc@montana.com
WEBSITE pictorialhistoriespublishing.com

Contents

BOOK THREE: GOVERNMENT WOLF HUNTER, 1937-55

Foreword

IN 1940, WHEN A LETTER ARRIVED at Fairbanks, Alaska, addressed to "The Wolf Man," it was promptly delivered to Frank Glaser, a wolf hunter (officially, Predator Control Agent) for the federal government.

Frank Glaser possessed encyclopedic knowledge of Alaska's wolves and other wildlife; he was also an expert at living in Alaska's wilderness. From 1915 to 1955 he led an adventurous life in Alaska as a market hunter, roadhouse operator, dog team freighter, big game guide, collector of wildlife specimens for the federal government, trapper, explorer, breeder of wolf-dogs, and federal wolf hunter.

Glaser's views on wildlife were those of the late 19th and early 20th centuries when hunting and hunters were respected as an important segment of society. During his time a primary goal of wildlife conservation was to eliminate predators, and the Territory of Alaska as well as most states paid bounties for the killing of "bad" wild animals in the belief that this would benefit "good" wildlife.

Glaser was fascinated by all wild animals, but he was especially drawn to the wolf. When wolves became abundant near his Savage River trapping cabin in the Alaska Range after the mid-1920s he had an opportunity afforded a privileged few—that of daily observing good numbers of wild wolves. For more than a decade as wolf howls resounded among the mountains and tundra flats around his lonely cabin, he watched the big predators hunt and kill, mate and raise young, fight, and kill and eat one another. Several captive wolves he kept also contributed to his knowledge, as did the wolf-dogs he bred. He admired wolves for their intelligence and skill as hunters. At the same time he was determined to kill as many of them as he could to protect caribou, moose, and wild sheep.

Comments of his associates give some insight into Frank Glaser, the man, the woodsman, the companion, the hunter, the trapper:

Sam O. White, himself a top woodsman, once told me, "Frank Glaser was a loner. He much preferred to be in the woods and out on his own. He was one of the most skilled and toughest woodsmen in Alaska. He was tireless on the trail."

For many years White was a wildlife agent for the Bureau of Biological Survey in Alaska. For several years he and Glaser worked together for the Survey and its successive agency, the U.S. Fish and Wildlife Service (FWS).

"Glaser was an expert on extended trips through the wilderness, and always knew where he was. He knew how to use every little advantage the terrain or foliage offered. Frank was never at a loss in the woods; he was as much at home there as a wild animal. He was an expert at finding edible roots and bulbs and other plants to supplement his diet. He was also good with a soup bone," said White.

White added, "I searched for one of his camps once in a clump of spruce timber, and although I knew pretty well where it was I was hard put to find it. Another of his skills was being able to call just about any animal in the woods.

"He could gain the confidence of captured animals very quickly. He trapped a huge black wolf on Goldstream [near Fairbanks] one winter. That wolf had a head as big as a bear's—one of the biggest wolves I've ever seen. Frank kept him in an old cabin on a chain and he would walk nonchalantly into the cabin with water and food for the animal. While the wolf was mostly sullen, he never offered to attack. I wouldn't have ventured into that cabin unless that wolf had been trussed in chains," claimed Sam.

"Frank killed a lot of wildlife, but he used it all. He was a natural conservationist. He did not ordinarily kill for sport— only for food and clothing. Even when it made no difference legally he always killed bulls rather than cow moose or caribou; the same with sheep—he shot rams, not ewes," said White.

Dr. Wilson L. Du Comb of Carlyle, Illinois, engaged Glaser as a hunting guide in September, 1935. In 1978, Du Comb wrote me, "We were both young men then, I was 34 and Frank was in his early forties. I slept in the cabin on Savage River that Frank built alone in ten days. Sod roof and dirt floor, but with a good stove and plenty of firewood it was very comfortable. It was with Frank that I killed my first grizzly, in fact my first bear of any kind. I cannot praise him too highly. Frank Glaser was a gentleman, an excellent guide and a fine companion."

Oscar H. Vogel, trapper, guide, premier outdoorsman and long-time Alaskan, met Glaser in 1934. He told me, "During the years from about 1930 to 1940 when wolves were ravishing Alaska, Frank was wolfing the whole northern part of the Alaska Range east of McKinley Park. He worked the year around getting rid of wolves, digging dens in the spring, trapping and snaring in winter. At the same time I was trapping, shooting, and snaring wolves in the Talkeetnas.

"Frank knew wolves just about from A to Zed, living with them year in and out. He was well established when I was only beginning and he gave me many valuable tips on trapping, every one of which proved effective," said Vogel.

Dr. Neil W. Hosley, a FWS employee and one-time Leader of the Alaska Cooperative Wildlife Research Unit at the University of Alaska, Fairbanks, and later the Dean of that university, made field trips with Glaser in the late 1940s and early 1950s. He told me, "Frank Glaser was a careful observer and his stock of information, particularly on wolves, led to his employment as a Predator Control Agent of the FWS. He worked with Adolph Murie during the studies which led to Murie's classic book *The Wolves of Mount McKinley*, and Murie included Glaser's observations in the volume."

Hosley, referring to Glaser's years as a government wolf hunter, said, "Frank's first three days in the office after a field trip were at least tolerable to him since reports had to be written. But then he got itchy to get out in the boondocks again. In midwinter with deep snow and temperatures well below zero, he would decide that the wolves somewhere, perhaps in the Alaska Range, needed control. A pilot with a ski-equipped plane would set him down at the selected place with his pack, rifle and snowshoes. Then for a week or so, he was alone in his element and happy."

Tireless on the trail, Frank had an energetic rolling gait that came from years of following dog teams, snowshoeing, and traveling over the rugged outback of Alaska. He drifted along seemingly with little effort. When afield his rifle was a part of him, and his shooting was that of an expert. A good rifleman needs superb eyesight, which Glaser had; even in his 60s he did not wear glasses.

In the early 1950s, drawings were held for permits to shoot bison bulls in the herd that roams near Delta Junction. Frank, in his 60s, was one of the FWS officials who accompanied lucky permit holders. A university professor drew a permit and was accompanied by Frank. Dr. Hosley went along as an observer. "I've never shot a big game animal," the professor admitted.

"That's all right. I'll help if necessary," Frank smiled.

Frank found a suitable bull for the professor and told him to shoot it. Two shots rang out at almost the same instant; the professor's bullet went into the bull's chest, and Frank's hit at the base of the ear.

Jim King, now of Juneau, recalled for me some of his memories of Glaser. "I went to work in Fairbanks for the FWS as an Enforcement Agent trainee in the fall of 1951 at the age of 23 (King retired as a biologist from the FWS in Alaska after many years of mostly waterfowl studies; for years he was a Flyway Biologist stationed in Alaska). Frank was 62 then and had been working as a Predator Control Agent for 14 years. That fall Ray Woolford, Agent-in-Charge, was assigned to a three months detail in Louisiana, leaving Frank and me and a secretary as the only staff at Fairbanks.

"During November and December Frank and I patrolled together, making wolf sets, and talking to people everywhere. Frank, like many old timers who have spent months alone in the wilderness over a period of many years, took advantage of any audience for exercise of the language, which he used with great color.

"He would arise in the morning and immediately check the weather through window, door or tent flap. This routine would call to mind an event and he would begin to talk. His stories would string together naturally through breakfast and into the car or plane and on through the course of the day.

"In the evening he would usually retire with a magazine but I never saw him get past the first paragraph without making a comment which would flow into a monologue that continued until cut off by sleep. Such a habit in most people would become exceedingly tedious, but not with Frank. Unlike most monologuists, Frank wasn't boring. He had a marvelous memory for names, dates and places. He had a great sense of the ridiculous. Humor punctuated his yarns. He was an audible text on the history, geography, climate, personalities, and wildlife of Alaska. He was a natural story teller. His yarns had a beginning, a middle, and an end. No professional writer could have produced better plots.

"Frank Glaser was universally respected by oldtimers who knew him for his ability as a woodsman. Wherever we stopped, everyone within earshot, oldtimer and newcomer alike, gathered to listen.

"When he trapped at Savage River some fox skins brought up to $700 each and he was able to produce a large income for the time in two or three months of early winter. He rented a room year-round at the Nordale Hotel in Fairbanks and boarded his big wolf-dog team nearby. Often, he had more money than he could spend. He bought every new rifle that came on the market, and provided liberal handouts to temporarily indigent acquaintances. He was free during summer and fall to join scientific or hunting expeditions of all kinds.

"After a few years of work in the Arctic controlling wolves around reindeer herds, he was well known to many Eskimos who respected his remarkable ability to catch wolves. In 1948 he spent much of the year on Nunivak Island, protecting and investigating the embryo muskox herd there. He traveled mostly by dog team, and spent weeks camping out each winter. Before he arrived on Nunivak, reports had drifted in that some of the resident Eskimos were killing the introduced muskox; Glaser talked kindly with them about it and there has never been a problem of that kind since.

"Wolf control has a bad name now with many, but it was absolutely necessary in the days when large numbers of Alaskans supported themselves by trapping and raising reindeer. Wolves, singly or in packs, are attracted to such enterprises and can be very destructive. It takes a real expert to consistently trap or shoot wolves. By those who needed his services, Frank was accorded all the respect of a doctor or any other essential highly trained specialist.

"In spite of his lifetime contest with wolves, he had the sort of love and respect for the creatures that develop between strong antagonists. He controlled wolves where they were out of hand but the idea of an Alaska without wolves was as abhorrent to Frank Glaser as to anyone in the land today," said King.

Another former FWS associate of Glaser's was Fairbanks-raised Charles "Chuck" Gray. In later years Gray became a respected executive with the *Fairbanks Daily News Miner* and a successful part-time big game guide. In the early 1950s Chuck, then in the army, was assigned to the military game warden detail and he often worked out of the Fairbanks office of the FWS. He was (and is) a pilot, and Frank frequently flew with him. "Frank was full of nervous energy, and was always restless. He loved to be on the go. He was also insecure about his federal job, always afraid of being fired. But Clarence Rhode, Regional Director of the FWS, once told Frank, 'As long as I'm director, you'll have a job,'" Gray told me

"It seemed to me that Frank knew everything about all the game in the interior of Alaska. College-trained biologists often asked him about the habits of animals, for they learned he knew the answers. He was a walking wildlife encyclopedia," said Gray.

"Frank was like an Indian at picking up wolf sign that was all but invisible to me. He knew which clump of grass they urinated on and which little ridge they preferred to travel on. I was always in awe of his knowledge of wolves, for he was almost always right.

"By the time Frank had the use of coyote getters [a lethal cartridge-loaded cyanide gun] along with strychnine baits and aerial hunting, he knew he was out of the dark ages and in an era where he could become effective; he knew he could never have really controlled a significant number of wolves with traps, snares, and rifle.

"Frank accomplished what the residents of the Fortymile country considered a miracle. As the 175-mile road was pushed through from the Alaska Highway to Eagle, wolves made use of it. Wolf tracks were everywhere each morning in the smooth fill following the grader. Frank had a heyday for a couple of years, killing wolves with getters along the new road.

Within five years there was an abundance of moose in the Fortymile country. Old-timers said there had never been so many. Game check stations revealed large takes and a high hunter success, which was surprising, for much of the Fortymile is covered by scrub spruce.

"The moose didn't last though. When predator control work ended in 1957 the wolves returned and today there are few moose left. Old-timers in the Forty-Mile long for another Frank Glaser," said Gray.

Frank was an inveterate "snoose" (snuff) chewer. He was usually healthy, but occasionally he had a debilitating gastric upset and had to go to a hospital. Usually after a hospital visit he would heatedly denounce snuff. "It ain't fit to put in a man's mouth," he would say with some vigor.

He always went back to it, however, usually within a few weeks.

When Frank went to work for the government in 1937 he had never driven a car. Sam White spent a week teaching him how. "He had quite a time keeping between the ditches on both sides of the narrow roads of the time, but eventually he became an adequate driver," Sam remembered.

On July 25, 1938 while looking for wolves along the Steese Highway north of Fairbanks, Glaser drove off the road and the car rolled. His diary entry for this event reads: "We [he was alone] drove around a bend and the sun was shining on the windshield. Before we could stop the car we went over the grade. Rolled over three times. I received a cut on the head and rib injuries. Sam White came out and brought me to the hospital at headquarters."

The broken rib healed but it was some time before his supervisors were willing to again release one of their precious autos to Frank.

When living at Savage River, and later as a government agent, Glaser hunted wolves with considerable success (in contrast to trapping them)—a feat that few other Alaskans have accomplished. He gained the admiration and respect of Eskimos who herded reindeer in northwestern Alaska when he repeatedly caught wolves preying on their herds. The many years he spent pursuing reindeer-killing wolves in arctic and sub-arctic Alaska were strenuous, but the wiry Glaser, then in his late 40s and early 50s, was up to it; he often out-Eskimoed the Eskimos, who are masters at surviving this unforgiving land.

In a 1934 letter to Alaska Game Commission Executive Officer Frank Dufresne, he wrote, "I don't mind shooting wolves but every time I find one in my traps I feel ashamed and can hardly get up nerve to shoot them. They are the real gentlemen of the predatory animal family."

That view didn't stop him as a federal employee from using every means possible to kill wolves. Federal policy was to reduce wolf numbers in Alaska, and he supported that policy.

Glaser's happiest years were from 1924 to 1937 when he lived alone in his log cabin at Savage River in a wild and beautiful setting near Mount McKinley National Park (recently renamed Denali National Park). More than half a century afterward it is difficult to fully describe the free and easy life he led there—a life that would be impossible today. Often, months passed without Glaser seeing another person. In the shadow of the towering Alaska Range, he lived alone with his beloved wolf-dogs among caribou, moose, grizzly bears, mountain sheep, and wolves, his little cabin a tiny island in the vast wilderness. Wild game and fish provided a limitless supply of food. He chose to live in this paradise because he loved the wilderness, he loved hunting and trapping, and he was, by preference, a loner.

—JIM REARDEN

Preface

I FIRST ENCOUNTERED FRANK GLASER (1889–1974), a slim, rather small, weathered man in his early sixties in 1952 when I was shopping at Frontier Sporting Goods, a small shop in downtown Fairbanks. He started talking as he entered the store, addressing remarks to me and five or six other shoppers; none of us knew him. He spoke of moose hunts, charging grizzly bears, driving a team of wolf-dogs, market hunting in the "old days," and other intriguing Alaska wilderness experiences.

After talking nonstop for 10 or 15 minutes he bought something and left.

"Who was that?" I asked Dick McIntyre, the store owner.

"He's that federal wolf hunter," Dick told me. "A genuine sourdough. An oldtimer oldtimers respect."

In time I learned Frank Glaser was even more: he was a living Alaska legend.

A compulsive talker, Frank was probably making up for years of living alone in Alaska's wilderness; some called him "Silent Frank." We became acquainted and in 1953 I proposed that we collaborate in writing about his adventures; he would tell his yarns, and I would write them.

I used a tape recorder at our yarning sessions (they weren't interviews; Frank didn't interview well), a new technique then, transcribing 588 typewritten pages and selling eight of the stories I wrote with Glaser, mostly to *Outdoor Life* magazine. Decades later I reviewed the transcript and discovered many fascinating footnotes to Alaska's history; I was new to Alaska in 1953, and didn't understand the significance of many of Frank's observations.

Forty years after my interviews with Glaser I decided to write *Alaska's Wolf Man.*

As a government wolf hunter, Frank kept daily field diaries which he was supposed to turn in to his supervisors when they were completed. They were federal property. I needed them to write the book. But where were they? They weren't in federal archives I arranged to have searched, and Glaser's former associates had no idea where they were. Through coincidence, wildlife photographer/writer Tom Walker learned that Dr. Louis Mayer of Anchorage had a collection of Glaser's diaries. Walker was aware of my search.

When I called him, Mayer responded enthusiastically. "Sure, I have Glaser's diaries. I cared for him during his last months and he left them to me when he died." Dr. Mayer generously loaned me the diaries and they provide much of the texture of this book.

In Alaska, but before working as a góvernment wolf hunter Glaser sporadically kept a diary with entries for 77 months out of 259 (May 1915–April 1937). Most entries were weather observations, for to a lone man in the wilderness weather overshadows all else. Here and there, though, in the pre-government Glaser diaries I found pithy comments summarizing wildlife encounters, wilderness escapades, and the world of wolves. Entries were typically low-key. A harrowing near-drowning while crossing Savage River in below zero weather rated only, "*Had a hell of a time crossing river.*"

During his federal employment Glaser made diary entries in all but 38 months of 218. This should be qualified, for the Mayer collection may not represent all of Glaser's federal diaries. It is possible, even likely, he turned some in.

Alaska's Wolf Man, written in first person, is an amalgam of my tape-recorded interviews with Glaser, his diaries, historic facts, edited stories I wrote that were published, and information provided by his former co-workers. Using italics, I have quoted Glaser's diaries here and there, believing readers will enjoy seeing what Glaser wrote about a subject or event.

Every professional writer is aware of the gap between spoken and written English. Frank, a colorful speaker, often repeated himself, saying the same thing several ways. If *Alaska's Wolf Man* were written as Frank spoke, this book would be repetitious, unreadable, and at least four times its present length. Nevertheless, wherever possible, I have used Glaser's matchless expressions.

Otherwise, I have written *Alaska's Wolf Man* simply, in a way I believe Frank Glaser would have appreciated and approved.

—JIM REARDEN
Sprucewood
Homer, Alaska

Acknowledgments

THIS RECOUNTING of Frank Glaser's adventurous career in Alaska couldn't have been written without help. I am indebted especially to former U.S. Fish and Wildlife Service associates of Frank Glaser who shared their memories of him. These include Ray Tremblay, of Anchorage; Jim King of Juneau; Charles "Chuck" Gray of Fairbanks, who shared memories and photos; the late Sam O. White, of Fairbanks; and the late Dr. Neil W. Hosley, of Golden, Colorado.

M.W. "Slim" Moore, and Oscar Vogel, both of Anchorage, and both deceased, were helpful in remembering Glaser's early years.

Writer/photographer Tom Walker, of Denali Park, who told me where to find the Glaser diaries, also shared hard-earned research; he was especially helpful with background on market hunter Harry Lucke. Tom also spent many hours reviewing an early draft of the manuscript. His expert eye brought about many improvements.

Without the generosity of Dr. Louis Mayer, of Anchorage, heir to the Glaser diaries, much of this volume could not have been written, for Mayer allowed free access to these diaries, the basis for much of this book.

Bette Wright, of Oregon City, Oregon, provided background information on Nellie Glaser.

Governor Jay Hammond's memories of Glaser, written in the inimitable Hammond style, add a special dimension to the Glaser story.

Veteran editor Cliff Cernick, Anchorage, used his red pencil on the manuscript to immeasurably improve my syntax.

To all of these, my heartfelt thanks.

—JIM REARDEN

Introduction

By GOVERNOR JAY HAMMOND

LONGTIME PROFESSIONAL WOLFER Frank Glaser bore out poet John Donne's assertion, "Each man kills the things he loves." Though Glaser waged relentless war on wolves for almost half a century, his admiration, if not affection, for the beasts was clear. It came through when he spoke of wolves, as well as in his preference for wolf blood in his crossbred working dogs.

Some who knew Frank best proclaimed him to be at least quarter wolf himself. Lobo lean, his keen, brown, "gun bore" eyes missed nothing, whether on the trail or confined to town. When the latter, Frank's discomfiture with "civilization" was evident in the way he loped about like a caged animal. Though not given to howling at the moon nor trying to establish territory by creating scent posts, he was not averse to verbally lifting a leg and raining criticism on those bent on over-taming the Alaska wildlands that he loved. For like his feral fetishes, it was in the deep bush among their company where Frank felt most at home.

With the advent of statehood in 1959, which Frank like many other reclusive Alaskan bushrats ardently opposed, he wishfully predicted Alaska would soon go broke. Then the tide of cheechakos (newcomers) would abate, moose would be seen scraping antler velvet off on down town parking meters, while bears roamed deserted hotel lobbies.

Had it not been for the discovery of oil, Frank's prediction might have come to pass. During the first five years of statehood Alaska tottered on the brink of bankruptcy and more folk left Alaska than arrived via any means save the birth canal.

Of course by the time oil spewed upon the scene to sluice away his wistful thinking, Frank's day was done. Gone was the "wild" from much of the back country Frank had coveted...or cursed; rubbed off by sportsmen's boots, loggers' hobnails and tourist birkenstocks and sneakers. Journeys into remote locations which had taken Frank days to accomplish now took no more than an hour or so by the armada of small aircraft which invaded every creek and corner of Alaska.

Some might say Frank was born much too late; that he should have lived through the heyday of the western fur trade when loners such as he could attempt to loose the bands of civilization and move on to ever wilder country, unaware they'd not really slipped those bands at all. Instead, one foot yet entangled, they pulled into virgin country much of what they had deplored and hoped to leave behind. They too helped kill the thing they loved.

No, Frank was born precisely at the proper time. I suspect the old American West would have proved much too confining. His ventures and incredibly rigorous hundred mile treks rivaled those of old-time Mountain Men. Moreover, Frank precisely reflected the attitude of his day which was "kill off all the varmints." It was not until the 1950s the pendulum swung the other way and the fearsome wolf of Red Riding Hood metamorphosed into the benign creature found in latter day fables such as Farley Mowat's *Never Cry Wolf.*

I first met Frank in the late 1940s when as a fellow government hunter I was assigned to join him in assessing wolf predation in the Katmai National Monument of southcentral Alaska. It was subzero when I flew into his camp to find Frank had pitched his tent *inside* an old Bureau of Fisheries summer cabin. The tent's fly was positioned to catch reflected heat from the woefully inadequate fireplace.

During the next few days I learned almost more about wolves and wolf trapping than I cared to. Like many who spend weeks in the bush alone, Frank would uncork when a willing receptacle appeared on the scene. And while I found his font of wood's lore fascinating, at two in the morning I must admit it began to slosh over just a tad. Our boss, Maury Kelly, later told me my erstwhile tentmate was not known as "Silent Frank" for no reason.

Most biologists spend at least a hitch or two patrolling ivory towers. Some, of course, fail to descend at all and may go into teaching. Those who take to the field and root about almost always reach the same conclusion when it comes to predators: wolf fact belies wolf fiction, though each is begrimed by politics. Ironically those who most decry political manipulation of fish and game management are the first to apply such pressure when it comes to wolves.

Today wolves in Alaska are far from endangered. There are more wolves here now than in the 1940s when I first arrived. Back then they were subjected to intense trapping pressure, poison, and uninhibited aerial hunting. A bounty system was in place, and prey populations much less abundant over most of Alaska. Now, not only has trapping markedly abated, poison has been outlawed, along with aerial hunting. Moreover, even the most constrained proposals for limited predator control are met with violent opposition by those who would elevate the wolf to noble status far beyond any creature's due. Harm to habitat, not hunting, poses by far the greatest threat to Alaska's wolves.

Most ironic is the fact that many biologists who ardently condemned the practice while under federal management back in territorial days, subsequently were the very ones to propose some state predator control when they were forced to conclude such could indeed have great influence on prey populations.

These days few professional biologists deny that under some circumstance a limited control program may be warranted. The dispute comes in determining precisely what those circumstances be. To compound the problem, the least expensive and most surgical procedures to remove wolves are deemed "unsportsmanlike", requiring bizarre alternatives, such as sterilization, to appease the "politically correct."

That many find admirable the wolf's extraordinary strength,

endurance, cunning and ability to survive despite onslaught by those bent on their destruction is not surprising. The surprise is that they should find the same traits in men like Glaser despicable. Of course, it's how those traits are applied which earns credit or condemnation.

To those who have seen wolves bring down a caribou calf to feed on while it is still kicking, the claims of apologists that wolves are "simply doing their own thing" will no more obliterate the horror of that calf's cruel demise than would apologies for those who hunt or trap change the attitude of those despising such activities.

Too often the degree of expertise exhibited by each faction seems inversely proportional to the amount of time spent afield with either wolves or wolfers. Truth, as usual, is lodged between the two extremes. Too bad so few of us are privileged to visit its encampment. Like or not the man's conclusions, almost none have pitched their tents so often and so close to that encampment as did Glaser. That upon occasion smoke may have gotten in his eyes does nothing whatsoever to obscure that fact nor diminish the man's remarkable accomplishments.

—JAY HAMMOND

Jay Hammond was Alaska's governor from 1974 to 1982. He holds a degree in Biological Science, and during the 1940s and 1950s worked for the U.S. Fish and Wildlife Service in Alaska.

Book One

MARKET HUNTER, 1915–1924

Frank Glaser, market hunter, at Black Rapids Roadhouse in 1921. That's a Dall ram on his packboard. Between 1915 and 1924, Glaser hunted the Alaska Range near the Valdez Trail and sold the game he killed for twenty-five cents a pound. Game was plentiful, and there were virtually no sport or trophy hunters. FRANK GLASER

To Alaska

As a young man I worked mostly at farming and logging. In 1908, when I was 19, I owned a team of horses and had a contract to haul cordwood for Washington Brick and Lime, an eastern Washington firm for which my father was plant superintendent. Briefly, before dams were built on the Columbia River, I used horses to drag in a huge seine to harvest salmon there.

My father, an architect and an engineer, moved about to find work as I was growing up. From Boston, where I was born in 1889, we moved to Colorado, to Oregon, and finally to eastern Washington, where I spent most of my teens and early twenties. I was delighted with the wild western states where there was room to hunt, fish and trap.

Tales of Alaska always fascinated me. I was gripped by stories about Alaska's fabulous big game, its great caribou herds, its giant bears, huge moose, and the white sheep that roamed skyscraping mountains. Besides dreaming of hunting in Alaska, I yearned to trap the Territory for northern fox, mink, lynx and marten. Alaska's furs had to be finer than those I collected in eastern Washington.

Bill Larson, our neighbor for a short time when I was a teenager, had prospected for gold in Alaska. I pored over an Alaska map he showed me, and was caught up by the sheer size of the place, the great rivers, the mountain ranges, the strange-sounding villages: Unalakleet, Nome, Gulkana, Tanana, Tolavana. Many areas on the map were labeled "unsurveyed." What was there?

Mountains? Unknown rivers? Great valleys full of game? For years Alaska's unsurveyed areas challenged and haunted me.

In May, 1915 I was 26, single and footloose and decided to move to Alaska. This was by far the most important decision of my life. I traveled by train to Seattle where for $24.50 I bought a new box magazine .30-06 Winchester rifle. I already owned a pair of fine binoculars. With my new rifle and binoculars, two duffel bags containing everything I owned, plus a packsack, I embarked on the Alaska Steamship Company's *S.S. Mariposa*.

At Southeastern Alaska stops—Ketchikan, Sitka, Juneau, Petersburg, Wrangell—I went ashore and wandered about. The towns bustled with friendly fishermen preparing boats and nets for the upcoming salmon season. As the ship cruised through the narrow channels of the Inside Passage I could hardly leave the deck to eat or sleep. The steep, high, timber-clad mountains fascinated me. No one had to tell me that travel in those mountains was difficult, or more likely, impossible. The big game and fur I was after would be found I knew, in more open country, farther to the north.

I bought a ticket for Seward, but after the ship was under way I heard sourdoughs talking about gold mining at the interior town of Fairbanks. One told me the region around Fairbanks was fine big game and fur country. Most passengers bound for Seward were hoping to work on the 470-mile railroad to be built from that coastal port to Fairbanks. They expected the job to last five or six years (it lasted eight).

I wasn't interested in working on a railroad.

"How do I get to Fairbanks?" I asked one sourdough.

He smiled, "From Valdez. And at this time of year only 371 miles by shank's mare, young feller, by shanks mare. Just follow me." (Alaska's Valdez is pronounced Val-deeze).

Winter travel by the trail from Valdez to Fairbanks was by horse-drawn stage—sleds. At breakup in May the only way to get over the trail was on foot. Later, after the route dried, Model T Fords, Dodges, Jewetts, and other autos hauled a few passengers (mostly tourists) between Fairbanks and Valdez. Tourists arrived at Fairbanks by steamer that ascended the Yukon and Tanana Rivers.

Between Valdez and Fairbanks log roadhouses offered sleeping accommodations a day's travel apart—about 20 miles.

With about 25 others planning to walk to Fairbanks, I left the *Mariposa* at Valdez. I arranged to have my duffel bags hauled up the trail when horse-drawn stages started again in five or six months

A queer-looking duck, the old sourdough who said, "just follow me," was about 65. He walked around Valdez with his head to one side, nodding at this and that. We talked with the owner of one general store and learned that 2,777-foot-high Thompson Pass, 26 miles to the northeast, had more than 25 feet of snow.

As my sourdough friend and I sat on a couple of kegs contemplating food purchases, several others who had arrived with us on the *Mariposa* came into the store and questioned the owner.

"There is no place to buy food anywhere on the entire trail," the storekeeper cautioned. "Most of the roadhouses are closed. Glacial streams are too high to wade and most don't have bridges. There's too much snow in Thompson Pass to get through. And there aren't any horse or dog teams on the trail."

As he spoke he flashed a wink at my sourdough friend, who grinned at me. "They're cheechakos (greenhorns)," he said, quietly, "but they'll learn."

At another store the owner warned us, "Watch yourselves on the trail. Two men traveling the trail were murdered at Copper Center last fall."

My friend bought food for several days, and he asked a storekeeper for a gunny sack to carry it in. He cut a hole in the sack so he could hang it on one shoulder. I stuffed about the same amount of food into my packsack.

"We'll hike to Wortmann's Roadhouse," my sourdough companion said. "When it's cold tonight and the snow is crusted, we'll cross Thompson Pass."

I wore well-oiled shoepacks—boots with rubber bottoms and leather tops. My companion wore 10-inch well-greased leather boots. Many from the *Mariposa* wore leather shoes not suitable for the muddy road and wet snow.

At Wortmann's, a roadhouse 15 miles from Valdez, we learned there had been no travel over the trail for more than three weeks.

We left there at 9 p. m., hoping it would be cold enough to freeze a crust on the wet snow in the pass. In the subarctic twilight the steep, treeless, snowy pitch up to the pass was intimidating. Brush and scrub trees, where there were any, were burdened with deep snow.

Clouds covered the sky, and the temperature was just above freezing as we climbed single file, following switchbacks. In mid-trail was a narrow ridge of slippery crusted snow and ice. We frequently slid off waist-deep into soft wet snow, requiring a scramble to get back on the trail. The route was well staked, so there was no danger of getting lost.

Some men carried heavy loads. One had two rifles, neither equipped with a sling, in addition to a heavy pack. Those who believed the Valdez storekeepers were burdened with enough food for three weeks.

Everyone was thoroughly soaked before we were half way to the pass. Most suffered wet feet and the inevitable blisters. My sourdough companion and I stopped a couple of times to change our socks. I put strips of adhesive tape over the blisters my feet sprouted.

Ptarmigan Drop Roadhouse, the first habitation beyond the pass, was on an island jutting out of deep snow. It was a small place run by Charlie Norvilius, who was pleased to have 25 customers, most of whom ordered coffee.

"Snow is deeper six miles ahead," Charlie warned. "You'll never make it until it gets a crust."

Charlie tried to persuade everyone to lay over until the next night when it might freeze so we could walk on crust. There had been no business for weeks, and he wasn't going to miss a chance for income.

My sourdough friend and I continued on. Icy wind probed us, with no timber or brush to shelter us when we stopped to rest. We reached Beaver Dam Roadhouse, 42 miles from Valdez many hours later. It was there that about a dozen of the party from the *Mariposa* turned back. Among those who threw in the towel was "Knockout" Solomon, a professional boxer with a cauliflower ear, a bashed-in nose, and scars all over his face. Solomon was scheduled to fight in Fairbanks on July 4th. Before we left

Valdez I asked him if his new tightly-laced leather boots that reached almost to his knees didn't pinch his feet.

"No," he responded, "they're comfortable."

But now his feet were in terrible shape. Not having oiled or greased his boots, they soaked up water like sponges. Painful blisters forced him to lag behind. To add to his misery, nobody would wait for him, leaving him behind on the trail. Though I was more than a hundred yards ahead of him, I could clearly hear him cursing those who left him behind.

A sad-faced fellow who wore low oxford shoes and a rumpled business suit groaned, "If this is a sample of the 371 miles to Fairbanks, Fairbanks is gonna have to do without me. I'm going back to Valdez."

Nels Jepson, owner of the Beaver Dam Roadhouse, bustled about doctoring the cripples who had hobbled into his place with foot-torturing blisters. He warned, "There are no bridges or ferries at most of the rivers."

"How do we cross?" one anxious traveler asked.

"You wade, or you built a raft," Nels explained.

A few miles from Beaver Dam we descended from the mountains and ran out of snow, finding the trail to be a huge mud wallow. Two or three times my sourdough partner stopped at streams where water ran atop the ice. He removed his boots and socks and washed his feet in the icy water. Then he carefully dried himself and put on dry socks. I imitated him, and I believe the process toughened my feet.

My partner and I agreed it was best to rest days and travel the cool, perfectly light nights. We spent one day in bunks at Upper Tonsina Roadhouse, 52 miles from Valdez. The blankets on my bunk were dirty, but being tired and needing sleep I didn't think much about it.

After we left Upper Tonsina I began to itch. I thought it was from sweating. After watching me scratch for about ten miles, my partner grinned, "You're lousy, Glaser," he said. "You didn't pick the lice out of that bed before you slept in it."

I had never before had lice, and was horrified. I removed my shirt and wool undershirt and captured eight or ten big graybacks. After that I carefully inspected roadhouse bunks before climbing into them. If I was suspicious, I slept outside with my own blankets.

My partner stopped to visit friends at a mine, and I traveled alone for most of the rest of the way to Fairbanks, walking nights and sleeping days. Some roadhouses were open, some closed, for there was little travel at that time of year. I was surprised to find that the Army Signal Corps maintained good telephone communications between Road Commission camps, roadhouses, and Signal Corps stations all the way to Fairbanks. Telephone and telegraph wires dangled on poles and tripods beside the trail.

About 80 people lived at Copper Center, 66 miles from Valdez, where the trail followed the silty, roaring Copper River. Mosquitoes had become a terrible nuisance during days when I was trying to sleep, although in the cool of night they weren't bad. The mosquito bed net I bought at the trading post at Copper Center proved to be a lifesaver.

I spent a couple of days with the friendly McCrary family which operated a fox farm at Copper Center. Each spring they searched out fox dens, digging out the pups, keeping only the silvers and blacks. The animals were worth from $200 to $1,000 a pair (male and female) when sold as breeders.

I became acquainted with the oldest of their three sons, who was about my age. The family allowed me to look into the pens where they had 25 or 30 silver foxes, warning me to stand still and remain silent as we watched from a distance. Foxes are sensitive to strangers, and if a stranger got too close when they were having pups, the vixens would kill the pups. The same member of the family fed the animals each day, always wearing the same clothing.

The previous summer, one of the McCrary boys caught a Dall sheep lamb and brought it home to raise. I watched this tame white sheep climb steps into the hayloft of their large barn and leap onto the ground, which was about as near to life in its native mountains it could get.

At Copper Center a farmer, Mr. Bingham, told me about the murders that occurred in the late fall of 1914. His hired boy, after the cows for milking, found a man's pocket watch hanging on some bushes. Nearby he saw drag marks on the ground and following them, he came upon a man's body.

Bingham notified the U.S. Commissioner at Copper Center, who investigated and found a .22 rifle near the body. Seven or eight .22 bullet holes were in the dead man's back.

The Commissioner loaded the body on a wagon and started toward Copper Center. About a mile from where the body had been found, the Commissioner happened to look into a clearing near the trail and saw another body. Nearby were two spruce bough beds, bedding, and cooking utensils, as well as a bloody axe.

The corpses were those of two young Norwegians who had worked that summer at Fairbanks mines. Together they had been walking to Valdez to catch a ship to Seattle. Each had about $1,800 in cash when they left Fairbanks.

While in Copper Center, an Indian's sled dog returned home carrying a decayed human arm. Volunteers searched, and near an old campfire found what was left of another body that had lain there all winter. This too was a miner who had worked at Fairbanks through the summer of 1914. He had been walking to Valdez when reported missing.

The killer was never found.

"Musher's knee" struck me just beyond Copper Center. Both knees became exceedingly sore from constant walking in mud and on uneven ground with a 60-pound pack. "Take off your boots and pants and stand in an icy stream until your legs are numb," an oldtimer advised, "then rub your feet and legs dry, and keep walking." When I did that several times a day for a couple of days, the soreness disappeared.

Beyond Copper Center the trail was a slurry of mud. There were, however, bridges across the streams. Gulkana, about 128 miles from Valdez, was an Indian village of about 100 people.

Buck Hoyt owned a saloon, a store, and a nice roadhouse there. Someone was trying to raise marten in pens near the trail, and I stopped to admire them. They were the first of these quick-moving, fine-furred timber-living relatives of the mink that I had ever seen.

I walked into the Signal Corps station and was startled to see a lynx sitting on a desk. When it saw me it climbed onto a shelf and hissed. A soldier at the desk laughed at my startled reaction. The lynx was his pet and he told me how he had acquired it as a kitten and raised it. "When village dogs start after it, he jumps up on the station porch," the owner said with a smile. "If dogs get too eager he leaps on a dogs' back and rides it a short way. That usually scatters the pack for a while."

Stock for trading posts along the trail was freighted from Valdez in winter by dog team and horse-drawn sleds. There was no freight in summer. I could see why—the trail was virtually impassible.

At Gulkana I was surprised to find the Winchester .30-06 I had paid $24.50 for in Seattle sold for $26.50. Grocery prices were just as reasonable.

Beyond Gulkana the trail meandered across extensive flats where I walked on any firm off-trail ground I could find. There were many small lakes and mostly boggy ground. Clouds of mosquitoes followed me. Rain had transformed the trail into a thick soup.

Poplar Grove Roadhouse, 12 miles beyond Gulkana, was owned by oldtimer Dick Windmiller. I spent most of a day talking with him about hunting and trapping. He offered to stake me to a new .22 rifle and ammunition if I would hunt muskrats in the hundreds of nearby ponds, lakes, and swamps. "I'll pay you a buck a skin," he offered. I was tempted, but decided against it, mainly because of the clouds of mosquitoes.

Twelve miles beyond Poplar Grove I came to Sourdough Roadhouse. As I neared the low, rambling log building, an Indian ran out of the door and sped across the muddy trail, looking fearfully over his shoulder. A large white woman about six feet two, charged through the door blasting curses at the fleeing man. I stopped dead, and I'm sure my jaw dropped, for I had never heard a woman use such terrible language.

After a moment she spotted me. "What the hell you staring at, you scissorbill?" she yelled angrily, obviously still ticked off at the Indian. Then, in a more friendly voice, she asked, "You hungry? Come in and have some coffee, anyway."

This was Molly Yager, owner and manager of the roadhouse. The place astonished me. The floors were carpeted, there were several beautiful sofas, and the rocking chairs were cushioned. The windows had white curtains. She showed me one of the several private apartments, which was as nice as could be. The big combined kitchen and dining room was a model of neatness. I later learned that she was famous for her fine cooking.

Many Athapaskan Indians from both the Ewan and Tyone Lake country traded furs with Molly for food, guns, ammunition, and clothing. There were about 50 Indians camped at Sourdough that day. They had started hunting muskrats with breakup, and were bartering the skins with Molly.

"Swearing Molly," as some called her, had owned a roadhouse in Dawson, in Yukon Territory (Canada) during the great gold rush of 1897-98. She was tough and able to care for herself; she was also generous, hard-working, and well-liked.

Legions of stories were told about Swearing Molly. One involved Tom Gibson who had just started hauling passengers in Model T Fords over the trail between Valdez and Fairbanks.

Gibson promised Swearing Molly that he would stop regularly at Sourdough with his passengers since it was a likely stop— the road was usually pure mud on both sides of Sourdough.

On the first trip after his promise, Tom and his mechanic, Tommy Carr, who drove Gibson's second car, sputtered past Sourdough because it was mid-day and the road was dry. They wanted to put more miles behind them before day's end. Molly stood at the door watching glumly as they rattled by on the next trip, too. This time she angrily shook her fist at Gibson.

On his next trip, Tom stopped at Sourdough with both of his cars loaded with tourists. It was late in the day and he planned to spend the night. Molly stood in the doorway as the two Fords chugged up. She watched Tommy Carr and the tourists pile out and cheerfully bellowed, "Come in people, come in." Then she laid her eyes on Tom Gibson.

"Oh, you dirty sonofabitch!" she shouted. "You lowdown bastard! Wait 'til I get my hands on you, you damned lying dog turd."

Tourists who had started to file through the door reeled back in shock. Poor Tom ducked behind his car. Molly shoved a cowering woman tourist inside. "Come in, come in, damn you. I won't hurt you. It's that dirty sonofabitch I'm after," she said, pointing at Gibson.

Eventually Swearing Molly became a prime attraction. Tourists who traveled the trail all wanted to stop "at the place where the woman swears."

There were other hardy pioneer drivers, too, who challenged the old trail in those years. These included Bobby Sheldon, Billy and Grover Fraim, Joe Enos, and a fellow named Polistino. Most drove Model T Fords. "We'll get you there if you have to walk and push the car every foot of the way," was their cheerful motto. The fare was $125 one way, and passengers paid their own roadhouse bills. If the trail happened to be reasonably dry, or semi-frozen, the trip took at least a week. Otherwise it often required two weeks or more.

Sourdough was a regular stop for horse-drawn winter stages. Drivers would dive into the warm roadhouse with the passengers while the hostler, Frank Lampson, took the horses into the barn to feed and care for them. Then Frank harnessed a fresh team in their place. By the time the driver and passengers had eaten and were warm, the stage was ready to go on.

Swearing Molly and Lampson often had fist fights, which she always won. She would blacken his eyes, and bruise him up pretty badly. He would usually flee to the barn, or even to Poplar Grove Roadhouse. If he went to Poplar Grove, after two or three days Molly would get lonesome and telephone him. She'd promise not to beat him up any more if he would only come home. Eventually they married, but she never quit beating on him, and he never quit fleeing from her, something that each of them must have enjoyed.

At Sourdough overnight one spring, Road Commission teamster Jack Bishop, told Molly that if he ever found any rich quartz/gold deposits, he'd stake her in on the claim. That summer he worked at Delta River, some distance north of Sourdough. One day he was in the Road Commission horse barn keeping flies and mosquitoes away from the horses with a smudge. It was a boring job but his mind was busy. His eyes fell on a chunk of rust-streaked rock salt in a manger. It looked very much like quartz; the rust had a gold-like appearance.

Jack wrapped and boxed the salt carefully and had a teamster heading for Valdez take it to Molly.

"Tell her this is a piece of quartz, and that it runs heavy to gold. And tell her we've finally hit it big, because I've staked her to a half interest in the claim."

For a time whenever Jack saw anyone headed over the trail he'd tell them to ask Molly about the chunk of "gold-bearing quartz." "You'll point out the gold to her, won't you?" he would urge.

After a time travelers didn't have to ask Molly about the quartz. She would plop it on a table in front of visitors, saying, "Look what I've got. Jack Bishop staked me in on the claim this came from. Jack and I are really in the money."

That continued for most of the summer. In September, two mining engineers examining properties at Slate Creek northwest of Paxson's (there are 38 Slate Creeks in Alaska) stopped at Sourdough. They knew nothing about Jack Bishop's practical joke. Molly plunked the big chunk of salt on their table, saying, "What do you think of *this!* I own half interest in the claim it came from."

They thought she was kidding, but soon realized otherwise. Finally one suggested, "Lady, did you ever try pouring boiling water over this rock? Maybe it'll bring out the gold."

Molly took the chunk into her kitchen and poured boiling water over it. It started to melt. She then tasted the salt, and realized Bishop's scam.

"I'll kill that G. D. Bishop," she swore. But Bishop didn't stop at Sourdough that fall when he left for the season, instead staying overnight at Poplar Grove. When he returned in the spring he was with other teamsters who insisted on stopping at Sourdough. Bishop remained in the barn, fearing to go into the roadhouse.

"Is Bishop with you?" Molly asked the others.

"Yes. But he's afraid to come in," they told her.

"Oh, hell, go get him. I won't hurt him. Tell him to come on in," she urged.

Swearing Molly had a forgiving heart.

Fairbanks

Surrounded by huge bogs and many ponds, Our Home, the roadhouse at Hogan Hill, was a long 12 miles from Sourdough Roadhouse. It was run by a fellow named Gaby, who was married to a beautiful, dignified, extremely shy Indian girl. When I arrived there early in the morning after sloshing most of the night through sticky mud, Gaby and his wife were eating breakfast. Without a word she left for a nearby cabin. Other travelers later told me that she refused to talk to them also, and fled from the roadhouse when they arrived.

I had a meal at Our Home, then found a dry place under a big spruce tree well away from the trail where I spread my blankets and slept for the day. I walked all the next night, mostly on the edge of the trail. Since there was no easy way to drain water away from the trail here, the Road Commission had corduroyed it with thousands of spruce poles. Ditches were dug on each side of the trail, and the black muck that was dug out was placed on the corduroy. This worked for a while, but heavy horse-team traffic smashed the poles pretty fast, leaving mid-trail bogs in which you could mire up to your waist. Chunks of spruce poles appeared here and there, projecting from the mud at crazy angles.

Next morning I arrived at Meier's Roadhouse, on the shore of a small lake about mile 170 from Valdez. The fine two-story log building included a store and a saloon. Bedding in the roadhouse was so dirty the blankets looked shellacked.

"Meier, are those beds lousy?" I asked the owner.

"I don't know," he laughed. "Some bring 'em, some take 'em away!" I slept outside that day.

At Meier's I picked up a pleasant traveling companion, Matt McGovern, from Wallace, Idaho, who hoped to find work in the placer gold fields at Fairbanks. He was 52, and for 25 years had worked in silver mines. A doctor told him if he didn't get out of underground mines and get some fresh air he'd die.

"Mind if I travel with you?" he asked.

"Not at all," I said. "I'll enjoy your company."

As the two of us slogged along I could see the great snowy peaks of the Alaska Range. This encouraged me. At last I had reached the land of the grizzly, moose, caribou, and Dall sheep.

Travel was better for the 15 miles between Meier's and the next roadhouse, Paxson's, at the head of Paxson Lake. The trail ran along the shore of 10-mile-long Paxson Lake. Snow was gone except for occasional drifts. At the upper end of Paxson Lake we came to a three-mile-long slanting patch of ice glazing the trail, which was laced by three and four-foot-deep gullies carved by running water. About half way along this ice patch we came upon a Model T Ford, driven by Bobby Sheldon, who, in 1913, was the first to drive an auto—a home-made one at that—from Fairbanks to Valdez. He was engaged in a typical activity for Sheldon— getting a Model T Ford to go where it didn't want to go. When we came upon him he was cutting a trough for his upper wheels to keep the Ford from sliding sideways into the lake. Inside the auto was a woman passenger, with whom he had left Fairbanks two weeks earlier, bound for Valdez.

Matt and I spent several hours helping him get the rest of the way over that huge ice patch. We chopped ice and jockeyed the sputtering, skidding, bouncing Ford over the rough, slick surface.

I thought of what lay ahead of Bobby; jagged chunks of corduroy stuck out of the mud in many places, deep mud lakes hundreds of feet long, deep snow lingering in Thompson Pass.

I wondered how in the world he would ever make it. But he did. Bobby Sheldon was truly a pioneer.

At Paxsons we found a big roadhouse, a signal corps station, and an Indian village consisting of seven or eight cabins. Sled dogs ran loose in the village.

In the fall sockeye salmon ran into Summit Lake via the nearby Gulkana River after swimming up from the Copper River. Almost every year a huge migration of caribou passed nearby.

The trail climbed gradually to Summit Lake in Isabel Pass. Though it was after mid-May, seven-mile-long Summit Lake at 3,210 feet elevation was still frozen. It commonly remains iced over until July.

Matt and I rested at a relief cabin we found about two thirds of the way around the lake. A miner at heart, Matt commented, "Look around you, lad. There's nothing in this damn country but gold!"

Gold was the last thing I had in mind. We were above timberline. To the north, the huge peaks of the Alaska Range were stacked like ice cream cones. Game tracks were abundant. To me this was a wilderness paradise filled with wonderful big game animals—not one huge gold mine, as Matt thought. !

In the relief cabin I was bent over the wood stove, piling kindling. "Got a match, Matt?" I asked, turning to my companion. He was sitting, fiddling with a pistol. At that moment the gun went off. A bullet slammed into the wall next to the stove, missing me by about a foot and the cabin filled with gun smoke.

"My God, what're you trying to do?" I exploded.

Matt's face was white. He sat staring at the gun. "Sorry, Frankie. I didn't know it would fire. I wouldn't shoot you for anything in this world. I'm terribly sorry."

He had bought the pistol in Seattle, but had never handled a revolver. His new toy was a double-action Colt. Pull the trigger and the hammer rose and fell, firing the gun if it was loaded. He hadn't known that while playing with the gun.

Matt, who had started to fumble in his clothing for a match suddenly blurted, "Where's my vest? I had matches in my vest. Oh, my God, I left it in the willows down by Paxsons. The soldier's will get it. There's four hundred dollars in it."

He rushed for the door saying, "Frankie, you wait here for me, and I'll run down and get my vest."

We had spent most of that weary night walking from Paxsons, and were both tired. I waited anxiously all day and all night. Finally on the following morning Matt returned, wearing his vest and a big grin. His $400 was intact.

From Summit Lake north to Black Rapids many of the glacier

streams were unbridged and fording them was often perilous and chancy. When the snow and glaciers melt in warm weather, streams become swollen. They are usually at their highest at midnight, and lowest about noon, after the cool of night.

The Alaska Road Commission had graded a gentle slope on the banks of these streams so that high-wheeled cars of the time—as well as horse-drawn wagons—could cross. The cars usually took a run at it, and their momentum usually carried them across.

A few years later, when the old trail had been upgraded into a wagon road, many of the streams were still without bridges. I was at Rapids in 1921 when Bobby Sheldon arrived from Fairbanks with a Model T. He stopped at the roadhouse, tinkered with the car, ate a meal, then drove off. Within an hour he arrived back at the roadhouse afoot and dripping wet. He told me he had arrived at Gunnysack Creek, south of Rapids a short distance (named after the habit of a miner who worked there and made overalls from gunny sacking), looked it over, and decided it didn't look any deeper than usual. He backed off and ran at it, rolling off the sloped bank and hitting the stream with spray flying.

"It was deeper than I thought," Sheldon said. "I stalled in midstream. Water poured over the hood and washed gravel from under the wheels. Then she headed downstream."

Bobby managed to splash safely ashore, where he stood and watched his car disappear into the Delta River a few hundred yards downstream.

A few weeks later a note appeared in the *Fairbanks News-Miner* reporting that a traveler on the Valdez Trail had seen Bobby Sheldon working a gold pan just below the mouth of Gunnysack Creek. According to the traveler, Sheldon claimed he'd found color of his lost Ford. Bobby was kidded about his lost Ford for several years.

Yost's Roadhouse, a two-story log building 10 miles from Summit Lake and four miles north of Isabel Pass, was built by Charlie Yost about 1906, when there was only a sled dog trail through the mountains from Fairbanks to Valdez. A 20-foot-long log tunnel connected the roadhouse with the barn so that during blizzards it wasn't necessary to leave the roadhouse to feed horses or care for dogs. The Signal Corp's McCallum telegraph station was located a few hundred feet from the roadhouse.

Winter travel past Yost's was mainly on the ice of the Delta River. Blinding winter blizzards rage frequently here and in nearby Isabel Pass where wind blows almost constantly. Winter travel is especially hazardous. Below zero winds can whip up a wall of snow 20 to 30 feet high, making it impossible to see more than ten or fifteen feet.

Stakes marked the winter trail, but the roadhouse, about 200 yards to one side, was often missed by travelers during storms. It was 18 miles to Paxson's to the south, and 13 miles north to Miller's Roadhouse. Missing Yost's during a storm could put you in a bad way. In the winter before my arrival several travelers froze to death near Yost's.

During the winter of 1912–13 traffic bustled on the trail. One March day nine people riding in a stage coach left Yost's in the morning heading into a strong north wind. The wind blasted the sled sideways and turned it over, dumping passengers onto the ice. The teamster took the four horses and the passengers into a patch of sheltering timber. Some of the passengers thought they could walk back to Yost's, since their back would be to the wind. However, as they tried to walk, the powerful wind blew them off the river and into the timber.

Two of the men passengers managed to struggle through the storm to Yost's, and a husky young Signal Corp sergeant from the nearby McCallum telegraph station repeatedly went out and packed the other seven nearly frozen passengers in to the roadhouse.

Years later Charley Yost told me that the blizzard continued without break for nine or ten days. Some of the passengers who had been carried in had frozen feet and hands and were stuck in the roadhouse without medical care. Gangrene set in and hands and feet started to rot. Because of howling wind, blinding snow and 40 below zero temperature, no doctor could travel to Yost's to help, and no one could leave Yost's.

That awful winter twelve people died on the trail near Yost's Roadhouse.

The following summer, Lieutenant Dougherty, the Army Signal Corp commander, strung a seven-foot-high woven wire fence on posts from the roadhouse across the river to a bluff. Near the roadhouse he balanced a 150-pound bell on heavy timbers in such a way that it would ring whenever the wind blew, which was

Springtime about 1917, and an Alaska Road Commission crew digs out the Valdez Trail not far from Black Rapids Roadhouse. Note shovels leaning against the snowdrift. At the time, big crews with shovels dug through winter-formed drifts. There is no blade on the tractor in this photo. The crew is not only digging through at least 25 feet of snowdrift, they are bridging a small stream.

FORD MOTOR COMPANY ARCHIVES

most of the time. The fence and that tolling bell saved many lives.

In winter Yost's two-story log building was sometimes buried by a huge snow-drift, leaving only the stovepipe visible. Travelers had to look hard to find the stovepipe. Then they had to scout around to find the tunnel leading down to the roadhouse door. Log notchings at the corners of the building were beginning to rot and were mended with tin from gasoline cans. Gunny sacking chinked the logs.

As Matt and I walked near Yost's, I was thrilled to see big fresh grizzly bear tracks along the trail and on bars of the milky Delta River. They were bigger with more distinct claw marks than the black bear tracks I knew so well. I made sure my rifle was loaded and nervously kept my eyes open for the huge animal that had made those tracks.

Hundreds of snowshoe hares, still partly winter-white, swarmed among the willows along the Delta River, devouring bark from the low trees. As I plowed through willow patches, they leaped out in numbers that looked almost like flocks of sheep. I've never seen such numbers of rabbits since.

Twelve miles beyond Yost's near Miller's Roadhouse, owned by a man named Bowman, I lost my traveling companion when Matt accepted a job at a Road Commission Camp.

A few days before my arrival at Miller's Roadhouse, a big man with a long black beard remained there overnight. Next morning, heading for Fairbanks, he waded the first glacier stream he came to without difficulty. Then he came to Castner's Creek, which pours out of Castner Glacier. The water was high, with standing waves surging two and three feet. When high, that stream rolls boulders a foot and a half in diameter, and rocks as big as softballs are frequently flipped two or three feet out of the racing water.

Here Blackbeard removed all his clothing but his boots, rolled them into a bundle with a few rocks inside for weight, and tied the bundle with a string. Evidently he hadn't slept well, or he had poor eyesight. Maybe he spent the night scratching lice. He planned to toss the clothing across and then wade the stream so he'd be nice and dry on the far side. He threw as hard as he could but the bundle landed midstream and disappeared instantly.

Anna Greenberg, cook and housekeeper at Miller's, had heard of people going crazy from mosquitoes and tearing off their clothing. She told me she thought that was the explanation when she looked out the window and saw big, naked Blackbeard, tearing toward the roadhouse, yelling and slapping mosquitoes. It took a lot of sweet talk to get her to let him in and to provide him with clothing.

When I came to Castner's Creek I walked downstream to a

delta formed where it spread out into many channels, none very deep; I had no difficulty crossing.

From Miller's Roadhouse to Black Rapids Glacier Roadhouse I became very excited. This was the kind of country I had dreamed about. With binoculars I spotted white sheep skirting the high mountain crags. A yellow-backed brown-legged grizzly swaggered across a snow field high above timberline. Fresh caribou tracks pocked bars of the nearby Delta River.

Black Rapids Roadhouse lies opposite 29-mile-long hugely-crevassed Black Rapids Glacier; the roaring, glacial, Delta River separates them. Victor Columbo, a Frenchman everybody called "Victor Columbus," owned the roadhouse, but he spent most of his time hunting and trapping.

I remained at Rapids, as this roadhouse is commonly called, for five days, hiking into the mountains and peering through binoculars at distant caribou and at white sheep high on the greening peaks. I saw several more grizzlies, and checked out tracks of foxes, lynx, and other furbearers on sandy stretches of the river bar. This spectacular country, with its on-end sky-scraping, rocky peaks tempted me to settle there immediately, but I went on, for I was determined to see Fairbanks, now only 145 miles distant; I could always return to Rapids.

About four miles from Rapids the trail crossed a spruce-grown Delta River bar. A four mile section of the trail here was called the "race track" because it was the only place on the entire route where cars could speed. It was a marvelous natural highway needing no grading or ditching. Here drivers of Model T Fords could urge their black, spoke-wheeled, 4-cylinder tin lizzies up to all of 40 miles an hour, sometimes faster.

Ten years later, in 1925, the speed limit on the Richardson Highway (then still classified as a wagon road) was 25 miles per hour. Trucks of one ton or less were limited to 20 mph, and those over one ton were limited to 15 mph. It was illegal for any driver to exceed 12 mph when the road couldn't be seen at least 100 yards ahead.

Though the Model T Ford was the most common make of car, I remember Stanley Steamer trucks, Jewett, Star, Chrysler,

Chevrolet, Nash, Oakland, Oldsmobile, Buick, and Dodge cars on the Valdez Trail (later named the Richardson Highway) during the 1920s.

The "race track" was a natural crossing for caribou drifting to and from the Mount Hayes country lying to the west. In later years when I hunted the area, I could always find bull caribou around the "race track" after about July first. They liked to linger there over the abundant wild pea vine, which they love.

The trail climbed steeply over Donnelly Dome, an isolated 3,910-foot, round-topped peak rising from the flats north of the Alaska Range a few miles from Rapids. There again I saw thousands of rabbits (snowshoe hares). Donnelly Roadhouse, a very nice place with good horse barns and dog houses, perched on the bank of the nearby Delta River, but it was necessary to detour off the summer trail to reach it. The roadhouse was built on the winter trail where travelers to Fairbanks crossed the frozen Delta River and went straight across country to Birch Lake, cutting off 25 or 30 miles from the summer route.

In the fall of 1926 I happened to be on the west side of the Delta River opposite Donnelly Roadhouse, which had then been abandoned for a couple of years. The river had changed course, and was cutting into the bank next to the roadhouse. I wanted to cross the river, and hoped it would go down, for it was very high. While waiting I sat on a hill for a couple of days and watched the river carry that roadhouse and all of its outbuildings away. Within three days there wasn't a trace of that historic structure left.

As I came to Beale's Cache, the next stop, I found Charley Miller building a new log roadhouse with logs he had hauled by dog team eight miles from Jarvis Creek the previous winter. His building was five logs high. Tired of walking, and wanting to stop and talk to someone, I helped him until there were ten rounds of logs on his new building.

He was living mostly on canned food. When he opened a can, he used a butcher knife to cut a cross in the top of the cans, then he bent the four pieces of the lid back and tossed the empty cans behind the new building where he threw his dishwater. While I was there that spot was a moving mass of snowshoe hares where, unbelievably, the animals were eating the dishwater-flavored dirt.

The first evening I was there three or four of the rabbits caught their heads in Charley's empty cans and ran around bumping into things. Charlie turned one of his sled dogs loose and it caught and ate the "canned" rabbits.

Several times I tossed green willow clubs into the massed rabbits, killing two or three with each throw. We fed the rabbits to Charley's dogs.

The village of McCarty, and McCarty Roadhouse, stood at the junction of the Delta and Tanana Rivers, 18 miles from Beale's Cache. A telegraph station was established on this site in 1904. Later, and some distance from the river, McCarty grew into the community now known as Big Delta. I crossed the Tanana River here on the captive ferry that could carry a four-horse team or two Model T Fords. The ferry slid along on a cable, with the angle of the hull in relation to the current powering it both ways. Now, Fairbanks was only 90 miles away.

I walked on to Tenderfoot, 15 miles north of McCarty, a cluster of 15 or 20 log cabins. Tenderfoot Creek was the attraction. Here frozen earth was thawed from bedrock in 80-foot-deep shafts, hoisted to the surface, then put through sluice boxes. It was difficult, dirty, and dangerous work.

Emard's Roadhouse was at the upper end of Tenderfoot. Emard, a bald old goat of about 55, had some land under cultivation and a barn. He couldn't keep a cook at his roadhouse. In response to his newspaper advertisements, the stage would bring a woman out from Fairbanks. She'd work for an afternoon perhaps, cooking supper, then Emard would show her where she was to sleep. After she was in bed he would walk in on her declaring, "I always sleep with my cooks."

The women usually left through a window, or shoved by Emard and fled to Hern's mine a couple of hundred yards away.

Emard was finally put under observation at the Fairbanks hospital. He tried to commit suicide, which convinced authorities that he was insane and he was committed to an institution.

The 1,500-resident town of Richardson, just over the hill from Tenderfoot, had four streets of high front business houses, dance halls, and saloons. There was also a post office, a two-story Army Signal Corp station with three or four soldiers, a

U.S. Commissioner, and several general stores. The town was named for Wilds P. Richardson, the first president of the board of the Alaska Road Commission who established the trail between Valdez and Fairbanks.

The town of Richardson died a few years after my arrival. Shortly after it was abandoned, the Tanana River changed course, washing it away. By 1950, only one building remained.

As I walked into Richardson I saw a flower-surrounded house near the road with one plot of multi-colored flowers spelling "Jesus Loves Us." It was the home of a middle-aged missionary woman.

Residents were laughing at how the missionary lady had trapped her new husband. She had taken a liking to a Signal Corps sergeant who had shown little interest in her. Then the lady began to grow larger and larger, and it appeared she was pregnant. She told the U.S. Commissioner the sergeant had wronged her. Miners always stuck up for the few "nice" women in town, and called a meeting. The sergeant was instructed to marry the woman or be tarred and feathered and run out of town.

He married her.

Immediately after the ceremony the woman removed the pillow she had tucked into her clothing, and the couple settled down to new-married bliss. Everyone thought it a great joke. I don't know what the sergeant thought.

I stopped to talk with Jack Taylor at his fox farm 52 miles from Fairbanks. His pens brimmed with beautiful silver foxes. Taylor was angry and upset about an incident of the previous day. He had owned an unusually tame vixen silver fox. When she had pups, he could handle them, and he could pet and handle the vixen. When her pups reached good size he let her out every evening and she would run off to catch a rabbit. When she returned carrying this food for her pups, she would bark, and he would open the door to her pen and let her in.

The previous evening a traveler on the road shot and killed the vixen, then brought the animal to Taylor and asked him to skin it for him since he didn't know how.

Jack snatched the man's rifle and kept it after telling the traveler he had just killed his most valuable fox. He kept the dead fox, telling me that the unhappiest job he ever tackled was skinning his beloved pet.

I walked the last 40 miles of muddy trail from Salchaket to Fairbanks in ten and a half hours. Fairbanks, according to local boosters, was "The Heart of the Golden North," and "the biggest log cabin town in the world."

When I arrived there in 1915 Fairbanks, population 3,500, was a 13-year-old frontier mining camp of log cabins and dirt streets. Excitement was in the air, and everyone seemed to have a sense of purpose. The town lived on gold and fur. Gold, discovered there in 1901, was king during the brief summer. Miners wanted to take advantage of every hour.

Stores carried the finest quality clothing, hardware, and groceries. Alaskans wouldn't buy shoddy goods, for they needed the best in challenging this remote, harsh-climated land.

Many men wore breeches and knee-high laced boots that clattered on the board walks. Teams of horses plodded the dusty dirt streets. Occasionally, a high-wheeled Model T Ford, or a Dodge touring car, putted by. Carts could be seen pulled by teams of panting sled dogs. Eight or ten sternwheel steamers were crowded in the Chena River below the Cushman Street bridge. Most heavy freight arrived in Fairbanks aboard these steamers; from Seattle it took a week for a steamer to reach the mouth of the Yukon River, where the freight was transferred to paddle-wheelers for the 1,000-mile journey upstream. The sternwheelers burned wood, replenished at woodcutters' camps on the banks of the broad, silty Yukon.

The town had a telephone system, and the Northern Commercial Company's power plant provided electricity. A great ship's whistle mounted on a stack above the N.C. power plant resounded four times daily with a deep melodious tone that drifted far across the wide Tanana Valley. The whistle was always echoed by the howling of hundreds of sled dogs.

False-front frame buildings lined Front Street and Second and Third Avenue—the main business part of town. A nearby sawmill was busily making lumber, and frame buildings were springing up.

There was a ballpark, two sets of tennis courts, and a roller rink. "The Row"—a red-light district—was situated in town center. The business district consisted of dry-goods stores, bakeries, laundries, hardware stores, two banks, and seven good restaurants. In summer the Waechter Brothers shipped in live cattle, sheep, pigs, chickens, ducks, and geese via sternwheeler riverboat. These were butchered and sold to town residents and to surrounding mines. During the six months or more of the year when the Yukon River shipping route was frozen, market hunters hauled Dall sheep, caribou, and moose meat by dog team from the Alaska Range, selling the meat for fifty cents a pound.

Low on money, I easily found a job at a placer mine at Cleary, a mining camp 20 miles northeast of Fairbanks. While aiming a high pressure water nozzle to wash away the overburden so the gold-bearing layer could be mined, I dreamed of Rapids and the wonderful game country around it.

After payday in mid-July I quit mining and walked back down the Valdez Trail to Rapids.

Market Hunting

I MOVED INTO BLACK RAPIDS ROADHOUSE and looked for a way to make a living. My problem was solved in a few days when Colonel Wilds P. Richardson of the U.S. Army Corp of Engineers, on an inspection trip, arrived on horseback. He needed a hunter to provide game meat to feed Alaska Road Commission construction crews then developing the Valdez Trail into a wagon road. I convinced him I could do the job, we made a verbal contract, and as simply as that I became a market hunter.

Market hunting for game was common, despite a 1912 federal law prohibiting sale of game meat. For many residents wild game was the only dependable source of fresh meat in interior Alaska. The Road Commission wanted mostly Dall mountain sheep whose meat is almost always tender and mild-flavored, and considered by most interior Alaskans as the finest game meat available.

Market hunters regularly hunted in the Alaska Range. Most of the meat was hauled by dog team, sometimes by pack horse, to Fairbanks where it was sold to restaurants, meat markets, mine owners and individuals. In addition, the Army Signal Corp advertised for bids to supply moose, caribou, and sheep meat to its men stationed along the telegraph and telephone lines between Fairbanks and Valdez. Of course, in remote areas of Alaska people lived off the country to a large extent, killing game year-round as needed.

Caribou and sheep were especially abundant; moose were plentiful in some vicinities. Some caribou remained year-round in the Rapids area where I hunted. Annually, the great Fortymile caribou herd migrated into the nearby mountains and valleys for the winter, returning north in the spring. There were few sport or trophy hunters and local residents who hunted did so mostly for the meat.

On my first day of hunting I walked from Rapids south on the Valdez Trail scanning canyons with binoculars. I soon spotted a band of about 20 white sheep high on the mountain. Keeping out of their sight, I climbed a rough, steep canyon, eventually working my way above them, since wild sheep are most alert to danger from below. I then crawled down through a dense stand of alders to within easy range.

I selected a large ram bedded at the base of a cliff about 75 yards away and fired at his neck with the .30-06 box magazine Winchester I had bought in Seattle. The ram's head dropped, a splotch of blood appeared on his white neck, and he kicked a couple of times.

The other sheep stood up, and came together in a loose band, staring my way. Taking my time, I selected another large ram and also shot him in the neck. He dropped without even kicking. I shot only two animals, not wanting to kill more than I could pack out of the mountains before the meat spoiled. Confused and alarmed, the remaining sheep didn't run until I stood up.

I gutted the two rams and removed their heads and legs. I lashed one to my packboard, carried it to a nearby glacier, and cached it on the ice. It took the rest of the day to pack the other ram down the steep mountain and along the trail to Rapids. I telephoned the nearest Road Commission camp, asking them to send a horse-drawn wagon to pick up the sheep. They agreed to come for the second animal the next day after I packed it out. There were a number of camps within 50 or 60 miles, and if one camp had a surplus of meat, they'd send it on to another.

I got twenty five cents a pound for sheep, caribou, and moose. Those two rams brought me more than $50, big money in 1915. The same meat delivered to Fairbanks restaurants and meat markets would have brought fifty cents a pound, but the problem was getting it there.

My first hunt set the pattern. I usually killed two sheep at a time, commonly caching one at a glacier, which are plentiful in the mountains near Rapids. Willow trees normally grow near the face of a glacier and I learned to lay a willow branch across an ice crevasse and swing the sheep from it on a rope—a perfect place to cool and to preserve the meat. This also protected meat from prowling grizzly bears.

The sheep lived at an altitude of 4,000 to 5,000 feet, and even when a glacier wasn't near, meat I cached was usually safe from blow flies, for it was too cold for them.

I killed mostly rams. They were the fattest during the spring, summer, and fall when I hunted, and they are also larger than the ewes. In July, a dressed two-year-old ram weighed 100 to 110 pounds (age is determined from the annular rings on horns). As fall approaches, sheep put on more fat, and by September a large five-year-old dressed up to 120 pounds. The largest ram I ever killed weighed 140 pounds minus the hide, head, legs below the knees, and entrails. Alive, that animal probably weighed about 300 pounds. Sheep continue to build fat until mid-October. Breeding season starts the first week of November, when the old rams lose weight rapidly. By then freeze-up halted road construction, and my market hunting was largely over for the season.

In a way I was like a rancher who raised animals for market; only my "livestock" weren't fenced in. The rams I killed didn't affect production of lambs, for one ram can cover ten to fifteen ewes, and plenty of rams were left. Few others hunted where I did, and game was wonderfully abundant. The Road Commission bought all the meat I could deliver, and during construction season I hunted full time, weather permitting. My hunts generally went smoothly, but I did occasionally have problems with the abundant grizzly bears. On a day's hunt I commonly saw four or five of these big predators. I often returned for a carcass only to find that a grizzly had dragged it off and eaten or buried it. At the time, like most Alaskans, I saw no value in grizzlies. They were simply dangerous pests that stole my meat.

These big bears were especially troublesome if I killed a caribou in the bench country bordering sheep range. I'd pack half of the caribou to the roadhouse, and return the next morning for the other half. Often a grizzly would have gobbled up much of the meat I left, covering the rest with moss, twigs, dirt, and leaves.

The bear would sprawl behind the pile to keep other bears, wolverine, ravens, and whatever else, away from *his* meat.

After a few encounters with grizzlies, I learned to always carry my rifle when returning for cached meat, even though it was a hindrance and extra weight. If I approached from upwind so a bear could smell me, he'd usually stand, look me over and get out, even if guarding meat. If he couldn't smell me, but heard me coming, he wouldn't know what I was. Such bears often stood and approached to look me over. Usually a loud yell and maybe a shot fired into the ground sped them on their way. Sometimes they wanted to argue, so I always had to be prepared for these aggressive fellows.

Mountain-killed grizzly hides were prime after the first week of September, and at first I sold many. In later years, I saved grizzly skulls and hides and sent them to the U.S. Biological Survey, which requested specimens from me.

After I had hunted for the market for a few years I developed strong opinions about rifles. I wanted the lightest weight rifle I could find. The .30-06 box magazine Winchester I brought to Alaska in 1915 was a heavy, clumsy thing, and I used it only a short time. When carrying a packboard, a pair of binoculars, an axe, extra clothing and a bit of food, a nine or ten pound rifle is simply too heavy.

For a time I used fine Mannlicher rifles which I could buy from Smith Brothers Hardware at Fairbanks for $35. I used the 7mm model, which is about like the .30-06 in hitting power. I even tried a .405 Winchester, thinking it would be a good bear rifle to back up bear hunting sportsmen I occasionally guided. I never did kill a bear with it. It had a terrific recoil, and was heavy and clumsy. I didn't like it very well.

The Savage .250-3000 was my favorite all-round rifle for market hunting. I also liked the killing power of the .30-06, of which I owned several. I had good luck with a cut-down sporterized .30-40 Krag. In the late 1930s and into the 1940s I had a Winchester Model 70 .220 Swift, and killed everything with it—moose, grizzly bear, caribou, sheep. However, the little 48 grain bullet didn't perform well on grizzlies. But with a lung shot on hoofed game the Swift killed quicker than any other gun I ever owned.

The last heavy rifle I owned and used on big game, during the 1950s, was a Winchester Model 70 in .308 caliber, which performed about like the .30-06.

Rifle caliber is less important than marksmanship. A properly-placed shot with almost any reasonably powerful centerfire rifle will efficiently kill any of Alaska's hoofed game, with the possible exception of the bison, which calls for at least a .30-06 or equivalent.

The big bears are also difficult to kill, and no hunter should tackle a grizzly (brown bear) with anything less powerful than a .30-06 using 220 grain ammunition.

In the late fall of 1916 when the road construction season ended and the Road Commission had no more need for meat, I moved to Darling Creek, just below the Rapids Roadhouse, and built myself a log cabin. In late December, with a team of three dogs and a sled I mushed about 30 miles west to a high bench on the north slope of the Alaska Range where I built another log cabin. While building, I lived in a wall tent heated with a wood stove.

After I'd been on the high bench for a day or two the temperature plummeted to 60 below zero. I had little food and needed meat for the dogs and myself. In reaching the site my dog sled had been filled mostly with axe, saw, chisels, hinges, a window, spikes, a stove and stove pipe and my tent; there wasn't much room for food.

I left my rifle outside in the cold, for I had learned that moisture condenses on a cold-soaked rifle taken into a warm tent or cabin. When it is again taken into the cold, the moisture may turn to ice, jamming the rifle. Despite the deep cold, with my frigid rifle I sought one of the many caribou feeding on a nearby flat.

On snowshoes, I approached several caribou. The animals saw and heard me and fled. Frustrated, I floundered through deep snow for the better part of an hour. Finally with my .30-06 I aimed above the shoulder of a caribou a good 400 yards away and fired. I was amazed at the lack of sound when the rifle fired; it sounded almost like a small firecracker. In later years I heard others shoot heavy caliber rifles in deep cold, and the sound was more like that of a .22 rimfire than a heavy rifle.

Black Rapids Roadhouse on the Valdez Trail in 1922, when it was owned by Frank Glaser. Note the carbide lights on the Model T Ford, and the shovel. The shovel is a good indicator of trail condition.
FRANK GLASER

Although the .30-06 made little sound when fired, the distant caribou collapsed with a bullet through the lungs. Now the dogs and I had meat.

In two or three weeks I completed the cabin, and for the rest of the winter of 1916-17 I ran a trapline between it and my cabin at Darling Creek.

Red and cross foxes were abundant; the black and silver color phases were less so (all are the same species), and their furs brought the best prices. On Christmas day, 1916, I caught two foxes; one was a black, the other a silver. I sold the fur of the black for $800, and the fur of the silver for $600. I could have easily lived a full

year on what I received for either of those furs. I snared a few
lynx, and caught a dozen marten as well.

A herd of about 10,000 caribou wintered in the region, so I
had no difficulty in feeding the dogs and myself. That winter I
never saw a wolf track or heard a wolf howl. I wondered about
that, for I had heard wolves were plentiful in Alaska. Eventually
I learned why the animals were scarce.

Market hunters operated in practically every major drainage
on the north slope of the Alaska Range within dog team freighting distance of Fairbanks. In 1917 a Fairbanks warden estimated
that during the previous four years 2,800 sheep had been killed
for the market within 200 miles of Fairbanks. Sheep were far more
abundant then than they have ever been since.

Between 15,000 and 20,000 people lived in and around
Fairbanks. Most were miners, living on the creeks, and in little
towns on the creeks like Olness, Cleary, Fox, Gilmore, and
Chatanika. Fairbanks itself had about 5,000 residents.

I met many market hunters. C. J. Johanson, the "Hunker
King," he was called, hunted in the Richardson-Tenderfoot area.
Another was Phil McGuire, a blond Scot, who used a poling boat
to ascend the Tanana River to get to his hunting area. McGuire
was drowned in the Tanana shortly after I met him. Bill
Eisenminger and Frank Gillespie also market hunted up and down
the treacherous Tanana.

Then there was Little Herman (Herman Kessler), and Big
Herman, his partner, who hunted the country that became Mount
McKinley National Park (now renamed Denali National Park).
Kessler later ran a trading post at Northway. A little guy called
Bill the Turk also market hunted in the McKinley Park country.

Harry Lucke and Tom Steele were big time hunters who killed
hundreds of wild sheep as well as moose and caribou. In summer
they ran a ferry across the Chena River in mid-Fairbanks until a
bridge was built a few years later.

Annually when the Chena froze over so residents could safely
cross on the ice, Lucke and Steele drove big dog teams from
Fairbanks into the Alaska Range, where, within a few weeks they
commonly yarded up several tons of sheep carcasses. The meat
froze, or at least chilled, as they hunted.

To keep foxes, wolves, wolverine, and other animals from eating the meat, they, like other market hunters of the time, scattered little pill-like balls of sheep gut-fat laced with strychnine around their meat caches. This at least partly explains the scarcity of wolves when I arrived. When the Tanana and Nenana river ice was solid and the trails were good, Lucke and Steele hauled the meat to Fairbanks with dog teams.

I spent a lot of time with Lucke, a charming, handsome, rawboned man who was born in Vechta, Germany in 1875 and emigrated to the U.S. as a young man. His German accent remained with him all his life, although he was fluent in English. For a time he worked as a woodcutter, providing cordwood for river steamers on the Yukon and Tanana. He once said his profession was "ice-man," because for a winter or two he sawed ice from a lake and insulated it with sawdust for sale during summer.

He was a crack woodsman and a wonderful shot. In his later years he was looked upon as an outlaw hunter who ignored the new bag limits and big game hunting seasons. Lucke and Tom Steele were once caught with several sheep they killed illegally in McKinley park. There was no jail, so they remained at liberty awaiting trial while the confiscated sheep were held on a cache high off the ground.

During a howling snowstorm, the two sawed the legs off the cache, tumbling the sheep to the ground. They loaded the carcasses into big freight sleds and drove their dog teams off. Snow covered their tracks, and they got away. No evidence, no prosecution.

Once Lucke and I mushed two dog teams into the head of Riley Creek which flows into the Nenana River. Here we killed a couple of sled loads of Dall sheep for the Fairbanks market. Our dog teams were pretty crazy as we careened down the mountain on our heavily-loaded sleds. We wrapped dog chains around the runners to slow them, and continually rode brakes; even so we sped down that mountainside at perilous speed. On some of the really steep slopes the dogs had to sprint all-out to stay ahead, and we had to throw our weight this way and that to keep the sleds upright.

Suddenly we came to a bench just above Riley Creek where about a thousand caribou were gathered amidst brush and dead

A scenic view along the Valdez Trail, probably about 1925.
FORD MOTOR COMPANY ARCHIVES

spruces. When we skidded and lurched into sight, the caribou stampeded, their hooves sounding almost like thunder as they charged across the bench toward Riley Creek, toppling spruces, charging through brush and tossing up clouds of snow.

My dogs wanted to chase the caribou, but I turned my sled over and climbed on top of it to stop them. Lucke, however, whooped wildly as he rode it out. His dogs almost caught several caribou.

He was still laughing when I caught up. He said, "If caribou had any brains, a bunch like that could kill every wolf in the country. Trample 'em to death!"

In the 1920s Lucke wrote some true outdoor stories and sent them to *Outside* magazine. They were rejected. He then fabricated a series of outlandish adventure yarns which the editor promptly bought. Lucke told me, "They wouldn't buy the truth, so I started writing bull, and they bought it. Others write about hunting, and tell how far it was they shot the game, where they hit it, and all that. But after you've shot 400 moose, how in hell can you remember how far they were and where they were hit? Better I write bull."

Though Lucke guided a few non-resident sportsman on big game hunts after market hunting ended, he never settled down to one job. During World War II he drove cab in Fairbanks, but was harassed because of his German heritage and accent. He couldn't stand that.

"I was an American soldier," he told me, "I fought in the Spanish-American War. And yet they come at me with this Nazi stuff."

About 1944 he went to Salchaket, where the Richardson Highway crosses the Salcha River. Here he lived in a little log cabin with two Indian women. He died of tuberculosis in 1947.

Another market hunter I knew well was Henry "Butch" Stock, who hunted at Jarvis Creek and other areas on the north slope of the Alaska Range. Occasionally we hunted together.

When I first knew Butch, who couldn't read or write, he was probably around 55, although it was difficult to determine his age because, strangely, he didn't know it himself. He was a ruggedly built 5' 10" and weighed about 175 pounds. Because he habitually squinted and blinked, I believe his vision was blurred.

He acquired the nickname "Butch" when he first arrived in Alaska with a herd of cattle that he drove from Valdez to Fairbanks and butchered. At one time he owned valuable gold placer ground at Slate Creek, a tributary of the Gakona River; he also owned two roadhouses on the Valdez Trail.

Butch was one of the most durable men I've ever known. When we hunted together I carried a packboard with broad shoulder straps to which I lashed the meat I carried out of the mountains. Butch, on the other hand, carried a length of quarter-inch rope around his waist which he used as shoulder straps. We once killed a big bull caribou a good distance from the Valdez Trail. Although 25 years older than me and without a packboard, he insisted on carrying the 175-pound front half of the caribou while I packed the 150-pound hind half. He tied his skinny little rope around the meat and when the weight of the meat was on him the rope sank out of sight into his shoulders. It looked painful to me, but he never complained.

After a long climb up a steep ridge I was ready for a rest. Butch was staggering along all bent over. "How about resting, Butch,?" I asked.

"Oh, we're doing all right, Frankie," he said in his hoarse voice, and he kept staggering along so briskly I had trouble keeping up with him.

Butch always camped under a tree, depending on a fire for warmth, even after freeze-up. Many times young Signal Corps soldiers asked to hunt with Butch, and he was always happy to take them along. One hunt was always enough for them. He carried very little grub and no bedding, and he'd slog them across rugged mountains for 20 or 30 miles. On such hunts he planned to kill a sheep and pack it out as I did. But I never packed a sheep 30 miles, like Butch did sometimes.

After hunting with Butch, many of the young soldiers could hardly pack themselves out of the mountains, much less carry a sheep. When they started out they felt sorry for the "old man," but it didn't take long for such sympathy to disappear.

When I first met Butch he owned a horse, a mule, an old cart, and a buckboard. Sometimes he took both animals with him when hunting, one pulling the cart, the other tied to the rear of the cart. He always walked, leading either the horse or the mule with a halter. When he came to a caribou or a moose he would drop the lead rope and shoot. Often the horse and the mule would run off. Butch would generally find the cart stuck between two trees, with the animals waiting for him. Most horses get skittish around bear hides, but Old Joe was unusual in that it didn't upset him when a fresh, bloody grizzly hide was put on his back.

A 50-pound Airedale named Bear, and a long-legged white Malemute named Talks accompanied Butch wherever he went. Sometimes the dogs deserted Butch for days, usually chasing game. Many times they came to Rapids where they'd rest for a day or two while I fed them, then they'd light out for McCarty which Butch called home, although he wasn't there much.

Once when the Road Commission urgently needed meat,

The Valdez Trail, renamed the Richardson Highway in 1923, sometime after 1929. Even in the 1930s the old trail was little more than a wagon road.
FORD MOTOR COMPANY ARCHIVES

Butch and I worked together. I was to go ahead and kill a couple of caribou and sheep. Butch was to follow with the mule and his cart. As I climbed a high ridge I saw the mule, the cart, and Butch far below, slowly heading my way.

I killed two caribou. By the time I had them dressed Butch arrived with the cart. He loaded them and headed back to Donnelly, while I climbed higher to shoot two sheep. Butch was supposed to return to help me with the sheep. When he arrived at Donnelly, the tailgate had fallen out of the cart and he had lost one of the caribou. He had to backtrack ten miles to find it. It was two days before he caught up with me, and by then I had relayed the carcasses of the two sheep almost all the way down to the Valdez Trail.

No one could live in a cabin that Butch used for any length of time. He never washed a dish or swept a floor. He piled garbage in a corner. He seldom changed his clothing. He didn't care whether he had bedding or not, commonly sleeping in his clothes.

The Valdez Trail at Summit Lake, probably in the 1930s. Note the telephone and telegraph poles. FORD MOTOR COMPANY ARCHIVES

About 1920 when Butch was at least 60, he acquired Jenny, a mail-order bride. He had a friend read the "Mate wanted" section of a magazine to him, and then had the friend correspond with Jenny. When Butch announced her imminent arrival, no one believed him. But Jenny, probably 30 years younger than Butch, duly arrived, and they were married at Richardson. The bridal couple drove Old Joe back down the trail to McCarty, stopping at every cabin along the way so Jenny could become acquainted with the locals.

From McCarty, Butch and Jenny often drove Old Joe to one of the dozen or so lonely cabins Butch used as hunting and trapping camps. They would spend a night and often wake up to find Old Joe gone. "Now, you wait here, Jenny, and I'll go and get Old Joe," Butch would say, and he'd start out. He might walk to Rapids and ask me, "You seen Old Joe?"

"No, Butch. Is he lost again?"

"Naw, he's not lost, Frankie, just wandering. I'll find him."

Then he'd suggest we go hunting for a couple of days, and we'd climb into the mountains and kill a couple of sheep. We might sit around a campfire all night. Next day we'd pack the sheep out. He wouldn't mention he'd left Jenny at one of his cabins somewhere back in the hills.

He'd go back to McCarty, maybe finding Old Joe somewhere along the way. People at McCarty would ask, "Where's Jenny?"

"Oh. Jenny. My God, the poor girl. She's at Jarvis Creek," Butch would say. "I'll have to go get her." Such afterthoughts happened repeatedly.

Once while hiking up Ober Creek, which flows into Jarvis Creek, I passed a little cabin nestled in a bunch of cottonwood trees and heard a phonograph playing. Looking through my binoculars I saw Butch's buckboard.

I decided Butch was there, so I walked to the cabin and hollered. Jenny came to the door.

"Hello, Frank. Do you know where Butch is?" she asked.

"Isn't he here?"

"Oh no. He left a week ago looking for Old Joe."

She still had grub, but was tired of being alone.

A couple of days later as I walked back to Rapids I met Butch leading old Joe. I returned with him for Jenny, and with Old Joe and the buckboard the three of us went to Rapids. Butch and I hunted for a couple of days while Jenny worked at the roadhouse.

Jenny was usually fairly content wherever she was, and a good thing, too. For several winters Jenny was housekeeper and cook at Gordon's Roadhouse a place owned by Butch on the winter trail halfway between Birch Lake and Donnelly. He also owned a roadhouse at Beale's Cache where he and Jenny sometimes stayed.

After about ten years, Jenny went Outside to live with her mother, never returning to Alaska. I guess she was tired of being misplaced, and probably tired of cleaning up after Butch. She died within a few years.

One icy winter day about 1950 while I was driving on the Richardson Highway near Donnelly I saw a familiar figure shuffling along the side of the road. It was Butch with a seeing-eye dog, its leash snapped to a broad leather belt he wore around his parka. Though legally blind, the old man had walked 25 miles from Big Delta to Donnelly that day and was headed for Rapids.

I gave him a ride, and we had a nice visit, remembering the old days. He must have been close to 95 years old. He died two or three years later.

During the years I market-hunted, from 1915 through 1923, I killed about 280 sheep. I didn't kill that many caribou; no matter how I handled a caribou, it was heavy. The front half of the resident caribou around Rapids commonly weighed 165 pounds; the hind half 150. That's a lot of weight to pack out of the mountains. I preferred to hunt sheep, and the Road Commission preferred the sheep meat.

I was virtually the only one hunting around Rapids in those years. During that period probably fewer than a dozen other sheep were killed there by other hunters.

The Alaska Railroad was completed in 1923, making it practical to ship meat by sea from the states to Seward and on to Fairbanks by rail, ending the need for market hunting for Interior Alaska. In addition, the Alaska Game Law of 1925, enacted by Congress, legally ended commercial market hunting in Alaska.

This law also created the Alaska Game Commission, which recommended to Congress annual seasons and bag limits for game and fur animals, and started the long trail toward modern game management for Alaska.

The Chetaslina Grizzly

BY THE SPRING of 1917 the Valdez Trail in the vicinity of Rapids was in fair shape for a winter trail designed for horse-drawn sleds. Most construction crews had moved on and the demand for game meat had dwindled.

Walking over the Valdez Trail on my arrival in Alaska I had admired the great Wrangell Mountain Range, dominated by 14,163-foot Mount Wrangell and 16,237-foot Mount Sanford. In my two years of hunting and trapping from Rapids I had heard of the beauty of the Wrangells, and had heard it was great game country.

That June I walked from Rapids to Chitina, an Indian village on the bank of the Copper River, looking for work, not necessarily market hunting. Someone told me that Billy Cameron, a Road Commission foreman, was taking a crew to Tonsina to build a bridge. I went into the Overland Saloon and found Billy and several Road Commission teamsters I knew, including Jack Bishop.

I approached Billy, who often pretended to be hard of hearing. "How about a job, Billy?"

"Sure," he answered. "Are you a cook?"

"No, I'm not a cook."

"I'm glad you're a good cook," he came back.

"I'm *not* a cook," I yelled back.

He leaned closer, cupping a hand to his ear as we yelled back and forth. The teamsters were grinning broadly, aware that Billy was baiting me. They knew there was nothing wrong with Billy's hearing.

"Jack Bishop will help you pick out a cook's outfit," he said finally. "We leave tomorrow morning." Then he turned his back on me.

Whether I liked it or not, I was hired as a cook.

Jack Bishop took me to a Road Commission barn and dragged out a huge box of tin and enamel dishes, pans, meat saws, cleavers and butcher knives.

"Frank," he suggested, "why don't you go talk to Tex, our regular cook? Billy fired him for getting drunk, but drunk or sober, he knows cooking. Maybe he can give you some advice."

Bishop was looking out for his own stomach; he knew I wasn't a cook.

I found Tex in the Overland Saloon. Though pretty drunk, he gave me some basic recipes and told me how to bake bread, pies, and cakes. I wrote as he talked and kept buying him drinks as he gave me recipes. When I left him late that evening he was in bad shape.

At Tonsina we set up a big cook tent and a huge woodburning stove, with tables and benches where the crew ate. I did all right cooking meat and such things as rice and beans, but my breads weren't very good. My doughnuts came out heavy and soggy— real sinkers. My first pies and cakes were awful.

I was wrestling with a batch of bread dough one day after I had been on the job for about a week when two men rode up. They dismounted and came in. "We hear you're a market hunter," one of them said.

It was hot inside the cook tent, with the big woodstove blasting heat, which augmented the heat radiating through the canvas from the summer sun. I had tied the walls up, the doors were open, and I had removed my shirt. Mosquitoes were a plague, and to challenge them, I had several piles of smoldering Buhach, a pyrethrum insecticide. Sweat poured off my brow. Now and then I slapped a mosquito with a floury hand, and I waved others off.

I dropped the bread dough. "Yeah, I'm a market hunter, and a good one," I said. I sensed that the conversation had the potential of ending my career as a cook.

Jim Galen and Dave Compets were mining engineers. With a crew of 15 miners they planned to drive a tunnel in the Wrangell

Mountains to evaluate a copper deposit. They needed a hunter to provide meat for their camp. I agreed to hunt for them for $250 a month, plus board and room. The "room" was a tent.

The Alaska Road Commission paid workmen (and cooks) $4 a day, and took 60 cents out of that for board, thus paying a wage of $3.40 a day. That made $250 a month look pretty good.

After peaking in 1906, Alaska's gold output was on the decline. Gold mining had supported more than half of the 64,000 residents in the Territory, but with the failing mines, many residents were being forced to leave Alaska. Miners were searching for other minerals. Copper was one possibility.

The exploration tunnel was drilled at the head of the Chesnina River, six miles above the last timber. Pack horses carried tents, tools, dynamite, food—everything needed by the 17 men—about 30 miles from the 170-person Native village of Chitina on the Copper River. A Chitina Indian with a poling boat ferried the freight across the swift Copper River. The all uphill trail to the proposed tunnel was long and difficult.

Sheep ranged the ridges and across the big basin where the tunnel was being driven, so my first month of hunting was easy. Then the crew started blasting. This drove the sheep off the watershed, forcing me to hike about ten miles to the Chetaslina River watershed to find more sheep. That ten miles of rough mountainous country was a long way to pack meat. I generally killed the sheep near glaciers, for these white mountaineers seem to have an affinity for these great rivers of ice. Slopes next to an active glacier are almost invariably rugged, steep, and broken-up with sheared-off rocks and boulders, the residue of glacial action.

Wrangell Mountain Dalls ranged at higher altitudes than those in the Alaska Range around Rapids. At mid-summer I found them as high as 6,000 feet. Often I climbed to a mountain rim where I could sit and glass for sheep on and around a glacier that lay 2,000 feet below me. A surprising number of times I spotted them bedded on clear glacier ice a mile or more from rocks or dry ground. I suspect that mosquitoes drove them there, for those tiny pests were fierce that summer.

I used to get angry with the hard-working men driving the tunnel who seemed to gulp down the meat faster than I could shoot it. The two packers, Ed Young and Jorgeson, usually took a sheep or two to their cabin near the Copper River so they could have meat as they hustled their pack horses back and forth. That seemed excessive to me, but the bosses let them get away with it.

I weighed about 155 pounds, and in those steep, rocky mountains I regularly packed sheep weighing from 100 to 120 pounds, strenuous, dangerous work. Daily I risked falling. At times I balanced myself precariously with a sheep on my back next to sheer cliffs that dropped hundreds of feet. If I had stumbled or tripped I'd have died. In such places I walked *very* carefully.

The only other game I saw that summer was an occasional grizzly, but for some reason the bears didn't give me the problems those around Rapids had.

There was one exception. The packers, Ed Young and Jorgeson, were repairing harness at their cabin near the Copper River one October afternoon when they heard two bears growling and roaring a few hundred yards from their cabin. They ran outside and saw two big brown (grizzly) bears trying to kill each other.

They were so busy calming the pack horses upset by the roars and growls of the bears that they didn't get to watch much of the battle, which continued off and on most of the night. Neither of them got much sleep, and when morning came they were glad to throw pack saddles and loaded panniers on the horses and head for the tunnel camp.

Before leaving, however, they cautiously walked around the torn-up ground where the fight had taken place. Their only rifle was a .30-30 carbine, too light to be effective on a big brown bear, so they were afraid to do more than walk to the edge of the area to look. Leaving the battleground, they faintly heard a strange whistling-gurgling sound in the nearby spruce timber. They moved off quickly, peering uneasily back over their shoulders.

At the tunnel camp, they excitedly told about the big bear fight. One of the bears, they thought, had stampeded the pack train a couple of times, and either the same bear or another, had broken into one of their grub caches and destroyed a lot of food. They wanted those bears dead. Would I kill them? The bosses agreed that I should try to help the packers.

Carrying the remodeled light, short-barreled military .30-40

Krag Jorgenson rifle I used that summer, and wearing a packboard (I lived with that packboard on my back) I hiked to the place the packers described. A tremendous battle had obviously taken place there, for the ground in an area about the size of a football field was torn up. Grass and bushes were flattened, and there was much blood and bear hair scattered about.

Cautiously, I sneaked around, listening and watching. Near the edge of timber I found the body of a large adult brown bear with deep bites around his head and neck.

I started to roll him over to inspect the damage on the underside when I heard a strange whistling-gurgling noise in the dense timber perhaps 30 feet behind me. I grabbed my rifle, whirled, and threw off the safety, expecting the other bear to appear. Twigs cracked, and the strange whistling-gurgling sound gradually receded. I circled the timber patch and found a fresh blood-spotted trail leaving it. I was pretty sure the peculiar sounds came from the badly-hurt victor of the bear fight who had apparently winded or seen me and sneaked off.

I followed his tracks and drops of blood for eight miles along a deep, centuries-old bear trail to the Chetaslina River and lost the trail on a gravel bar near the Chetaslina Glacier, which flows off Mount Wrangell.

I had a hunting camp at the face of that glacier. It was only a tarpaulin spread over some willow bushes, with a little grub cached in a five-gallon can. There I remained for the night. Next day I hunted for sheep, but didn't see the injured bear. Late in the day I shot a large Dall ram and packed it back to the main camp the next morning.

A few days later I was again hunting in the Chetaslina drainage. I located a band of sheep on a cliff near the glacier about two miles from my camp, made a stalk, and killed a large ram. I dressed it, lashed it to my packboard, and started to pack it out.

The glacier moraine was too rough for me to cross, and the cliffs were too steep to climb. But between the glacier and the cliffs was a fair-sized stream I could walk beside. Even there the going was rough; it was one step or one jump at a time, from rock to rock.

I heard rocks rolling behind me and turned to look. There,

about 60 feet away, on his hind legs stood a huge brown bear. As I turned, he dropped to all fours and galloped to within 30 feet, where he again stood up, shaking his head and growling. It was then that I heard the same strange gurgle-whistle sound I had heard at the site of the big bear battle.

The bear was above me, and he was close. Too close. He was obviously unfriendly. Should I shed my packboard before I shoot? Or should I just shoot?

The bear dropped to all fours and bounded to within about 15 feet, where he again stood on his hind legs. I heard him growl with a humming sound almost like a hive of bees. He appeared to be working himself into a rage, for the volume and pitch of the strange whistling sounds and the growls rose.

Now I had no time to shuck my meat-heavy packboard—my life depended upon quick action. That bear could have been upon me in about two jumps. Sheep blood had soaked my overalls as I had dressed, handled, and packed the sheep; I must have smelled like a freshly killed mountain sheep. That meat smell could have attracted the bear. He could also have been an old sorehead with a grudge after being torn up by the bear he killed.

I noticed a spot of white fur on his neck—a good target. "I'll just kill him with one shot into his neck before he gets to me," I decided. I threw the Krag to my shoulder, held on the white spot, and fired.

That huge bear stood and absorbed my 180-grain bullet. His only reaction was to bring both front legs up and to make a half-choking, half-roaring sound. I fired again, aiming for his chest. He still stood on hind legs. By the third shot I was panicky, and I threw off to the left. This broke his shoulder and off-balanced him; he collapsed, falling backward. In moments he was dead.

I climbed out of the packboard, wiped sweat off my forehead, and examined the bear. In addition to the bullet holes I had put into him, he had deep wounds on his chest, neck and head. I stuck my fingers into them. One of the wounds led to a gash on his windpipe. No doubt that was what had caused the peculiar whistling-gurgling noises.

A patch of hide as big as a man's hand was missing from one shoulder. Myriads of whitesocks—tiny biting flies—were working on the raw flesh. He must have hurt all over from his wounds and from the bites of the flies. Apparently he had been in the high cool mountains for some time, for, although it was only early October, his rich dark brown fur was quite heavy. Stretched after I skinned him, the hide squared 10 feet 4 inches (average of greatest length and greatest width). His brown and yellow discolored teeth were worn nearly to the gums and he smelled strongly of salmon. No doubt he had been feeding on the fish on one of the tributaries of the nearby Copper River. He was far larger than most interior Alaska grizzlies, and he more resembled a big coastal brownie.

I packed the sheep to my jack camp and returned for the bear hide. Later that day I packed the sheep to the main tunnel camp, and returned to retrieve the bear's enormous skull, thinking the U.S. Biological Survey would like to have it. I often sent skins and skulls to add to their scientific collection.

To my surprise, the entire carcass, including the skull, was gone. Nothing remained but the entrails. Dried blood stained the ground and rocks. My three .30-40 cartridge cases stood neatly on end on a nearby rock. That wasn't where I had left them. I cast about and found moccasin tracks.

A year or so later Harry King, a Copper River Indian I happened across, told me that he and several other Copper River Indians hunting in the nearby mountains, heard my three hurried shots when I killed the big bear. "White man shoot awful fast. Maybe in trouble down there," Doc Villums, leader of the band, commented. "We better go see."

The Indians started looking for the white man in trouble, and soon located the dead bear. By then I was gone with the hide. They had cut the carcass up and packed the meat down into the timber where they camped for several days feasting on it.

I hunted for the mining crew until the end of October when tunneling ceased. The ore they found was rich, but as far as I know nothing was ever done about that copper deposit.

I returned to Rapids, and during the winter of 1917–1918 I again ran my 30-mile trapline between Darling Creek and my bench cabin in the Alaska Range.

In the Army

By 1918 THE ERA of horse-drawn sleighs on the Valdez Trail was nearing an end. The Alaska Railroad was near enough completion so that horse and dog teams, and an occasional tractor, were hauling freight and passengers between ends of steel. Track had been laid from Fairbanks south, and from Seward north.

The Valdez Trail was no longer the only route Outside from the Interior—in fact, now it wasn't even the preferred route. Much of the impetus to upgrade the old trail was gone, and construction on it went slowly. The need for game meat for roadhouses and for Road Commission crews dropped off.

The "War to End All Wars," was roaring full-blown in Europe, and the United States had been in it since April, 1917. In July, 1918, when I was 29 years old, I walked from Rapids the 220 miles to Fort Liscum at Valdez and enlisted in the Army. I was assigned to C Company, 14th Infantry, which shortly was taken to the Presidio in San Francisco by the Army transport *Sherman* , then by train to Camp Dodge, Iowa, to form a division.

That August, while at a target range, I managed to outshoot most of the other troopers, and the Colonel in charge asked me if I'd like to volunteer for sniper school.

"Mortality of snipers is very high," he warned. Nevertheless, I volunteered and spent six weeks at sniper's school at Camp Dodge.

Sniper trainees went to a firing range built in a former cornfield five days a week. A four-mule team arrived with a load of ammunition, which came in bandoleers of 60 rounds. We'd each hang two or three bandoleers over our shoulders and go to assigned sectors to shoot.

Each trainee had a telephone operator to report hits. Targets were at unknown distances from a trench or from behind some kind of a barricade. A pop-up target in the shape of a man would appear to be walking along a trench at anything from 100 to 500 yards. Perhaps just the head of the "man" would appear. Sometimes I'd have as much as a minute to get off a shot; other times I had to fire within seconds.

We used heavy-barreled .30-06 Springfield rifles equipped with Swazy prism telescopic sights, which resembled half of a pair of prism binoculars. They were good scopes, but not as good as the fine sporting scopes that became popular after World War II. Eye relief was very short—in fact, it was necessary to put your eye right up to the rubber cup on the scope. This wouldn't work, of course, except on a heavy rifle; the recoil from a light rifle would have jammed the eyepiece into your eye.

Nels Gilbertson and I were the only two from the 14th Infantry to attend sniper school. Gilbertson had been a market hunter in the Knik River and Matanuska country of Alaska. We often made a game of our target shooting, referring to our targets as "mountain sheep," or "grizzly bear," or "wolf." We'd yell back and forth to each other, challenging each other on difficult shots. In retrospect, I think the idea of shooting men bothered us; it was more acceptable to shoot at game animals.

Three evenings a week we attended class where we were lectured to by a Frenchman who had fought the Germans on the Western Front; his main theme seemed to be the short life span of snipers in the trenches of France.

I was still in sniper training at Camp Dodge when the great influenza epidemic of 1918 struck. It prevented the 87th Division we had formed from being shipped overseas. For a time I was assigned to help nurses tend to flu and pneumonia patients. Then for eleven nights I worked with Shorty, the driver of a horse-drawn ambulance.

"What do we do, haul sick people?" I asked him.

"Nope. Dead people," he replied.

We drove the ambulance around the base hospital. When a doctor came out and held up his hand we'd go inside with a stretcher and pick up a body and put it in the ambulance. I heard the death rate at Camp Dodge was the highest of any army camp in the United States.

Shorty was a career soldier with years in the service and he knew his way around. A solicitous nurse once asked us if we would like to have a little of the special flu medicine they were giving to patients.

"Yes, sister, we'd love to have some."

She took us into a dispensary where there were cases of bonded whiskey that was given to the flu patients. She poured each of us a drink and left. I'd have been satisfied with that, but not Shorty.

He shoved a bottle into my hip pocket and pulled my coat over it, and then tucked one into his pocket. We walked out past the nurse without her noticing the bulges.

For a time as we carried bodies out of the various wards we weren't very steady. The nurses and doctors probably assumed we were affected by the flu. We were, in a way.

Later that evening Shorty and I were sitting on the steps in front of the hospital. Business was slow, with no one dying. A colonel stopped and asked, "Are you working on this dead wagon?"

"Yes, colonel," I answered.

"That's a pretty terrible job you boys have," he commented.

"It's not too bad," I slurred, still feeling the effects of the whiskey.

I turned my back on him and took a big chew of Copenhagen snuff. Soon I leaned over and spit.

"What are you chewing?" the colonel wanted to know.

At my response, he said, "You'll never get the flu. That stuff'll kill the bugs before they get to you."

When the November 1918 armistice came I was transferred back to Fort Liscum, Valdez, where I had enlisted. I was discharged April 22, 1919, and I immediately walked back to Rapids, which I now regarded as home.

Many of the roadhouses along the Valdez trail were abandoned. The Northern Commercial Company had halted its winter stage line route to Valdez, as well as the dog team freighters they had maintained on the old trail. Practically all travel to the coast from Fairbanks now went via the Alaska Railroad route, even though the railroad was not yet completed. Horse and dog teams hauled people and freight the 122 miles between ends of steel at Healy and Talkeetna.

Black Rapids Roadhouse was for sale, and I bought it. I had saved some money while market hunting, and I had put some aside while I was in the army. I ran the roadhouse and market hunted until the spring of 1924. I needed meat for meals served at Rapids, and there were several Road Commission crews still working on the trail. I also sold meat to the few other roadhouses that remained. A loophole existed in the game laws; though a 1912 law forbade market hunting (a law that was largely ignored), it was legal to kill game to be served at roadhouses. When north-bound cars had room for it I sometimes sent meat to Fairbanks restaurants.

The Valdez Trail changed little during those years. Even when completed as a wagon road in the 1920s it was rough and difficult for summer auto travel. Its main winter use was for horse-drawn sleds and dog teams. Much of the summer traffic was by Alaska Road Commission horse teams driven by construction crews, although a few pioneer auto drivers like Bobby Sheldon, the Fraim brothers, and others, continued to tackle the rugged trail each summer.

As late as 1940, after 25 years of improvement, the trail was still not much more than a wagon road.

I frequently hired others to manage the roadhouse and do the cooking so I could spend my time hunting and trapping. Roadhouse business on the Valdez Trail was pretty leisurely in those years.

The sniper training I received in the army taught me the value of a telescopic sight. I never again owned a rifle that wasn't equipped with one. This made an immediate difference in my success as a market hunter, and it forever changed my hunting skills.

I remember one shot I made with a scope-equipped rifle that would have been extremely unlikely without the scope; in fact, it was an unlikely shot even with a scope.

Frank Glaser, hunting ptarmigan on Mount Wrangell, 1917. Fall is near, for the ptarmigan held by Glaser have started to turn from summer brown to winter white. Frank Glaser

*Frank Glaser
1917*

It happened in the spring of 1920, when the Road Commission moved into the Rapids area with about 50 men to clear snow from the road between Paxson's Roadhouse and Rapids. In those days there were no bulldozers; men with picks and shovels cleared the snow. Big, hard-packed slanting snowdrifts had built up on the trail, and that crew shoveled and picked their way through drifts so that a team of horses could pull a wagon through.

I had been out all day trying to find a caribou to take to the Road Commission camp to feed this huge crew. I walked along the trail, glassing as I went, but I saw nothing. Returning discouraged, I came upon the crew at the Glory Hole, a windy spot near Rainbow Mountain. Their camp, near a favorite caribou crossing, was nearby.

It was late afternoon, and as I came upon the digging men, one called, "Frank, we've been watching two caribou here all day. Look."

He pointed to two tiny spots—caribou lying on a snowdrift across the river. I looked with binoculars, and saw they were adults, and there was no calf near. Just what I wanted. But the creek was high, with water running on top of the ice—a hard place to cross. I decided to try a shot from where I was. If I killed an animal, then I could struggle across the creek and get it.

I carried a six and a half pound Savage bolt action .250/3000 with a three power telescopic sight, my favorite at the time. I sat and put the sighting picket far above the back of one of the caribou, thinking the distance was at least 500 yards. I eased off a shot. In a few moments we heard the bullet hit, and the caribou slid and rolled off the drift, dead.

The other caribou stood, staring.

"We can use two caribou," one of the men called.

"No," I said. "The one I killed is a pretty good-sized animal. He'll keep you going for a while."

I didn't dare shoot again. My chances of dropping the other caribou were too small. Those men didn't know how far above the back of that caribou I had held.

When I went to retrieve the animal, I roughly stepped the distance off at 750 yards.

Freighting with Dogs

THE TEMPERATURE HOVERED around zero, and daylight was just breaking when I stepped out of the roadhouse and watched Frank Tondro, otherwise known as the Malemute Kid, as he harnessed up. The Kid was about five feet three inches tall, weighed maybe 100 pounds, and was about 50 years old. He was a squeaky voiced, dried-up little fellow always dressed fancy. He resembled an arctic explorer with his elaborate squirrel skin parka, fur pants and fur mukluks, a show-off. But he knew how to handle dogs.

His dogs howled and barked with excitement as he went from animal to animal putting harness on while they were still tied to their houses. When harnesses were on all 27 dogs, he turned them loose. Then he stood by his towline, holding a big blacksnake whip, ready to stop fights. He called each dog to the towline, leader first. His leader leaned into the towline, keeping it taut as he snapped the other dogs into place one by one.

The Kid's 18-foot freight sled was loaded with more than 1,000 pounds, but when he yelled, "Come alive, there Tony," to his leader and the team leaped into action, it skidded down the trail almost as if it were empty.

Tondro stampeded to the Klondike in 1898. He walked over Chilkoot Pass and boated across Lake Bennett, shooting through the dangerous rapids of the upper Yukon. He started mining on Dominion Creek, and in the winter he hauled goods with a dog team for the store his father, Lyman Tondro, established in Dawson.

The Kid liked dogs. While at Dawson he picked up every stray that came along, eventually accumulating 30 or 40, which he liked to harness all at one time. This earned him his nickname. Author Jack London met and talked with the Kid, then used the name "Malamute Kid" in one of his stories, giving the Kid immediate fame.

The Kid drove his dogs to Fairbanks about 1915, and for several years he had a contract to haul mail in interior Alaska. He was working for the Alaska Railroad when I met him during the winter of 1919-20.

During the first third or more of this century sled dogs were the most important method of moving people and freight around mainland Alaska during winter. Sled trails spiderwebbed the land, with roadhouses about a day's travel apart where travelers could eat, rest, or sleep. The roadhouses provided individual doghouses or dog barns and stocked bales of dried salmon for dog food, as well as dried grass for bedding. Dog sled and dog harness makers made a nice living. Fishwheel operators on the Yukon and Tanana Rivers caught, dried, and sold tons of chum salmon for dog food. One dried salmon a day fed a medium-sized working dog. Chum salmon were (and are) called "dog" salmon—largely because it was the species most often dried and fed to dogs. Dog liveries were found scattered across country, where for a moderate price, dogs could be boarded through the summer. Fairbanks had two of these, and both were big businesses.

In addition, horse-drawn stages and double-ender sleds handled some routes. But horses couldn't handle many deep snow trails as well as dogs.

For a time, during winters, dog teams hauled freight and passengers between steel when the Alaska Railroad was under construction. The 470-mile railroad from the coastal town of Seward to the interior town of Fairbanks was built by the federal government during the years 1915-1923. Horses hauled much of the heavy freight along the right of way until steel was laid, when the railroad itself could do the hauling. But sled dogs also played a part.

During the winter of 1919-20, steel extended from Seward to mile 236, near Talkeetna, and from Fairbanks to Healy at mile

358, leaving a gap of 122 miles where dog teams, horses, and an occasional crawler tractor hauled freight and passengers.

There were many temporary construction camps and road-houses in this gap while the roadbed was being prepared. Dog teams driven by mushers from all over the Territory hauled passengers and light freight to these camps and roadhouses. The route led through 2,363-foot-high Broad Pass in the Alaska Range. For a time that winter I left my Black Rapids Roadhouse in the hands of a manager, and contracted with the railroad to drive a dog team between steel. While there I became familiar with the capabilities of working dogs, and at the same time I met some fabulous characters, including the Malemute Kid.

Hundreds of miners from the interior wanted to go Outside (to the states) in the fall to wait out the long Alaskan winter. By 1919 the Alaska Railroad route was favored over the Valdez Trail. This slowed business at my Rapids roadhouse almost to a standstill.

Passengers traveling by dog team from Healy to Talkeetna paid a fare of $100 one way. They often had to walk a good many miles in deep snow and on steep climbs. They paid their own roadhouse expenses.

That winter the Malemute Kid owned three huge dog teams—the team of 27 he drove, plus two others for which he hired drivers.

When spring came and dog team freighting ended for the season, the Kid had to find a place to feed his dogs for the summer. He considered too expensive the fish camps along the Tanana and Yukon Rivers where salmon were caught and fed to boarding sled dogs. Instead, he got a job as a bull cook at the railroad construction camp at Healy. A few days after he went to work, the construction crew got up in the morning to find nearly a hundred sled dogs tied up around camp. That didn't endear him with the workers. The dogs were noisy, made messes, and attracted flies.

Being bull cook, he had access to food scraps, which went to his dogs. In this way he managed to keep them alive through the summer. However, that fall, before snow fell the foreman blew up. "Get those damned dogs to hell out of here," he ordered the Kid. "You're fired."

Come snowfall, the Kid again ran three dog teams between

steel. But the following spring all the foremen were wise to him, and no one along the line would hire him as a bull cook. That didn't stymie the Kid. Just before the last snow melted, when winter freighting was at an end, he hooked up all his dogs and left Healy, heading for Talkeetna. That must have been some sight— around 90 dogs yelping along in one team. At every construction camp he turned a bunch of dogs loose.

Naturally, the pooches ran to the camp's garbage dump and hung around the cook shack. By the time the Kid reached Talkeetna he had a sled full of harness and no dogs. Construction workers at the various camps almost invariably adopted the dogs. Many built houses for them and fed them through the summer in the belief they were lost. Some started planning to develop their own dog teams.

After first snowfall the Kid showed up and "found" his dogs. He called them by name, petted them, and made a big fuss, explaining that the dogs had gotten away from him the previous winter, and that he'd been hunting them ever since. After that song and dance, he hooked his dogs into the team and happily drove away with all his dogs fat and in good condition.

The construction workers were afraid to object, because stealing a man's sled dog in those days was a terrible sin—almost like horse thievery in the days of the Old West.

When his dogs were working the Kid fed them well and took good care of them. But feeding the mob through the summer when they didn't work was a real problem.

The Kid was a kind owner and didn't abuse his teams, although he expected every dog to work when in harness. Like almost every other musher he carried a whip, mostly to prevent and break up fights. Hollywood movies and cartoons to the contrary, when there are 15 or 20 dogs strung out ahead, it's impossible to reach all of them with a whip. Some dogs are lazy, though, and they'll trot along all day with slack traces. Such dogs need special attention.

Until the Kid came up with the idea of using a BB gun on lazy dogs, they were pretty safe until it was clear they were non-workers. Then, sadly, they were usually put down. The Kid bought a spring-powered BB gun and carried it in a scabbard on his sled. When a dog wasn't working, the Kid would call his name and put a BB into his rear. Most dogs would shape up and start pulling. Next time the Kid called his name the dog usually responded without use of the BB gun. The low-velocity BBs didn't penetrate a sled dog's heavy coat—they just stung.

The idea spread until almost every dog team driver freighting and hauling passengers between steel carried a BB gun.

Some time in the 1920s the Kid guided a woman lawyer from Holland around Alaska. They made several long trips with his dog team. She was an attractive lady in her 30's and after several weeks the Kid proposed to her. She turned him down, and caught a train for Seward to return home. The train broke down, and as it sat idle on the tracks the Kid drove up with his dog team. He proposed again, and the lady decided he was such an unusual man she couldn't refuse him again. They were married and lived in Fairbanks for a time. As late as 1925 the Kid was running "Dog teams for hire" advertisements in the *Fairbanks News Miner*. The couple lived in Anchorage for a time, then moved to California and later to Texas. Sometime during the 1930s while his wife and daughter were visiting abroad, Tondro disappeared. It was assumed he was murdered.

One cold morning when I was on that dog-team-freighting job between steel, I watched the tiny Kid try to break his loaded sled free after it froze down overnight. He lunged against the gee pole and bounced back. Again and again he threw his hundred pounds against the sled, only to bounce back each time. Disgusted, he finally said "To hell with it," and harnessed his dogs, but instead of laying the towline out straight ahead of the big, heavily loaded freight sled, he layed it out at a 90 degree angle to the sled. When the team was all hooked up, he yelled, "Ok Tony, come alive there," and the team lunged against the frozen-down sled.

It didn't move. The dogs were jarred to a stop, and looked back in confusion. Three more lunges by the dogs failed to break the sled loose. Finally the Kid gave up and rounded up three or four other mushers, including me, to pry and heave on the sled to break it loose.

Except on an unusually smooth and straight trail, the driver of a heavily loaded freight sled doesn't ride on the rear, as depicted in some movies. He has to be at the front of the sled in order to guide it and keep it on the trail. For this he uses a gee pole—a three-inch diameter spruce pole lashed to the sled and projecting forward at almost shoulder height. When the sled freezes down overnight, a quick jerk with the gee pole usually loosens it. When the sled refuses to track behind the dogs, or threatens to turn over on a steep pitch, the driver manhandles it with the gee pole.

In the early years, dog team freighters often rode a short pair of skis with simple loop bindings as he hung onto the gee pole or the towline and the team dragged him along. Then, about 1920, the weegee board appeared. This was a sled-like ski, about 18 inches wide and three feet long. A line from the front of the weegee board was snapped into the towline. The musher balanced himself on the board and worked the gee pole as needed.

There were many good sled builders in those years, and they were kept busy. Building a dog sled is an art as much as a science. Split birch sleds have always been the most popular in Alaska because they are tough and light. A properly made, limber, sled, lashed together with babiche (rawhide) will ride over tussocks, up and down stream banks, over logs, adjusting to bumps. A sled that is bolted together is too stiff, and will soon break; a dog sled must give with the unevenness of the trail.

Freighting sleds up to about 20 feet in length sold for about $200 in the 1920s. Lightweight 12 to 14-foot sleds were about $150. Some hickory sleds were built, but they are heavier than the birch, and when the temperature drops to 40 or 50 below, a sudden jolt sometimes snaps hickory stanchions or runners. Not so with a properly-seasoned birch sled.

The Malemute Kid wasn't the only unusual character freighting between steel when I was there. Geepole Larson was another. He owned a team of big, powerful, quarter-breed wolves, one of the craziest dog teams I've ever seen. All the drivers knew about Geepole's team, and did their best to avoid it. The moment they were harnessed, hooked up, and turned loose, that team lit out in whatever direction they happened to be headed, and nothing would stop them.

Maurice Moreno, who owned a roadhouse at McKinley Park, grew a little garden each year. He kept a pole fence around it.

Invariably when leaving Moreno's, Geepole's dogs ran under that fence and pulled it down with the sled. Moreno would patiently rebuild it, but the next time Geepole was there, his dogs would tear the fence down again. Moreno was angry at Geepole all the time.

One spring, Geepole talked Moreno into taking care of his dogs for the summer while he went off to work at a mine in the Kantishna country. Moreno tied Geepole's dogs in front of the roadhouse. They were noisy, and that upset Moreno, because his guests complained.

Harry Lucke and I often stayed together in a cabin near Moreno's Roadhouse. When Moreno took care of Geepole's dogs, Lucke and I started to needle Moreno. Around midnight I would step outside of our cabin and cut loose with a wolf howl. Geepole's nine wolf dogs would open up and answer me, and the roadhouse would almost vibrate with the noise. Moreno would rush out angrily in his nightgown and slap some of the poor innocent wolf dogs. Lucke and I, usually relaxed and happy from the effects of prohibition days fig wine, would go to bed chuckling.

We teased Moreno like that for some time. Then he outwitted us. He built a four-foot-high board fence and drilled holes in it, then threaded the dogs' chains through the holes, and tied a rope to each dog chain. The ropes ran to the roadhouse door. When a dog let out a peep, Moreno pulled a rope, yanking the dog against the fence. The dog would scream, of course, and as often as not Moreno would punish the wrong dog. When a dog made a noise, he'd simply start pulling ropes.

He succeeded in curing those dogs of making noise. In the end I could howl all I wanted, but those nine big dogs would simply sit there quietly, glumly eyeing the roadhouse door and Moreno's ropes.

Some drivers abused their dogs. I'll never forget the Swede we called "Laughing Ole" who freighted between steel. He had a team of 20 small Indian or Native type dogs weighing 35 or 40 pounds each. They always looked about half starved.

I had known Ole several years earlier when he worked on a Road Commission gang on the Richardson Highway near Rapids. I often visited the bunkhouse where he stayed. One evening when I was visiting, George, one of the workers, told a funny joke. At the punch line all but Ole roared with laughter. Ole didn't get it, and sat sadly staring at George.

Next morning after breakfast Ole started laughing. He laughed until he was weak, and his sides pained him.

"What are you laughing at now, you crazy Swede?" someone asked.

"Oh, dat yoke George told last night," he replied.

Laughing Ole.

One day when I was on the trail between steel with my dog team I was stopped, resting the dogs. It was calm, and sounds carried a long way in the 30 below zero air. I heard Laughing Ole coming for a couple of miles, for he was yelling and screaming at his dogs. Now and again I heard a dog yelp.

When he came into sight I saw him run up beside his moving team, kicking dogs. He started at the wheel dog and kicked each animal in turn, right up to and including the leader. Other drivers also reported seeing him do that. Ole had no business handling dogs.

A few days later I was at a bunkhouse near Hurricane Gulch. My dogs were tied up for the night. Snow 15 or 20 feet deep had completely buried the bunkhouse. A sloping runway had been dug from the door of the bunkhouse to the top of the snowdrift. Perhaps 20 men were sitting around on straw-ticked three-decker bunks, and at tables, talking, playing cards, relaxing. It was warm inside, and the door had been propped open.

We heard Laughing Ole coming up the trail, hollering and cursing at his dogs as usual, and we expected that he and the team would go by. Instead, his leader dashed down the snow ramp and into the bunk house, followed by the team of 18 or 20 dogs. Dogs crawled under bunks and tables as they pulled and scratched on the wooden floor. Laughing Ole, yelling, jammed the sled across the doorway so it couldn't go any farther, then he climbed over it and into the melee of scrabbling animals, kicking and yanking and screaming at them. He fished his leader out from under a bunk, lay down on the floor, and started chewing on one of his leader's ears.

He couldn't have done much damage to the poor dog's ear, for Laughing Ole had few teeth.

The crew took to the upper bunks when the dogs arrived, but soon a couple of men climbed down with me and we yanked Laughing Ole off of his leader. Others pitched in to straighten the mess and we got the team and the sled with Laughing Ole back on the trail.

Long before the Alaska Railroad was built, mushers all over Alaska held contracts to haul the winter mail. I knew Bill Burke and Fred Milligan who hauled mail the 300 dogteam-miles from Nenana to McGrath. To support their dogs, they owned salmon-catching fishwheels at Nenana on the bank of the Tanana River and each year hired men to operate them. The salmon were split and dried, and then tied in bales of about 50 pounds. They often hauled nothing but dried fish so they could have dog feed along the trail when hauling mail.

They usually made a monthly trip with anything from 500 to 1,000 pounds of mail, driving one or two teams of 25 to 30 dogs. Often they carried passengers.

The Nenana to Nome winter mail route, part of which Burke and Milligan plied, was made famous by the spectacular relay of dog teams that hauled serum during the Nome diphtheria epidemic of 1925. The drivers who participated in that 600-mile dash traveled mostly in short relays, carrying a single box of serum on their otherwise empty sleds. Yet they were acclaimed heroes by the outside world. The heavily loaded mail teams traveled the same route and carried the bulk of the serum. They bucked the same storms and survived the same temperatures, but were hardly noticed.

Gradually through the 1920s and into the 1930s airplanes took over the mail routes, and the picturesque mail team dogs disappeared, along with most other freighting dog teams. With them went dog liveries, now-unneeded roadhouses and government relief cabins, harness and sled-makers, and the business of producing tons of chum salmon for dog food. By the 1950s most of the old winter trails were unused and overgrown, discernable only from the air.

Dog teams hung on in remote Indian and Eskimo villages until the late 1950s and early 1960s when practical snow machines appeared, so that for two to three decades, most of Alaska's working dog teams were Native-owned. Dog teams were capable of wonderful feats.

Years after I drove dogs between steel, I lived in the coastal arctic Eskimo village of Kotzebue and watched the spectacular arrival of the biggest dog team I ever saw. Bush pilot Archie Ferguson had been forced down 200 miles east of Kotzebue in the Zane Hills while flying a four-place Stinson airplane on skis. He and his passenger were rescued a few days later by another pilot. Archie hired a group of Kotzebue Eskimos and their dog teams to retrieve his plane.

They drove their teams to the downed Stinson and hooked them to it, then headed for Kotzebue. Days later they arrived in Kotzebue after dark and most of the villagers, including me, turned out to watch. I'd have given a lot to have been able to take a picture of that scene.

The team of nearly 70 dogs was stretched far ahead of the airplane, moving it swiftly over the snow. Seven or eight dog sleds, carrying tents, tools, food, bedding, and extra clothing, were strung out in tow behind the airplane. Eskimos sat inside the airplane, while others skied alongside and at the head of the dog team. It was a spectacular and triumphant arrival.

The Box Canyon Grizzly

IN 1918 A TOW-HAIRED PROSPECTOR named Elmer stampeded from
Valdez, Alaska, to Fort Norman in the District of Mackenzie,
west of Great Bear Lake, where an oil strike had been made, and
there were rumors of gold. He spent the summer, fall, and winter
there seeking gold before he became discouraged and decided to
return to his placer diggings near Valdez. A number of Eskimos
were freighting for the stampeders, using their teams of powerful, wolf-like dogs. Among the latter were several teams from
Victoria Land, more than 100 miles to the northeast.

Elmer bought one of these teams and started homeward. He'd
never handled such fine dogs and was amazed at their power and
endurance. They were far bigger than the 50 and 60-pound huskies of Alaska, and when he arrived at Valdez after a lengthy trip
he was in love with them. Nothing could have persuaded him to
part with these magnificent animals.

One day in August, 1921, I sat on a mountainside near my
Black Rapids roadhouse, training my binoculars on one of the
biggest grizzly bears I'd ever seen. He was not only big, but he
was black, an unusual color for a grizzly in that part of the Alaska
Range. I had seen the big bear several times during the summer
across the Delta River from the roadhouse and became excited
every time I spotted him. Little cream-colored Toklat-type grizzlies were fairly common in that country—in fact the region was

known for its bears. One day in the nearby Granite Creek country I counted 11 grizzlies in sight at once. But I had never seen
one nearly as big as that black animal. Butch Stock was with me
on two occasions when the bear was visible. "That's an outstanding bear," he concluded, after we had watched it for a time from
about a mile away.

I'd tried several times during the summer to ford the river so
I could hunt for him, but the Delta is a deep, swift glacial stream—
a mean river to cross—and I was forced back every time. The
river remained high until freeze-up that fall, too, but that August
day I made up my mind to get that black bear, and began by
trying to figure a way to cross the river. As it turned out, I never
did make it that fall.

One morning that fall I heard my three sled dogs barking. Occasionally a grizzly bear or a caribou wandered near the roadhouse,
so I grabbed a rifle and stepped outside. Instead of game in the
yard, there were two dogs. But what dogs! Big, long-legged and
wolf-like, they weighed about 120 pounds each - twice the weight
of the biggest of my sled dogs. Both were males and I thought they
might fight my chained dogs, so I decided to run them off.

"Git," I yelled and heaved a rock at them. They dodged and
sat looking at me. After they had dodged two or three more rocks
and showed no sign of leaving, or of fighting, I gave up.

"C'mere, then," I called. They ran up to me, wagging their
tails as though they'd known all along they'd be welcome. I tied
them, thinking their owner would soon be along looking for them.

That fall, three Ford Model Ts managed to bounce their way
over the rough trail. I asked the drivers to spread word up and
down the road about the dogs. Freeze-up came and no one had
claimed them. I needed a couple more sled dogs anyway, so I
didn't really mind. I named them Yukon and Red.

The first time I harnessed them with my three dogs the big
dark fellow, Yukon, calmly trotted to the leader's position. None
of my dogs was much good as leader, so I left him there. We
started off, and to try him, I softly called, "Gee!" He didn't hesitate a second, but whirled in his tracks. He made a fine leader—
always picking the best going and promptly answering commands.
Besides, he pulled like a horse and somehow pepped up the whole

team. Ordinarily, pushing a sled and yelling at mule-headed sled dogs is hard work, but with Yukon in the lead and Red pulling at the wheel (next to the sled), I actually enjoyed traveling.

That winter, as usual, I trapped across the Delta River. Fox skins brought good prices, and I enjoyed getting out despite the cold. One day along in February, when patches of fog lay here and there, as they always do when it's real cold—it was at least 45 below that day—I was across the river driving the team up a box canyon. Almost always there's enough breeze in a little canyon like that to keep the willows free of frost, but this day I noticed a little patch of frost-covered willows on the side of a steep slope. I couldn't figure it out, so I stopped and looked it over with my binoculars. There was an opening right below the willows—a bear's den, I realized. The bear's breath was freezing and piling up on the willows. "Now, I wonder . . . Maybe it's the big fellow," I thought. "I'll just watch and see."

From then on, every time I went past there, I'd stop and look with the glasses. The bear stayed denned up through February, March, and April.

On the morning of May 6, 1922, I stepped out of the roadhouse, rifle in hand and a light pack on my back. Winter was leaving the rugged Alaska Range; snow was melting, it was warm, and I wanted to be out in the hills. Any excuse would do. I told the Hammonds, the couple operating the roadhouse for me, that I was going to cross the river to see if the bear was still in his den. I habitually took a couple of dogs with me on my hikes, so I turned Yukon and Red loose.

There was still good ice on the river, even though several inches of water was flowing over it, so I crossed and started up the mountain. Long before I got to the den I saw fresh tracks coming out of it. The bear had cleaned his den, and part of the dirt had rolled down the slope onto the snow. The tracks at the den were so enormous I was sure they had been made by the big black grizzly.

I spent ten minutes reading sign at the den. He'd loafed around for several days after emerging—probably coming out and lying in the sun during warm days, then crawling back and sleeping in the den at night. Fresh tracks, looking perhaps two hours old, led up the box canyon. Sheer cliffs rose from both sides. I knew that within a mile the canyon ended abruptly in a wall. The bear was trapped.

Three inches of snow had fallen during the night, making for good tracking, but fresh snow on top of the hard-packed old drifts also made the floor of that steep canyon slicker than grease. I buckled on steel ice creepers I always carried in my pack, and started on the fresh trail. That bear laid the biggest tracks I had ever seen. He walked kind of pigeon-toed, and the tracks were spaced almost two feet apart. He had a good three-foot stride, too.

His huge claws showed in every track in that fresh snow. I regretted bringing the two dogs. I figured if I jumped the bear they'd be an awful nuisance. I considered taking them back to the roadhouse and returning alone. Then I decided not to, for if I jumped the bear at close range they'd probably high-tail it home anyway—sled dogs usually don't care much about fighting bears.

The dogs kept trying to break ahead of me and then seemed anxious to take off on the track. I couldn't figure that out, and began to get a little anxious for them. The canyon narrowed to about 25 or 30 feet in width. The bear was in it, I knew, and couldn't get out except by passing me and the dogs. I didn't know where I'd run into him, but I sure hoped I'd be able to drop him before he got to a dog if they were foolish enough to tackle him.

The tracks led up the center of the canyon for about half a mile. I saw where the bear had tried to climb out; there were steep gulch-like chimneys here and there in the canyon wall and the bear had tried them all. He had gone up each chimney as he came to it until it became too steep for him, and he had to turn and slide down; then he'd try another.

It was getting more difficult to hold the dogs back. I didn't want to make any more noise than necessary, so I had to "shout at them softly" as they crowded me. I began to get keyed up. I wanted the bear, but didn't want the dogs to get hurt. Once in a while the warm sun caused a rock or a bunch of snow to slide down the side of the canyon. Every time that happened I whirled, expecting the bear. What confused me, though, was the way those dogs behaved. They dashed right at each slide, bristling and growling. They sure didn't act like any sled dogs I'd ever seen.

We came to the last bend in the canyon. The bear wasn't in sight. I could see all the lichen-encrusted walls that formed a tight box out of which *nothing* could climb. The floor of the canyon was 25 or 30 feet wide at the end, and there was absolutely no cover.

Puzzled, I stood looking at the tangle of fresh bear tracks. He had gone to the end of the canyon and returned half a dozen times, circling and looking for a way out. Opposite me was a narrow gash in the wall, where another chimney went up out of sight. It had a good 35 degree slope four or five feet wide. I knew from once climbing it that it ended in a sheer cliff.

"Damn!" I said as I looked closer. The bear's tracks were in the chimney—going up, but not coming down.

I heard a clatter, then saw loose snow and stones bounce around the bend in the chimney, right above me, not more than 30 feet distant. Suddenly, heading straight for me, almost filling the chute, came the bear, sitting and sliding. He evidently didn't realize I was there. That black, silver-tipped, skidding bear looked absolutely gigantic. I lifted my .30-06 rifle, but before I could shoot, Yukon and Red bounded past me to meet the bear head-on.

"Yukon, Red, come back here, damn it!" I yelled, at the same time trying to get a bead on the bear. I'd probably have managed a good shot, too, because the bear was sitting, and his chest was up where I could hit it. But those crazy dogs got in the way and I had to shoot to one side.

Wham! the echoes in the canyon almost deafened me. I broke the bear's left shoulder with that shot. Yukon met him head-on just as I fired, and the startled bear swiped at him with a snow-shoe-sized paw—and missed.

The bear roared with surprise as the slug and the two dogs hit him at the same time. Bear and dogs rolled onto the floor of the canyon, right at my feet. It happened in a flash. I was so amazed I didn't have time to move, and probably couldn't have if I'd tried.

The bear picked himself up, looked around as though he couldn't believe what was happening, shook himself, and beat it down the trail as fast as he could, with the dogs swarming around him. I could see for 70 or 80 yards down the canyon, and tried to line the rifle on him. Every time I did a dog flashed by, so I didn't get to fire. Then, bear bawling and dogs growling, they disappeared around a bend.

I started to run toward them and had gone about 50 feet when I saw the dogs coming back, running hard, with the bear behind them. They were heading right for me.

I skidded to a stop, raised the rifle—and one of my creepers slipped. I landed flat on my back, both feet in the air. I expected the dogs to dash in behind me, trying to get me to pull the bear off their tails, and for the bear to climb all over me any second. It was a lucky thing I'd broken one of his shoulders with my shot —now the dogs could outrun him. Otherwise I think he'd have caught them in that narrow canyon.

Instead of leading the bear to me, they took the angry and bawling critter right past me to the head of the canyon. I twisted around as they passed within 15 feet and fired without aiming. The bear lurched at the shot. Gosh, he looked big! He kept right after the dogs—just boiling mad and blaming them for his troubles. They ran to the end of the canyon, where the bear sat up and faced them, swatting at them with his one good paw.

I got to my feet, set the creepers firmly in the packed snow, and watched for an opening. Every time I was ready to shoot, a dog got in the way.

I groaned in exasperation and stood watching. Neither dog had been touched, and they were having one hell of a good time. Red would work behind the bear and actually leap on his back, slashing at him all the while; Yukon danced back and forth in front, keeping him busy. And then it dawned on me: these were experienced bear dogs, working as a team! One dog kept the bear busy while the other leaped in and slashed.

I figured the bear would make another break for it, so I backed up to the canyon wall to give him plenty of room to go by. I still couldn't line the sights up on a vital spot. Once I threw the rifle to one side just as I fired, for Red dashed into my line of sight. I didn't miss that dog by two inches. The slug caught the bear in a hind foot.

The bear started down the canyon again, the dogs growling at his heels. I swung and snapped a shot as they went by. Before long they returned, with the bear again chasing the dogs. He bounded along on three legs, his lips curled back, his white teeth showing with every jump. Again I slammed a shot into him as he ran by. He passed so close I could see individual hairs in his rippling, silver-flecked hide.

This happened twice more and I got in two more quick shots. One time the bear would be in the lead; next the dogs were hotfooting it out in front, tails between their legs and heads over their shoulders. They actually egged the bear on!

Every time I fired, loud echoes slammed back and forth in that little canyon. The roaring and bawling of the animals sounded unreal. Finally they stopped not more than 20 feet from me and the bear sat up to face the dogs. He was weakening. He squatted, mouth open, left leg dangling. Blood oozed from his black hide, and the floor of the canyon was bloody where he had passed. I could hear him panting, and every few seconds he let out a loud bawl.

Red climbed on his back, growling, dancing, and slashing with those wolf teeth. "Easy, boys, easy! Let me have him. Get back Red, Yukon. Get out of the way," I yelled, anxious for an opening as the dogs danced in and out, slashing at the reeling bear. I saw my chance and got in a good chest shot and the bear dropped, belly down. A final shot in the neck quieted him for good. The two dogs climbed atop him and wooled him some more.

"Where'n hell did you dogs learn to fight a bear like that?" I burst out at them, relieved. "You two crazy mutts damn near got us all killed!"

That bear was a monster. The hide, after I peeled it off and packed it home, squared out 10 feet 8 inches (average of greatest length and greatest width). The dark, lustrous fur was tipped with silver, and was as fine a trophy as I've ever seen. The skull, cleaned later and measured while it was still green, was 17 inches long. I didn't measure the width.

As I skinned the bear, Yukon and Red curled up in the snow with their tails over their faces, and went to sleep. Now and then rocks clattered and rolled off the walls of the canyon; each time they'd bound to their feet and rush toward the noise, and then they'd run over and bite the bear again. I had a difficult time skinning that bear on the steep, slick slope; by the time I finished the bear and I both had rolled and slid about 50 feet downslope.

About the middle of June I was replacing some chinking on the front of the log roadhouse when a Model T Ford pulled up and stopped. I looked up, waved, and started towards it. In those days cars were few and far between. The driver—a fellow with straw-colored hair—climbed out, then stiffened suddenly as he saw Yukon and Red tied nearby. He ran over to them, stooped, and hugged them to him, petting them and making a big fuss. I walked over, and the guy stood up with a grin on his face.

"You know those dogs, mister," I asked.

"Sure do," he said. "They're mine. My last name's Elmer, from down Slate Crick way. I've got placer diggings there and these dogs followed Wilson Miller, my packer, out to the trail. He tried to drive them back, but I guess they wandered this way instead. I've wondered ever since what happened to them. Looked all over for 'em."

They were part of his team of Victoria Land dogs, and he'd kept them at the mine as watchdogs for his kids. They ran loose, played with the children and kept bears from wandering too close to camp. Elmer had left the rest of the team at Valdez, where he lived winters. The one I called Yukon had been his leader. After following the packer and his horses from Elmer's mine to the Valdez Trial, they wandered down the trail 40 miles or so to my place.

When I told him how they had handled the grizzly Elmer said, "That's nothing. You ought to see the whole team tackle a polar bear. Those Eskimo dogs from the Canadian arctic are the best damn bear dogs in the world. They have to be or they wouldn't last long."

I hated to see them go. Until some years later, when I had my own wolf-dog leader, Yukon was the best leader I ever had.

Several people who saw the bear hide wanted to buy it, but I wouldn't sell. I was willing to part with any hide I had—except that one. An Alaska Road Commission superintendent offered me $150 for it, but I turned him down.

That fall I guided a party of sheep hunters into the Jarvis Creek country, and when I got back, Mrs. Hammond met me at the door.

"I sold that big bear hide to the editor of *Outlook* magazine," she said proudly. "He was traveling through and happened to see it. Here," she said, handing me a slip of paper, "I've got a $100 check for you!"

Doctor's Orders

BILLY FRAIM WAS HAULING PASSENGERS—or trying to—from Valdez to Fairbanks. The trail was a veritable quagmire—suitable, really, only for horses. One spring day in 1921 Billy drove up to Rapids in a Model T Ford, having taken all day to drive from Yost's, 25 miles to the south. Yost's had been abandoned for two or three years.

As he pulled to a stop the mud-spattered Ford was spouting steam two feet into the air. And Billy was excited.

"Frank, you've got to do something about those bears down by Yost's," he said.

"Who, me?" I said. "That's way out of my territory, Billy."

"But somebody's got to do something. It isn't safe to travel that road." Billy almost shouted.

The three passengers, two women and a man, stood next to Billy and loudly agreed with him. They kept shaking their heads and looking at the hood of the steaming Ford.

I wasn't too surprised to hear Billy's complaint. I'd heard that the grizzlies near Yost's were thicker than fleas, and every now and then someone traveling the trail was frightened pea-green by one or more grizzlies there.

"Frank," Billy said, "this morning I came around a bend near Yost's, and one of those white-colored bears—a reg'lar monster—was right in the middle of the road. I guess I got excited, and instead of slowing down I yanked the throttle and went faster. You know, the road's pretty good there for a ways.

"I scared the bear all right—at first. He ran down the road ahead of us, but I gained on him. That was a mistake."

The three passengers stood behind Billy, nodding and looking solemn.

"All of a sudden," Billy continued, "he stopped running and stood up. Lord, man, he must have been eight or nine feet tall—I looked *up* at him—and he wanted to fight the car!"

Billy reached over and patted the Ford like it was a horse or something alive.

"I slammed on the brakes and the reverse pedal both at once. Practically threw my passengers through the windshield."

By then Billy was waving his arms in my face and the passengers were all talking at once, trying to help Billy tell the story.

"I'll bet I wasn't five feet from that monster when I stopped. The women screamed and I yelled and honked the horn and raced the motor—and that bear, on his hind legs, snarled and walked right up to the car! It happened so quick I didn't have time to back up. He swatted the hood once, then I guess the noise scared him and he took off into the willows. I got out of there fast, believe me!"

I looked at the hood of the Ford, and sure enough it had been bashed in and there were deep claw scratches in the metal.

I didn't dwell on Billy's problems—I was busy with my own life, and didn't think it was my place to go to Yost's to shoot grizzlies because they upset travelers.

That fall, Dr. E. W. Nelson, chief of the U.S. Biological Survey which loosely regulated hunting and trapping in the Territory, spent about a week at my Black Rapids Roadhouse collecting small bird and mammal specimens. He was a tall, gray-haired, distinguished-looking man in his 70s.

I was interested in his work and took time off from my market hunting to show him around. One day, as he was searching the country with his binoculars, a cream-colored grizzly wandered out along a gravel bar of the Delta River.

"Frank, isn't that an unusual color for a grizzly?" he asked.

"Gosh no, Doc. Most of them around here are that color," I told him.

"How common are they?"

"Too common, as far's I'm concerned. They give me a scare every now and then. Why, there's a place up the road that's just alive with 'em," I said, and mentioned the river bar near Yost's, and I laughingly told him about Billy Fraim's experience.

Dr. Nelson became excited and made me tell him more. This was 1921, and science was still finding new species of birds and mammals in Alaska. Expeditions were being made to Alaska simply to collect birds, mammals, and fish.

As a rule the cream-colored grizzlies were not large, I told Dr. Nelson, but they were often nasty tempered. I told him about some that had charged me while I was hunting, explaining, "Most will high-tail it when I yell, or fire a shot. But now and then one will decide to attack. They're mostly a nuisance," I said.

The Alaska Road Commission teamsters hated them and complained about the runaways and near runaways—especially around the river bar near Yost's. They didn't enjoy trying to rein down four terrified horses that bolted when they saw or smelled a grizzly.

Dr. Nelson asked if I'd collect a large group of these bears for the Biological Survey. The Survey had bear specimens from other parts of the Alaska Range, but none from that particular area. I agreed to collect some grizzlies for him at Yost's the following spring.

"How many do you want?" I asked.

"All you can get," he said.

That winter Nelson wrote me, repeating his request for "a large representative series of those straw-colored grizzly bears." He would pay me $50 for each specimen, which was to include the hide, the clean skull, measurements, and weights. He told me how to take the measurements he wanted.

There was little traffic over the Valdez Trail that winter of 1921–22, and the ammunition I ordered from Fairbanks never arrived. Come spring, I rummaged around the roadhouse to find ammunition for my bear hunt, finally accumulating an assortment of about every kind of .30-06 cartridge then made. Some of the stuff was at least 10 years old. I had a few 220-grain loads, some 180s, and others of 150, 145, and 172 grains. Some way to start a grizzly hunt!

I started out May 15 by dog team and drove up the Delta River on the ice toward Yost's. It was about noon when I pulled into the McCallum Signal Station a couple of hundred yards from the abandoned Yost's roadhouse.

Jim McHenry and McCann, the two soldiers stationed there, were just leaving to visit another station 20 miles down the trail where they planned to stay a while. I told them why I had come and got their permission to tack hides on the side of the Signal Corps station buildings. These included a log telegraph station, a log barn, and an oversize cache.

As usual huge snowdrifts had built up around Yost's old road-house, and I drove my dog team right up to a second-story window, removed it, and stepped inside. I could have easily driven the dog team over the roof where the winter's snow had drifted to the eaves.

The downstairs was filled with snow. Evidently someone had left the door open the previous fall. I found where the kitchen stove pipe ran through an upstairs room, disconnected it, and hooked up my little Yukon stove. I was perfectly comfortable there for the two weeks I hunted. When I left I stood on the drifted snow and replaced the window I had removed without even having to stretch.

Yost's is gone today, likewise the fence and the bell. As I hunted there in 1922, both the two-and-a-half-foot-high bell and the fence were still there; whenever the wind blew more than about 10 miles an hour, an insistent clanging filled the air. That was most of the time, and it could be heard for miles.

The mile-wide river bar where I planned to hunt was blown almost clear of snow. That made it easy for the bears to dig the plentiful pea-vine roots that attracted them to the place. Spruce timber and thickets of sapling birch grew right to the bar on each side of the river, and snow lay in big drifts here and there in the dense growth.

A long ridge poked up between the bar and the Valdez Trail. After fixing up a comfortable "camp" in the empty upper-story room at Yost's, I climbed this ridge to look at the flat.

I had no sooner reached the top and glanced at the bar than I saw three cream-colored, brown-legged grizzlies, the kind that

Dr. Nelson wanted. I glassed them for a few minutes and decided it was a female and twin yearlings.

I wasn't keen to shoot yearlings or cubs, but Dr. Nelson had specifically requested a representative series—young as well as old. I made up my mind it was for the good of science, so started out to collect the three if I could.

The wind was in my favor, and I waited until the bears went into a dry wash, then I walked to within 40 or 50 yards of them. I gathered them in with three shots as they came into sight. It was as simple as that.

I measured them carefully, as Dr. Nelson had instructed, recording the figures in my notebook, then skinned them and packed the hides back to the roadhouse. I left the skulls, which are important for scientific specimens, planning to pick them up the next day.

Next morning I fleshed the three hides clean and nailed them to the buildings at the signal station. Then I went after the skulls. First, I walked up on the ridge for a look-see at the flat. I hadn't gone 100 yards along the crest when I saw three more grizzlies in about the same place the first ones had been. Two of these were also cream-colored and apparently they were another sow with yearlings. One of the yearlings was almost white, with blackish legs—kind of a freak.

I worked in close and collected the three with three shots again. I was pretty cocky that night—six grizzlies with six shots was fair shooting, even if four of them were yearlings.

It was near midnight and barely dark when I finished skinning those three and packing the six skulls and three skins back to the roadhouse. I cleaned skulls and fleshed and nailed up hides all the next day. A snowstorm set in then and I didn't get out for two days.

The next day was clear and I sat atop the ridge glassing the flats for a couple of hours before I spotted a single big cream-colored bear digging roots. I had a lot of confidence in my luck with the first six bears, so decided to see how close I could get to him. It was the largest grizzly I had seen on my hunt, and I was sure it was a male.

I moved down into a dry wash and worked upwind toward

him, bending over to keep out of sight. Now and then I went to the edge to look at him. He was more cautious than the others had been, for occasionally he stood up to look around, then calmly went on feeding.

After half an hour of alternately sneaking and watching, I was surprised to find that I was within 40 or 50 feet of him. He apparently had moved toward me as I sneaked the last few yards. He was much closer than I liked, and he looked as big as a horse.

When I stuck my head up to look at him he saw me and stood still, staring. A spindly willow bush about four feet high was nearby—the only cover of any kind for some distance. That huge bear walked over and tried to hide behind it.

He was too close for comfort, but I had a 145-grain, bronze-tipped cartridge in the rifle chamber and I had had good luck with them. I thought they were pretty skookum grizzly medicine. One good chest shot should finish him off nicely.

I talked to that bear, trying to get him to stand on his hind legs. Instead, he crouched behind that skeleton of a willow, peeking around it at me.

"This is ridiculous," I thought. I talked, whistled, moved my head back and forth, waved a hand—did everything I could think of to get him to stand on his hind legs, as bears do when they are curious and want to study something. I wanted his chest exposed.

After what seemed like a long time of playing peekaboo, he did stand to get a better look. I usually line up a rifle with my right eye, then open my left and fire with both eyes open. I did this, and squeezed the trigger. As the rifle fired, a wall of flame hit my face. At the same time, my rifle twisted out of my hand and spun backward over my head. I thought both of my eyes had been put out. They were full of tears and I couldn't nerve myself to open them.

At that moment I didn't know or care where the bear was— he might have been breathing down my neck for all I knew. My eyes burned fiercely, and a continuous stream of tears poured out of them. All I could do was lie there and cover my face.

After a while I forced my eyes open, but all I could see was blackness and stars rolling around. I was sure I was blind. I wondered if I could get back to the Valdez Trail for help. I listened for

the bear. I felt he was still standing behind the lone willow looking at me. I began to panic, thinking I was blind, with an angry,
wounded grizzly ready to pounce on me any second. But I made
myself lie still and fight off the temptation to rub my eyes. Finally, after I don't know how long, I could see light and the pain
began to go away.

It must have been at least an hour from the time I fired until I
could see again. When I did see, my vision was blurred. I picked
up my rifle, expecting to find a hole blown in the side of it or
something equally serious, but it didn't seem to be damaged.

I managed to lift the bolt, but I couldn't draw it back with my
hand. I finally put the rifle butt on the ground and used my foot to
force the bolt open. The cartridge, split in three places, fell out—
and the primer fell out of the shell case. No doubt the aged brass of
the shell had caused the trouble. Fortunately, the gas port func-
tioned properly. I had never before been certain why that port was
there. I worked several shells through the action, looked it over,
and decided it was undamaged. Then I started looking for the bear.

He had been hit, for I found blood where he had stood behind the lone willow. I went toward the nearest patch of brush
about 250 yards away, looking for his trail. My eyes still watered
badly, blurring my vision.

He had crossed a snow-packed dry wash, leaving a clear blood
trail as he made for the nearest cover. I have often wondered why
he didn't charge when I crippled him; I've had many grizzlies
come at me for less.

The trail went into thick brush and I followed it carefully,
keeping my rifle ready. Ahead I saw a big snowdrift, and it looked
to me as if the bear had walked right next to it. I walked toward
one end, planning to climb the half-rotten snow and look around.
Just as I reached the end of the drift I heard a rumbling noise
behind me. I whirled, expecting to see the bear charging. But he
was standing on top of the drift, about 25 feet away, with his big
head swinging back and forth as he growled at me. I shot, and he
disappeared. The rifle performed properly this time.

He was dead when I reached him. He had originally turned
just short of the snowdrift, gone around to the other side, climbed
it, and dug a hole almost on top. I'd walked not more than five

feet directly under where he was curled up on the drift.

I quit using the old 145-grain loads.

That flat by Yost's was a bear hunter's paradise that year. I killed one or more grizzlies almost every time I went out. In all I shot three sows, each accompanied by two yearlings, plus eight males. All had cream-colored bodies, and brown legs. None of those bears was especially large, but I ran into a couple that *looked* awfully big for a while.

One day I had climbed the ridge as usual and watched the flat for a couple of hours before I saw two bears. They turned out to be big males, and when I first saw them they were fairly close together, working south, busily digging pea-vine roots. I decided to try to collect both.

The wind was in my favor, so I walked directly toward them. Every time either bear looked up I froze and didn't move until it went back to feeding. I had about 400 yards to go to put me in fair range. A deep dry wash ran between the bears, and I ducked into that, crouched over, and ran. I checked frequently to see where they were—I had learned my lesson about getting too close. Each of the bears was about 50 yards from the dry wash. While they were busy feeding I worked along the dry wash until I stood directly between them. There was no cover on the gravel bar and I could see them clearly. I was certain that I could drop one, whirl around and quickly drop the other.

I bellied up the bank of the wash until I could see over it, and drew a fine bead on one of the bears. He was standing still, broadside, clawing at pea-vines. I held for his shoulder, hoping for a heart shot. He dropped as I fired and I was positive that he was dead.

Without a second glance at him I whirled to see the second bear standing on hind legs, looking toward me. He had heard the shot, and was curious. His chest was exposed and I quickly fired before he could drop to all fours again. I must have fired too quickly because he was knocked sideways by the bullet—I was using the last of my 180-grain ammunition. He then bounced to his feet, biting savagely at his shoulder and running toward me. I was fairly certain he hadn't seen me, and I think he ran in my direction only because he was headed toward his partner; or possibly he just happened to be facing my way when he bounced up after being hit.

A grizzly can travel fast even on three legs. I rammed another shell home and carefully put another bullet into his chest. He was within 50 feet when he dropped, kicking and biting. It was then that I heard the noise behind me.

Something had gone wrong.

I whirled with another cartridge in the rifle, ready to shoot, and saw the first bear about 20 feet away, staggering toward me. He was looking at me, and his head was swinging from side to side, lips curled back in a snarl. Those big yellow teeth looked huge. I took a quick bead on his chest—I was low enough in the gully to shoot *up* at him—and pulled the trigger.

Snick went the firing pin. One of the old shells had misfired.

The next cartridgel *had* to be good—it was the last one in the rifle. I yanked the bolt open, slammed it home, and fired. The bear dropped, his nose plowing gravel and sand. Then he kicked a few times and lay still. After I got a wad of snoose in my mouth and calmed down, I measured the distance from his nose to the dry wash. It was just eight feet.

I think each of those bears, after being wounded, had headed for the other, and I was right between them. My first shot, instead of killing the bear, had glanced off his shoulder blade, gone forward through muscle, and come out of the lower part of the neck without hitting a vital spot.

When I had 12 hides nailed to the buildings at the signal station, Jim McHenry, one of the Signal Corp soldiers returned. I was there when he arrived. He looked at the hides and his jaw dropped and he swiveled his head back and forth, staring. Then he walked around each of the buildings, counting hides.

"Where did you get all those ?" he asked.

I had difficulty convincing him that I'd killed all of the bears right there in the seven or eight days he was gone. Next day he went to Fairbanks on Army business.

A day or so later Olaus J. Murie, a U.S. Biological Survey biologist, arrived at Yost's from Fairbanks. He had walked part of the way, and had caught a ride the rest. He helped me weigh the carcasses of the last few bears I had killed, using a beam scale I had brought.

The heaviest carcass, that of a full-grown male, without skull or skin, weighed 350 pounds. Its hide weighed about 75 pounds, and his skull around 20—giving the animal a total live weight of about 450 pounds. The carcass of one fat, nearly toothless old sow weighed 250 pounds; with hide and skull her live weight must have been around 350 pounds. The yearling carcasses weighed around 125 pounds each. The hide of the biggest bear squared around 7 1/2 feet (average of greatest length and greatest width).

I look back on that hunt with mixed feelings. Today it would be a terrible thing for anyone to kill 17 grizzlies for a scientific collection. Conditions were different then. Market hunters occasionally shot big bears and sold the hides, but not as a common practice. Practically no sportsmen hunted Alaska's interior grizzlies at the time. Consequently, grizzlies were extremely abundant and were generally regarded as dangerous pests. At the time, I received thanks from the Alaska Road Commission workers, and the teamsters and drivers like Billy Fraim who used the road, and of course Dr. Nelson. I also received a check from the U.S. Biological Survey for $850.

The soldier who had been so amazed to see all my hides talked to a reporter at Fairbanks. Not long after, someone sent me a clipping from the *Fairbanks News Miner* telling of the hunt. I'll never forget one line: "Glaser says there is nothing to killing grizzlies and he has not had a bit of trouble during his hunt."

Trapping Caribou

When Dr. Edward W. Nelson, chief of the U.S. Biological Survey, spent a week with me at Rapids in 1921 collecting small mammals and birds, he was impressed by the great number of caribou there. The following year Nelson decided that the Bureau should live trap some big caribou bulls in the Alaska Range. He wanted to release them on the Bering Sea island of Nunivak, where they could breed with the much smaller (domestic) reindeer on the island; the goal was to develop larger reindeer.

Olaus Murie, a slim blond blue-eyed biologist with the Survey, was given the job of trapping the caribou. In May 1922, at Dr. Nelson's suggestion, he came to Rapids, looking for a place to build a caribou trap. That was when he found me at Yost's, collecting grizzly bears for Dr. Nelson.

He decided it was much easier to transport the live animals from Mount McKinley Park than it would have been from Rapids or anywhere along the Delta River. Park superintendent Harry Karstens chose the site for the caribou trap in the park, and Murie hired me to help with the project during the summer of 1922.

Olaus and I spent most of the summer building the trap at the head of Savage River, about six miles above the last timber. Using some wire, but mostly poles that we cut and hauled to the site, we built a big circular trap with lead wings that ran about a mile up the mountainside. We caught no caribou with the trap that year.

That fall, at Rapids, without a trap, I caught my own live and healthy caribou.

The Fortymile caribou herd was at a peak. Each fall for the years I was at Rapids (1915-24), thousands of animals left the Yukon River and crossed the mountains heading south and southwest until they reached the Alaska Range, where they spent much of the winter between Hundred Mile (in the Mount Hayes area) and Rapids. They reached the Rapids area after the October rut and scattered out in bunches to settle down for the winter. In the spring they circled back into the Fortymile country.

During the winter of 1920, for example, there were perhaps 200,000 to 300,000 of these caribou. Those who tried to drive autos over the Valdez Trail in September and October occasionally found caribou as far as Paxson so thick on the road they sometimes had to stop for hours and wait for them to move on. When caribou are massed in such great numbers they have no fear of people or cars.

On October 8, 1922, Fairbanks attorney E. B. Collins and a U.S. Marshall friend of his were visiting me at Rapids. There were perhaps 8,000 to 9,000 caribou on the bars of the Delta River in front of the roadhouse. The rut was on, and bulls were grunting and fighting each other. Cows were running here and there, making an awful fuss, a regular circus.

As we stood a few hundred yards from the roadhouse watching these antics, I noticed a full grown cow caribou asleep on the river bar. She was lying with her head tucked toward her flank like a sleeping dog. I decided to take her picture.

I sneaked close and snapped the camera shutter when I was within 15 feet. She didn't even raise her head; just flicked an ear. Caribou bulls were noisily running around on the gravel. Perhaps that's why the camera click didn't make an impression.

I decided to try to catch her. I put the camera down and pounced on her, grabbing one antler with my left hand. She reared on hind legs and fell backwards. I hung on to the antler, and worked around in front of her and tried to get a knee on her neck. I was wearing a new pair of Filson woolen pants, and somehow she hooked her dew claws into them and started pulling them off. I kept working and wrestling, and, with pants half down, managed to get both knees on her neck. She really struggled.

Collins ran to the roadhouse for rope, and we crossed and tied her front legs, then did the same with her hind legs.

I thought we had her then, and stood up to pull up my pants and rest. As soon as I got off of her neck she jumped to her feet and bounded 20 or 30 feet, then stumbled and fell. I rushed over and pounced on her again.

Collins went for more rope while I held her. When he returned we made a hackamore for her. I then untied her legs and tried to lead her up to the barn at the roadhouse. This she didn't like. She braced her feet when I pulled on the lead rope. Collins pushed from behind. That alarmed her and she lunged ahead and ran by me clear to the end of the rope. Then I ran and caught up with her. Each time this happened she got closer to the barn.

Finally we dragged and pushed her over the cut bank in front of the roadhouse and across the Valdez Trail to the roadhouse barn where I tied her to a fence.

At that moment eight or ten big caribou bulls came rushing up, grunting, until they were within 15 or 20 feet. They threatened us—defending the cow in the only way they knew how. It was during the rut; no caribou bull would have behaved that way otherwise. I had a .38 revolver in a shoulder holster and I fired a shot into the ground near the bulls, which drove them off.

We pulled the cow into the barn and turned her loose. I picked a couple of gunny sacks full of white lichen for her, went into the barn with a bucket of water and the lichens, put them down, and walked about ten feet away. She immediately drank some water. While she was drinking I eased close and put my hand on her back. She stood still and trembled.

Horses had been kept in the barn, and there were several bricks of salt. She found and licked the salt, then headed for the bucket of water. Over the next hour she was busy between the salt, the water, and the lichens.

She soon recognized me when I arrived with water or lichens, and within a few days I could handle her without her showing fear.

The day after I caught her, Johnny Fox and another Road Commission man arrived from Fairbanks to repair a Dodge pickup stranded at the roadhouse. They knew nothing about the loose caribou in my barn. Johnny went into the dark barn for some reason, and the caribou immediately ran at him, stood on hind legs, and struck out with her front legs. She got both legs over his shoulders and pushed Johnny over backwards. Then she started to stomp him. He leaped to his feet and fled, not knowing what had attacked him.

I heard all about that attack from other Road Commission men the next summer when I happened to go to Fairbanks. Johnny Fox must have described the encounter pretty graphically, for he had been kidded about it all winter.

I didn't have any dogs that winter, so I made a harness for my caribou and hooked her to a dog sled. She made a good harness animal and I often drove her 12 to 15 miles up and down the Delta River. She made fair time going upriver, but was even faster on the return when she wanted to get back to the barn where the salt was.

On our drives when wild caribou were in sight she wanted to join them, and I had some wild rides until we'd get into woods where I could jam the sled into a tree to stop her. After a while she'd forget the other caribou and we'd go on.

One March day I drove her to Miller's Roadhouse for a visit. On our return home she ran all out. It was 40 or 45 below, and we traveled into a strong north wind. All seemed well until we were about a mile from the roadhouse. Dark was near, and I was eager to get home, and I thought she was too. But she stopped and simply laid down on the ice. I picked her up, but she immediately flopped down again. After several tries to keep her on her feet I gave up and tied her on the sled and pushed the sled home. I reached the cut bank of the river below the roadhouse, and got her off the sled. Only then was she was willing to walk into the barn on her own. She had simply exhausted herself.

During the summer of 1923 I was to again work at the caribou trap with Olaus Murie. I feared that my pet caribou wouldn't get fed or cared for properly while I was gone, so one day I opened both barn doors and led her outside. A bunch of caribou were on the nearby river bar, and I turned her loose, assuming she would run to join them.

Instead, she whirled and ran back into the barn. I got her out again and led her closer to the wild caribou before releasing her. This time she understood that she was free and ran to join the wild bunch. That was the last I ever saw of her.

Olaus' biologist brother Adolph joined us on the caribou trapping project during the summer of 1923 and I worked with them from July until late August.

When the trap was complete Olaus and Adolf climbed up the mountain beyond the wings of the trap, and concealed themselves. I tied a 100-foot rope to the gate, and hid myself in a shallow draw. Then we waited. Caribou had been moving through the area in increasing numbers for the previous several days.

Then, in the way of caribou, a band of several cows with calves and one young bull walked into sight, snatching a bite here, another there, as they traveled. Olaus and Adolf waited. When the animals were between them and the trap, they stood up, arms outstretched. The animals stopped, staring. A cow made an excitation leap—running on hind legs for about ten feet. She then ran a short way on all fours, and stood looking back. The others followed. Olaus ran to try to head them back toward the trap. This frightened them, and they fled, easily outrunning the frustrated Olaus as he tried to head them off.

After several such experiences, we learned to be more subtle. Instead of standing and showing themselves when caribou were between wings of the trap, Olaus and Adolf remained crouched and waved a hand at the animals to get their attention. This made them nervous, and they'd edge away from the Muries and toward the trap entrance. Another brief hand wave or two, and the caribou would edge closer and closer to the trap. When the animals were at the entrance, Olaus and Adolf would leap up and run toward the animals, and as often as not the deer would run into the trap. When they were well inside I yanked the gate shut.

The animals were terribly wild in the trap and most of them could climb the seven to eight-foot-high fence; they simply hooked their feet into the wire and climbed over.

Caribou are very quick. When the animals were inside the trap we had to rope the young bulls we wanted. I did most of the roping, using a regular lariat. Often, with the loop hanging right over the head of a bull, just about to drop on him, he'd leap to one side, and the loop would land on the ground. Then the animal would attack the rope with his sharp hoofs. If I did get the rope around a bull's antlers (which were in velvet), he'd usually lower his head and charge, and I'd have to dodge. I had some very close calls. In the end I had to snare most of the bulls by a front leg.

We sawed the antlers off of the half dozen young bulls we did catch, put halters on them, and staked them out around our camp with 40-foot ropes tied to heavy, movable, dry spruce toggles. We frequently moved the toggles to put the animals on better grazing. Surprisingly, they tamed quickly and were easy to handle.

None of those caribou tangled picket ropes. They were afraid of the rope, and wouldn't step across it, always keeping at the end. They learned to move the toggle a short distance with a sideways pull so they could get to fresh grazing. Then they'd feed in a wide circle as far as the rope would allow before yanking the toggle again. We kept some of them that way for more than a month.

The cows were even easier than the bulls to handle when first caught. When we roped them they usually stood while we walked down the rope and put our hands on them. The bulls, however, invariably tried to fight us. We didn't keep any of the cows.

The captured caribou were taken by horse-drawn wagon to the Alaska Railroad in McKinley Park, by boxcar to Fairbanks, and then down the Yukon River by steamer to the village of Kokrines. There they remained until 1925 when they were barged to Nunivak Island and released to mingle with the reindeer herd.

The experiment appeared to be a success. I first saw the Nunivak Island reindeer in 1946, and most of them resembled caribou. They are larger and longer-legged than reindeer in other Alaskan herds, and many the bulls are dead ringers for wild caribou.

The only drawback, I believe, is their wild character. The Nunivak Island Eskimos who own this herd have their hands full when they drive them into corrals for antler removal, castrating, slaughter, and tagging.

While the Murie brothers and I were trapping caribou in July 1923, President Warren Harding came to Alaska to drive a golden spike symbolizing completion of the Alaska Railroad. On July 15 the president stopped at Mount McKinley National Park on the way to Nenana, where the spike was to be driven. For the occasion Park Superintendent Harry Karstens decided a banquet would be appropriate, and he asked Olaus to kill a Dall ram for the feed.

Olaus, Adolph, and I shot a big ram in McKinley Park, and Mr. and Mrs. Wendler arrived from Anchorage to cook it. The meal was steaming hot and ready to eat when the president's train pulled into the park station. But first, the president had to meet everyone.

We all lined up beside the tracks, and the president, who looked unwell to me (he died in San Francisco on August 2 on his return trip), started shaking hands.

Just before the president's train arrived, Harry Lucke had rushed to his cabin and put on some old torn and beat-up clothes, an old slouch hat full of notches, and an old faded sweater. He usually carried a belt knife, but for this occasion he wore a much wider belt than usual, with a big butcher knife in a scabbard, which he placed square in the middle of his back. He looked like he had just come from a hundred mile hike across the mountains.

I was in line next to Lucke to shake hands with Harding. When Lucke's turn came, he bent his tall frame over, grabbed the president's hand, and pulled the president close, loudly saying how delighted he was to meet him.

A nearby secret service agent reached over and yanked Lucke's big butcher knife out of the scabbard, then stood there looking at it. This got a big laugh from everyone. As Lucke turned, the agent handed him the knife, saying, "That's a nice knife you have, Mr. Lucke!"

Mrs. Harding, a nice friendly lady, wandered around visiting and greeting everyone. I had sled dogs tied at a nearby cabin and she asked me if she could pet them. "How fast can they run, and how much weight can they pull?" she wanted to know.

A few weeks later a party of Congressmen arrived at McKinley Park. They too were celebrating the opening of the Alaska Railroad. Again Karstens decided to have a Dall sheep barbecue, and again the Murie brothers and I climbed into the sheep hills in the park for meat. We shot three rams, and packed them out. They fed about 70 people at the barbecue Karstens sponsored.

Soon after my job with Olaus Murie trapping caribou ended, big, strong Fred Mackwitz proposed that I accompany him to the Bearpaw River. I met Mackwitz at Nenana that summer of 1923, and we immediately became friends. In 1916 Fred ran a trapline on the Bearpaw River (which runs into the Kantishna River). I was at loose ends, and wanted to see more of that country, so away we went.

It was October when an Indian with a poling boat ferried us across the Nenana River at Kobi (now called Rex), and we walked west, following the old winter dog team trail, carrying bedrolls and grub. I had two big sled dogs and each carried a pack. After finding broad, shallow places, we crossed the Teklanika and the Toklat Rivers, and spent a couple of weeks in the Kantishna Country. While there we lived in a miner's cabin. One of the miners had hung up five fat bull caribou, and we were told to help ourselves. I found a meat-grinder in the cabin and ground about 15 pounds of meat, which I made into patties and fried in bacon fat. That was all the food we had with us when in late October we started our return to Kobi.

Some of the smaller lakes were frozen and we could walk on the ice, but ice on the big lakes was still unsafe. Slow-moving streams were frozen over solid, but we had to wade the big, rushing glacier streams.

We reached the Nenana River a mile from Kobi. Our choice was to cross there if we could, or walk upriver through the brush for about 20 miles to Ferry to reach the railroad and a bridge across the Nenana River.

Naturally we decided to cross the Nenana there. It is about 200 yards wide at that point, and slush ice had formed on the bottom, making it very slick. I removed the packs from the two dogs to keep them from getting wet, and piled them on top of my packboard, giving me a load of about 70 pounds. The dogs were young, not well trained, and I was reluctant to turn them loose. I had them both attached to one chain. Fred was making up his pack as I started to wade the river.

I was half way across and looked around to see if Fred was

coming when a dog bumped into me. My feet flew into the air, and I sat down in the water with my back to the current. The weight of the pack held me down, and I couldn't get out of it. I turned loose of the dog chain, got my hands on the bottom and started bumping along. I'd push my hands down, trying to get high enough to get my feet under me, but the current would push me, and I'd bounce some more, heading swiftly downstream. I didn't want to fall flat and wind up rolling under water.

Deep water lay about a hundred feet downstream, and I was being washed into it. I heard Fred yelling as he ran to my rescue. I glimpsed him out of the corner of my eye, but by then just my nose, mouth, and forehead stuck out of the water.

The water threw me astraddle a big rock, and my downstream journey stopped. The weight of the current held me, and water rolled clear over my face, but also pushed me to my feet. My hands hit a part of the rock that had stopped me, and with the current pushing, I stood up and discovered I was up to my waist in a roaring torrent.

The water was too swift for me to walk in. I could barely stand. But Fred arrived and braced me and we struggled the rest of the way across.

There was a little snow on the ground, and the temperature was around 10 degrees below zero with a strong east wind. I was chilled from the water, of course, and became doubly chilled when that icy wind hit me. We found a pile of driftwood, and within a few minutes Fred had a fire roaring. I stripped and waved my underwear and other clothing through the flames, and Fred helped me. My front would burn and my back would freeze. I'd whirl around, and freeze my front and burn my back for a while, then do it again.

When my underwear was warm I put it on, but the side away from the fire would freeze, and I'd have to turn it toward the fire. It took a couple of hours before I was warm enough to walk that last mile to the roadhouse at Kobi.

It was close. If I had been alone I probably would have drowned.

A Miner Alone

ALONE, NELS NELSON MINED FOR GOLD at Rainy Creek for 11 years, starting in 1911. Rainy Creek is 14 miles from the site of the McCallum Signal Corp station on the Valdez Trail. In winter, when mining was impossible, he trapped foxes and beaver along Rainy Creek.

I met Nelson in 1920, but we didn't get well acquainted. In May, 1922, I was visiting Jim McHenry and his partner, McCann, the U.S. Signal Corp soldiers at McCallum, when Nels arrived necking a Yukon sled loaded with a couple of suitcases and two duffel bags. He was husky, blond and blue-eyed and appeared to be in his late 50s. We spent a friendly evening together.

"No more mining for me after this season," he told me, in his pronounced Swedish accent. "Come freeze-up this fall I'm going back to Sweden." Then he added, "I'm low on grub, but I'm not going to buy much; I'll live on caribou meat this summer. No sense in getting a lot of grub when I'm going to leave."

I had reason to remember those words.

He didn't say so, but I got the impression that he had made his pile and planned to retire in comfort. We visited for several hours, talking mining, caribou, the weather, and other subjects. Like many who live alone, Nelson had saved up a lot of things he wanted to talk about. Next day he stored his suitcases and duffel bags at the McCallum Signal Corps station and returned to work his mine for one more season.

I walked the 25 miles back home to Rapids, then in June I left to work with Olaus Murie to build the caribou trap. I arrived back at Rapids in early October. That night I telephoned the Signal Corp Station at McCallum. The voice that answered wasn't familiar. I then learned that Jim McHenry and McCann had been replaced in September by two Signal Corps soldiers named Cohan and Exline, who had been transferred from New York State.

"Has Nels Nelson gone Outside yet?" I asked.

"Who?" they asked. They had never heard of Nelson.

I told them to look in the station cache for Nelson's gear. They told me his suitcases and duffels were still there. I knew then something was wrong. "I'll walk over there tomorrow and check on Nelson," I said.

Next day I walked to McCallum and met the new boys Cohan, 21, and Exline, 19. In the daily log we found that the last time Nelson had been to the station was August 4, when he picked up his mail.

I spent the night at McCallum, and next day headed for Rainy Creek. To get there I had to cross Phelan Creek and the Big Delta River. The temperature was about 15 above. Both streams are glacial, and during warm weather they usually run in flood stage. But with cooler temperatures both were down. I had rubber hip boots, and forded Phelan without getting wet.

The broad, roaring Delta River was another story. I found a place where it was a few hundred feet wide and appeared shallow, although it was very swift. Slippery slush ice clung to the gravel in the stream bed. When I reached midstream water sloshed over the tops of my boots and I skidded on the ice and fell. The swift current rolled me downstream several hundred feet before I was able to regain my feet. My clothes started to freeze before I reached the far bank. I needed a fire quickly or I'd die.

In my packboard, which remained mostly dry, I had a pair of rubber shoepacks and two pairs of heavy wool socks. I also had dry matches in two Marble waterproof containers. I cut a pile of dry willow, using the light axe I always carried, and had a big fire going within minutes. It took several hours to dry my clothes. By then a full moon had risen above the surrounding peaks, giving good light. It had also turned very cold.

It was probably about nine o'clock that night when I started up Rainy Creek. Nelson had told me his cabin was two miles up the creek, and his placer mine was beyond that.

I walked more than two hours with the moon lighting my way until I figured I must have passed Nelson's cabin, so I climbed a bluff next to the creek and searched up and downstream with binoculars. I soon spotted his cache roof sticking out above the spruce trees. After a long stumbling search through the dark spruces I found Nelson's one-room log cabin. The door was latched from the inside.

I forced the door open, lit a match, found a stub of a candle on the table, and lit it. Then I saw Nelson. He was dead, lying on the floor with his head propped against the bunk. He was fully clothed, including his old black hat, as if he momentarily expected to get up and walk out. His feet looked bare and shiny, even in the dim candlelight, and I moved the candle down to look.

I was startled to see a swarm of tiny black shrews. They had eaten all the flesh from his feet, leaving polished bones. By spring, the little carnivores would have eaten all of his flesh, leaving a clean skeleton.

On the table were six or seven sheets of paper covered with writing, which proved to be a daily diary. The first entry, dated August 4, told of his visit to McCallum to get his mail. The entry for August 5, the day after his return, detailed how he had suddenly become paralyzed from the hips down; he was unable to walk.

I remembered then his comment about not buying extra grub, that he planned to live on caribou meat that summer. Since he couldn't hunt caribou and he had no grub, he had starved. Strangely, he didn't expect anyone to arrive to help him; at least he made no mention of it in his diary.

His last diary entry was September 27. A few days earlier he had commented, "I cannot last long now." He was then unable to get back into his bed.

He had written a will, leaving everything to two brothers in Toledo, Washington, and a sister in Monroe, Washington. He listed seven sacks of fur in his cache, and on the table was a moosehide poke containing 52 1/2 ounces of placer gold. There were bank books showing he had $8,600 in a Fairbanks bank and $3,800 in a Seattle bank. I found $3,200 in government checks made out to him for gold he had sold to the San Francisco mint. Piled on the table was $320 in $20 gold pieces.

I sat there in the dark and cold cabin beside Nel's frozen body, reading the brief daily diary by flickering candlelight. I was near tears when I finished. It bothered me terribly that this good man had to suffer and die alone. If I had returned to Rapids early in September I'd have known something was wrong when I checked with the Signal Corps Station, and perhaps I could have rescued him.

To get drinking water he had crawled more than 150 feet from his cabin to the creek, dragging his paralyzed legs. He had no food in his cabin, nor in his cache. Absolutely helpless, he slowly starved for nearly two months. During late August and early September more than four feet of snow had fallen, adding to his hardship. By early October the snow was all gone.

After reading Nelson's diary I left the cabin, closed the door tightly, and climbed into his cache where I found a bedroll and spent the rest of the night. I lay awake for some time, acutely aware of the nearby dead miner. I thought sadly of his long, lonely harrowing ordeal. Then the lulling sounds of Rainy Creek and my tired muscles put me to sleep. At daylight I again searched the cache and the cabin for food, and found none.

I recrossed the rivers without getting wet, and encountered Cohan and Exline near McCallum's where they were hunting caribou. From the signal station I sent a telegram to the U.S. Marshall at Fairbanks, describing Nelson's death, then I walked home to Rapids.

A few days later the Marshall called me on the telephone at Rapids, saying he was going to try to drive to Rapids to investigate Nelson's death. It had turned cold, and the ground was frozen solid.

On October 17 Roy Lund drove up to the roadhouse in his Model T Ford. With him were Deputy Marshall Fred Parker and prosecuting attorney E. B. Collins (who helped me catch the cow caribou). In normal years during the 1920s snow closed the Valdez Trail to Rapids from Fairbanks by October 1.

Next day we managed by pushing and almost carrying the Ford to get it to a place called Casey's Cache; no buildings, just a name. Here Phelan Creek and the Big Delta River come together. From there we walked. Now the rivers were much lower due to the cold.

Caribou were everywhere as we crossed the Delta River. The rut was ending, but a few bulls were still clattering antlers in brief, violent battles. At the mouth of Rainy Creek we saw two bulls with locked antlers, yanking and straining, trying to pull themselves apart. One would shove the other, and they'd dance and fight. The antlers didn't clatter for they were too tightly locked. We decided to see if we could separate them, otherwise both were doomed to lingering death. As we approached, they redoubled their efforts to break free. Both bulls were on their knees, pulling and twisting, and rolling their eyes at us. When we were within 20 feet, they suddenly broke apart, leaped to their feet, and fled. It was the only time I've ever seen caribou bulls lock antlers.

At Nelson's cabin I made a stretcher for his body and the sacks of fur. We found Nelson's boat, a small scow, at the mouth of Rainy Creek, and put the body aboard. Parker and I sped downstream in the boat while the others followed on foot. By the time Collins and Lund reached the parked car, we had rolled the body in a tarpaulin and tied it on the running board; it didn't weigh very much, for Nels' body was just skin and bones.

We arrived at Rapids long after dark in a snowstorm. Next morning Collins and Parker asked me to accompany them the 70 miles to Richardson, where they planned to hold an inquest before the U.S. Commissioner.

Other than two flat tires, which Lund quickly repaired, and having to cut pry poles to move his car out of deep ruts where it high-centered several times, we reached Richardson with little difficulty.

The inquest was held next day, October 20, and I described for the Commissioner my finding of Nelson.

Next morning I started to walk back to Rapids. The ferry across the Tanana River had stopped for the season, but there was a cable with a little bucket on a pulley. I crawled into the bucket and pulled myself across. I spent the night at McCarty, 22 miles from Richardson. Overnight it had snowed about 16 inches. It was still snowing when I started out, with 48 miles still to travel, of which about 20 miles was above timberline, with only one relief cabin.

I was lucky on that walk. For about half of the 48 miles an enormous herd of caribou had followed the Valdez Trail, packing the snow, making for fine walking. That day I made it to the relief cabin at Donnelly's, only 13 miles from home. I was anxious to get home, because I had not yet killed my winter's meat.

Next morning I reached home early, and found the river bars and timber near Rapids alive with caribou. At that time of year the only animals fit for winter's meat are barren cows. I carefully picked out and shot two of these; both fine pieces of meat, for each had two and three inches of backfat.

A few days later a chinook wind blew up from the south melting away the snow in the foothills. With the snow gone, I took advantage and climbed into the mountains and shot two large rams. With the caribou, this gave me enough meat to last until spring. Hung in the barn near the roadhouse, the meat remained frozen all winter.

In June, 1923, I was notified by the U.S. Marshall at Fairbanks that Nelson's $26,000 estate had gone to his two brothers and his sister, thus complying with the will he had written during his last hours. I never heard from Nelson's family.

While at Nelson's cabin with Collins, Lund, and the Deputy Marshal, Collins found another, older diary, which indicated that Nelson had sold all his gold to the U.S. mint in San Francisco for $17.32 per ounce. It also made clear that the 52 1/2 ounces I had found on the table in the moosehide poke was the result of three summers of mining for Nelson.

In the cabin we found a moose skin sack holding a fist-size

piece of quartz. It appeared to have little value. "Keep it as a souvenir, Frank," Collins said, handing it to me. "It's probably all you'll ever get for all your trouble."

Years afterward I broke the quartz up. Inside were many little gold nuggets.

I've often wondered where Nels found that fist-sized chunk of rich gold-bearing quartz.

Book Two

At Savage River, 1924–1937

11

At Savage River

During the two summers I worked with the Murie brothers at the caribou trap in McKinley Park, we occasionally scouted for caribou some distance from the trap. On several long hikes I was impressed with the great high ridges near Savage River and decided to look that country over with the idea of establishing a new trapline.

In the spring of 1924 I turned my Black Rapids Roadhouse over to a fellow named Collins, and with several pack dogs walked to Savage River, 125 miles straight line, and about 250 miles by foot. I had to cross many large rivers, and was often soaked to the shoulders. I thoroughly explored the area that summer and early fall. No one lived in this region just outside Mount McKinley National Park. Caribou, moose, sheep, and grizzly bears were abundant. Three levels of mountain range tower nearby—the main Alaska Range, the foothills (where I eventually trapped), then the front range. From there a series of benches of decreasing altitude roll north toward the Tanana Valley.

Good spruce timber was plentiful in the Savage River valley. Foxes were especially numerous, and it was a time when some fox furs brought good prices. There were lynx and wolverine. Mink lived along the river. Healy, on the Alaska Railroad, the nearest town where I could get supplies, was 18 miles away.

It was a paradise, the land of my dreams, my Happy Hunting Ground.

That September, as slush ice formed on Fish Creek and Savage River, I watched school after school of grayling swim down

Fish Creek and into Savage River. The water of beautiful little Fish Creek is gin clear and flows over a fine gravel bottom. Had I wished, I could have killed a gunny sack full of grayling with a club at any one of a dozen riffles. They ranged from little six-inch fellows up to two-pounders about 20 inches long. Grayling are delicious, with white and mild tasting flesh.

I decided to build two log cabins, seven miles apart. The main cabin was on Savage River; the other downstream on Fish Creek, which runs into Savage River. I pitched a tent at Savage River, then went to Healy to wait about a month for snow which would allow me to use a dog team and sled to haul tools and building materials to the site.

I left Lignite four miles north of Healy on October 18, at 7 a. m. while it was still dark, driving a five-dog team. The temperature was 18 below zero with a foot and a half of snow. I had about 800 pounds on the sled, including tools, a stove, stovepipe, windows, bedding, food for me and the dogs, and various items a man needs to survive in the wilderness.

Five miles out of Lignite snow was four feet deep and going became tough for the dogs. At midnight I was a little over half way to Savage River. My load was too heavy for my five dogs to pull and to break trail in the deep snow.

I unloaded the sled of all but my bedroll, food for me and the dogs, and a few other things, and snowshoed ahead of the dogs the rest of the way. I had killed a few caribou earlier and cached them at my tent at Savage River, so there was additional food there for me and the dogs. When I got to my tent around three a. m., I knocked the snow off, fed the dogs, ate something, and crawled into bed.

I slept four or five hours and hooked up the dogs and re-trieved the things I had left on the trail, an easy job since the trail was broken.

Over the next two weeks I built a 14 by 16 log cabin. Using a good crosscut saw and a heavy axe I cut down, limbed, and peeled bark from straight spruce logs that were light enough for me to lift into place. Using the dog team, I skidded the logs to the cabin site. I laid spruce poles across the purlins to the ridgepole and built a ridge roof, covering it with unfrozen sod I uncovered after I chopped through a section of frozen ground. I dug through the snow and found sphagnum moss, which I thawed with a big fire, and used it to chink logs. The moss froze as fast as I chinked. The cabin floor was dirt, which eventually packed as hard as cement. Later I covered much of the floor with bear and moose hides. A good cast iron kitchen range provided plenty of heat, and was wonderful for cooking and baking.

Once the cabin was tight and livable I drove the dogs to Healy and hauled four loads of grub and other items to my new cabin. Then I drove the dogs seven miles downriver and lived in the tent while I built another, smaller, trapline cabin.

October 14, 1926: 20 above. East wind. See seven caribou, one red fox. Big display of northern lights at 6:30 p.m.

In mid October the Kuskokwim caribou herd of four to five hundred thousand animals moved in to winter on the north slope of the Alaska Range between the Savage and Toklat Rivers, which are about 50 miles apart. This, I learned, was an annual event. By the time I got around to building the second cabin, these animals were settling down for the winter on the high bald ridges I intended to trap. That winter it seemed as if every cow caribou had a calf, and every Dall sheep ewe had a lamb. The Savage River country is natural game country.

October 18, 1929: Caribou by the thousands going by the cabin, heading west. 6 below at 7 a. m..

When both cabins were completed, I put out traps. That first winter I trapped along the river between my two cabins as well as on top of one of the high ridges. The next winter I didn't bother to trap in the deep snow along the river; there was no point in fighting the snow with traps, and working on snowshoes, when I could walk without snowshoes and set traps on bare ground on the ridges. That's when I set up a second trapline.

One trapline, to the east, was on a 10-mile-long ridge at about 4,000 feet. From the cabin it was a 1,900-foot climb in less than a mile to the top, but the ridge top was level. When I ran that ten miles of trapline, I had to return by the same route, thus I walked 20 miles every time I ran that line.

The other trapline ran to the west over a series of three ridges. Although it was only six miles long, it was much harder to cover.

From my main cabin I climbed 1,100 feet onto the first ridge, made a big circle, and ended back at the cabin.

My main cabin fell under the shadow of the mountains on November 18, and the winter sun didn't hit it again until January 20. *January 23, 1934: Sun hit the cabin at 10:50 a.m., left at 12:25. 54 below zero. Calm.*

Accustomed to the almost constant wind at Rapids, I was amazed and delighted at the near lack of wind at Savage River. During most of November temperatures ranged below zero. December arrived with temperatures of 40 below and colder. Day after day in January the temperature was 50 to 60 below zero; once it reached 72 below. Because there was virtually no wind, it seemed warm to me, despite the deep cold.

I trapped only a short time that winter. Yet in March I drove my dog team to Fairbanks with a sled load of fox, lynx, and mink furs which I sold for $2,600. This was big money in 1925. Although I ran traplines almost daily, I never saw a wolf track, nor did I hear a wolf howl all winter.

From 1925 into the early 1930s the fur of an ordinary blond or orange red fox brought $15 to $100, while cherry reds (trade name Kamchatka red) brought $100 to $200. Cross fox furs brought from $15 to $100; in the early years much more. Silver and black foxes were worth from $25 to $300. Later, fur farms flooded the market with silver and black foxes. Lynx furs brought $25. Wolf skins brought $15 to $18 from fur buyers, sometimes double that from local parka makers. In those years dog team-driving fur buyers often came to my cabin to buy my furs, paying cash.

After I became established, with two traplines producing, I figured on making at least $5,000 a year; in some years I made up to $7,000. That is, until fur prices took a dive in the 1930s. Trapping season opened in mid-November and closed February first.

My expenses were negligible. A box of shotgun shells sold for $1.50 at Smith's Hardware in Fairbanks; a .30-30 rifle, with several boxes of cartridges, cost $15. Hunting guides were paid $10 a day by the occasional trophy hunter who came to Alaska. I believe that $500 could have kept me nicely for the whole year. With my income I could buy anything I wanted. I always had eggs (a luxury in Alaska then) for I hauled a case of eggs to the cabin every fall. I bought canned salmon, canned peaches, pears, figs, grapefruit. I bought the best bacon I could find, plus lots of dried foods like apples, apricots, prunes. I bought canned and dry milk, and spices of all kind to liven up my cooking.

Caribou, moose, and sheep meat was my primary food. I could have easily done without most of the other foods I bought.

December 30, 1930: See about 2,000 caribou today. Shot three. Hard south wind. 30 above.

Here's one of my grocery lists from June, 1926.

Sweet chocolate, one lb can 5 lbs.	2.10
Postum, 5 cans	1.95
Mazola oil, two 1/2 gallon cans	1.95
dry corn, 5 lbs.	1.53
dry dates, two 5 lb. packages	1.20
dry pears, two 5 lb. boxes	2.90
black figs, 25 lbs.	4.35
peanut butter, ten 2 lb. cans	4.80
fig bars, 5 lbs.	1.19
oatmeal crackers, 5 lbs.	1.00
crackers, five boxes, 5 lb. each	1.18
walnut meats, 4 lb.	1.44
shredded coconuts, 3 lbs.	.73
Oregon walnuts, 10 lbs.	2.10
one half can sage	.23
celery salt, 2 small size	.18
cube sugar, two 5 lb boxes	1.00
dry vegetables, 10 cartons	2.00
peppermint extract	.25
vanilla and lemon	.69
shredded wheat, 10 packages	1.20
pimento cheese, 6 cans	.88
horse radish, 3 jars	.32
mustard, 3 jars	.31
macaroni, two 5 lb. packages	1.00
two dozen cans evap. milk	2.00
bacon, 5 lbs.	1.50
beans, 10 lb.	.90

I like rifles, and usually bought one or more new ones each year to try them out. For several years during the late 1920s when my income was far beyond anything I needed, I kept a room year-round at the Nordale Hotel in Fairbanks, the cleanest and best place to stay in town. It didn't cost much, and all the trappers and miners from the bush stayed at the Nordale. Often at the end of trapping season I'd drive my dog team to town, sell my furs, and board the dogs either at Van Bibber's or Ed Day's dog livery at the edge of town. Then I'd live at the Nordale Hotel while I shopped and visited for a month or more. Commonly, I went to Fairbanks three or four times a year. I often drove my dog team right into the business district. Traffic was no problem; in 1924 there were only 206 privately-owned cars in Fairbanks, and only 1,116 in the entire Territory.

When I was ready to return to Savage River I'd ship things I bought in Fairbanks on the railroad to Healy, then drive my dogs to Healy and make several trips to haul the stuff the 18 miles home.

I caught one cross fox for every three reds for the 12 years I trapped at Savage River—1924 to 1937. Some were silver crosses. I released from my traps many silver foxes, both male and female, as well as some black foxes. I figured they would mate with a red fox and raise crosses, which brought the best money. One female silver fox I knew was mated to a cherry red and lived at a den close to my cabin. For several years each winter I caught five or six of their dark cross pups. She finally lost her red mate and mated with a cross fox, and she still produced very good pups. It was almost like having a fur farm.

During my first winter at Savage River, I often took one or two of my dogs with me for company as I ran the trapline on the high bare ridge to the west of my cabin. The males insisted on leaving their sign at every clump of grass. Since the prevailing south wind blew the ridge bare, the few grass clumps that were there were always visible.

This was too good an opportunity to pass up. The following summer I dug about 70 high grass clumps from the lowlands and back-packed them onto the ridges where I transplanted them on every high knoll where I wanted to set a fox trap. As I transplanted each clump I dug a hole on the south side and about six inches away. Next I drove big steel spikes into the ground nearby. When trapping season opened, I fastened traps to the spikes, which had frozen into the ground, placed the trap in the hole, and covered it with dry dirt, which I took from nearby ground squirrel holes.

It was the only set I used on those ridges. It was perfect for catching foxes, and later, when they arrived (or increased enough to trap) for wolves and coyotes. Occasionally I caught lynx and wolverine in those sets, for they too like to visit clumps of grass.

December 6, 1930: South wind that I mean was a real wind. Had a hell of a time to get back home from trap line. Caught a fine silver fox. 36 above.

December 7, 1930. 41 years old today.

Snow, invariably coming from the north, would generally drift a little ridge on the south side of the grass clumps. But soon the prevailing south wind would knock the snow off. It was wonderful sight for me to stand in the cabin after a big snowstorm and watch the south wind come up. It would start at the bottom of the ridge, and take the snow right on over the top. I called it "the old man sweeping the ridges." The ridges were cleared of snow almost as if swept with a broom.

That's why those ridges were such good sheep and caribou winter range; there was plenty of feed, and the animals didn't have to paw through the snow for it.

January 25, 1934. 44 below for the last 24 hours. It has been 40 below or colder now for 16 days.

My new home had many other advantages. As I learned before settling there, each spring grayling migrated upstream in Fish Creek in great schools, only to return downstream in the fall when slush ice formed. Fish Creek was fed largely by springs. Where it ran into Savage River much of it came in underground through the gravel. The underground water was relatively warm and kept Savage River open for about a quarter of a mile downstream even during the coldest times.

In March, when air temperatures climbed to around zero I often stood on the anchor ice on Savage River above where Fish Creek entered and peered into a deep pool there to see hundreds of grayling swimming about. I used black gnat flies to catch them. For many years I caught and dried immense numbers of grayling, often catching more than 100 a day.

July 9, 1930. Was down to Fish Creek. Caught 20 grayling in 30 minutes.

Many times I tied my sled dogs to willows near that deep hole and I'd catch eight or ten grayling for each dog. They would eat them whole. Next I would fill their pack sacks with grayling and take them home to my main cabin to dry for later use.

By 1929 I had four different fly rod outfits. Whenever I stopped fishing I stood the rod I was using against the willows and left it there. When I returned to Fish Creek I seldom had to walk more than a few hundred yards to find one of my fly rods so I could fish.

Each spring I bought three or four dozen of the best quality flies. By fall they would all be worn out. I often put three flies on at a time, and commonly caught two fish with a cast, hooking one fish, and while working him ashore, another fish would take one of the other two flies. Occasionally I caught three fish with one cast.

I wasn't the first to be attracted by the abundance of fish and game at Savage River and Fish Creek. A year or so after I moved there, at Healy I talked with Titus Bettis, an Indian who was born at an Indian Village at Savage River near where I built my main cabin. He was blind, and at least 90 years old when I talked with him.

"Plenty moose at Savage River now," I told the old man.

"Yes. Long time ago many moose. We kill from blind in tree," he explained.

I had found one of their old blinds. The Indians had lashed dead spruce poles into a platform about 15 feet off the ground, using spruce roots for ties. From the platform they used a bow and arrow or a spear to kill moose that walked beneath them.

"What kind of arrow and spear point did you use?" I asked Titus.

"Copper," he responded. Somehow trade from the Copper River country brought raw copper to these Indians.

I found remnants of houses a few hundred yards from my

main cabin, and another dozen remnants along Fish Creek. Evidently the Natives lived underground, for the sites I found consisted of square holes in the ground. Whatever they covered them with and lined the holes with had rotted and caved in. They were probably covered with poles topped with sod.

Titus told me they built funnel traps out of willow to catch the grayling in Fish Creek. In the spring when the fish went upstream they set the traps facing downstream; in fall they reversed them. They must have taken a lot of fish. They dried the fish, of course, but also in summer they put them in pits in the permafrost (permanently frozen ground) to preserve them. I found those storage pits—they were two or three feet deep and a couple of feet across, with moss growing in them.

When Titus was in his twenties he made a spring trading trip with his father with two birchbark canoes loaded with furs. They traveled to an island in the Tanana River across from the site of the present town of Tanana. There the Natives had established a neutral ground trading ground where Titus' people, the Koyukons, the Tananas (all three are Athapaskan Indian groups), and the Eskimos from far down the Yukon River commonly met to trade. When the Russians arrived they established one of their trading posts on the site.

On that trip Titus traded furs for a muzzle loading rifle. He was a six-footer, and described the gun as taller than he was. "All gold, around the sides," he told me. It was brass, of course. When he returned to his Savage River village with the rifle he became a hero when he killed three grizzlies with it.

He had killed and dressed out a moose at a salt lick at Savage River. When he returned to the lick he came upon the three grizzlies. The Indians had great respect for grizzly bears; spears and bows and arrows are poor weapons against these powerful animals. But with the muzzle loader, it was another story.

Titus said he started shooting at the bears. As he told me about it he got down on one knee. He pointed, then pretended to shoot, and he motioned that the bear fell down. He went through the complicated motions of loading a muzzle loader, then he shot again.

"Bears *hiyusonic* (very angry)" he said.

He growled, and pretended to shoot again and again. He

wounded at least two of the bears. His story continued for a good ten minutes, and in that time he pretend-loaded and fired his muzzle loader six or seven times.

"All gone," he said, finally.

The Indians must have lived on Savage River for hundreds of years, for I found a 100-foot-long midden pile in an opening in the woods where there was no moss growing, just gravel. It looked like a five or six foot high dry river bar, littered with charred and broken bones, mostly moose and caribou.

I once dug down there with a stick and found charred wood and assumed it was a place where the Indians had feasts, and probably cooked entire animals.

A six-foot human skeleton partially washed out of a gravel bank of the Savage River while I lived there. It had to be one of those early Indians. I dug the skeleton out, and found it had been wrapped in birch bark. Birch roots had grown clear around the body, so it had been there for many years. I reburied it nearby, well away from the river.

There are three game salt licks near the old Indian village site on Savage River. Many times I quietly walked through the timber to one of them. As one walks through the dense timber, suddenly there is an opening with the game lick in its middle. I enjoyed finding moose and caribou there. If game was at the lick I would be within 30 or 40 feet when I stepped into the clearing. Caribou would leap into the air a couple of times and depart in a hurry. But moose commonly reacted differently. Whether it was a bull or a cow, they behaved alike. Here I would be within rock-throwing distance of the animal, and I would stand and watch as the moose would look around at me. Then it would turn its head away and look down at the ground for a while. Next it would swing its head to look at me again. Then it might stand and stare at the trees, as if it were pretending I wasn't there.

After a minute or two the moose would take a slow step or two, stop, and look back. In this manner it would take five minutes or so to reach the nearby trees. Once it was in the trees it would whirl quickly, take a last look at me, then jump behind a tree and disappear into the timber.

I never tired of watching this performance.

May 21, 1931. Shot a fine big grizzly, a fine skin. The only grizzly I've seen this spring. See lots of moose at Fish Creek..

During the twelve years I lived at Savage River I was a member of the National Geographic Society, and received the *National Geographic* magazine. Often on long winter nights I went to my cache and selected a dozen or so issues and settled down under my gasoline lantern near my glowing wood stove for an evening of reading and dreaming of the far-off places they told about. I read many of those issue over and over.

Joseph Rock was in northern China and Tibet in the 1920s and he took some wonderful photos of the Himalayan Mountains that I often studied. I followed Admiral Richard Byrd to the South Pole. I went to Africa with Martin and Osa Johnson.

I had a battery-powered shortwave radio and followed world and Alaska news. A lot of historic events rolled downstream while I was at Savage River. In February 1925 there was the famous 650-mile diphtheria anti-toxin sled dog dash to Nome. In May 1927 Lindbergh flew the Atlantic. In 1929 the Great Depression hit. In 1935 the federal government relocated 200 poverty-stricken farm families to Alaska's Matanuska Valley.

Visitors occasionally stopped at my Savage River cabin, which I never locked. Usually in April, a trapper from the Kantishna country drove his dog team through and stopped. If I wasn't home he'd stay overnight anyway. He'd use a little of my grub, and normally leave something in its place. He always split kindling and left it by the stove before he left. I never lost anything to those like him who used my cabin while I was gone, and I thought nothing of it, for that was the way it was in Alaska then.

Savage River Wolves

February 15, 1923: 22 below at 8 a. m. Shot at wolf on the bar. Did not get him.

I missed a long shot at that gray wolf, the first I ever saw.

While walking along the Valdez Trail near Rapids I saw movement along the Delta River far below. With glasses I saw the wolf, perhaps 400 yards away, trotting along, head and tail low. I had but a moment to lift my rifle and shoot, and I blew snow and gravel all over the animal. I went down to the river bar and found his tracks where he had sprinted into the brush after my shot.

Wolves were scarce in the Alaska Range where I market hunted from 1915 to 1924. In that time I saw a few wolf tracks, but I don't recall hearing a wolf howl.

I never saw a wolf track or heard a wolf howl during the winter of 1924–25 at Savage River. A few wolves showed up during the winter of 1925–26. By the winter of 1926–27 there were noticeably more wolves, and I often saw them chasing caribou.

November 9, 1926: 20 above. See seven wolves, six blacks and one gray. Shot two blacks. The gray wolf was a big brute. See one red fox.

November 13, 1927: Six below at 7:30 a.m., four below at 5 p. m., clear, calm. A band of wolves came close to the cabin and howled all last night.

November 19, 1927: Caught two red foxes. Wolves howled most all day. Foggy.

Wolf numbers continued to increase. By 1930 during the February-March mating time they were so numerous and so noisy with their howling that they often awoke me at night.

One clear moonlit mid-February night in 1930 when I had pulled all my traps, and my annual catch of furs was safely in my cache, I sat near my glowing wood stove reading *National Geographic* magazines until after midnight, when I went to bed. I had been in bed perhaps an hour when the musical sound of howling wolves awoke me. There were so many of them and they sounded so close that I got up, dressed, and stepped outside. My rifle hung on a peg outside the door, and I grabbed it as I stood looking and listening.

The sky was clear. There was no wind, and a full moon lit the snow-covered land so it seemed almost like daylight. The big thermometer outside the door read 30 below zero. My sled dogs were all awake. Some sat atop their houses, alertly looking into the distance. As I stood listening, a wolf howled off to the west, then another, and another, until at least half a dozen were howling. They sang for two or three minutes then suddenly their howls broke off. Moments later I heard a solitary wolf to the south. He was joined by second, and then a third. Like the first pack, after several minutes their howls suddenly stopped, and then, far to the north I heard another band howling.

The wolves to the west and south sounded close, but after listening for a time I realized that the still, cold, dense air carried sounds unusually well. The two nearest packs were probably a mile or more from my cabin.

After enjoying wolf music for a time, I howled myself a couple of times. That often elicited a howling response if wolves were near. That night it shut them up. After a time I went back to bed.

At daylight, which came about 10 a.m., I again heard two bands of wolves howling nearby. It was their breeding season, and I sensed excitement among the wolves. I dressed for a long, cold day in the hills. With binoculars and rifle I climbed a nearby ridge where I could overlook the flats where feeding caribou were scattered.

I scanned the flats with binoculars for a few minutes, but saw only caribou. Fog rose from each caribou as its body moisture condensed in the cold. A chill crept through my furs, so I moved to another spot. The walk warmed me. I had no sooner sat down again and braced my binoculars, holding my breath as they neared my face to keep them from fogging, when I saw a pack of eight wolves a couple of miles away, trotting single-file across the flats. Several caribou turned and stared as they passed, but the wolves ignored them.

I swung the binoculars, and was startled to see another pack of seven wolves moving single-file across the flat. The two wolf packs were headed toward each other.

"Now I'm going to see something," I told myself. I knew wolves had territories, and that fights between packs (generally family groups) are common. Several times I found the remains of wolves killed in fights with other wolves. Often the remains had been eaten, for wolves *do* eat wolves.

I swept the flats again with my glasses, and was amazed to see a third band of eight wolves, trotting single-file. Now there were three packs bound for the same general area. As I watched, a low howl came from one band, to be answered by a low howl from one of the others. Eventually all three packs stopped a few hundred feet apart, appearing reluctant to approach each other. Gradually then, the three packs, a congregation of 23 wolves, gathered in one furry concentration on the open, snowy flat. I had a grandstand view of this remarkable natural phenomenon.

The wolves milled about and mixed, I heard yips and growls. Here and there it appeared that wolves were challenging each other; several appeared to be fighting. I started making big plans, thinking that eight or nine of the wolves would be killed in the melee. I had in mind sneaking in and finishing off a bunch of cripples and I imagined I was going to collect a bundle of $15 bounties, and would have a bunch of wolf hides to sell.

I dashed onto the flats and hurried to the spot. Except for tracks and a little blood in the snow, I found nothing. All 23 wolves had sped off. They were high in the sheep hills howling in a low, sweet chorus. I watched them for a time with binoculars, puzzled. They had seen me and left, of course.

Then it dawned on me that it was wolf breeding season. Per-

Frank Glaser, about 1926, in Mount McKinley National Park.
FRANK GLASER

haps one or more females were in heat. Those wolves were just playing around at a time of excitement. All the growling, and bumping each other, and fussing was just posturing that didn't amount to much.

April 27, 1928: I saw three black and one gray wolf. Soon seven more black wolves joined them and they had the damndest fight I ever saw.

A female wolf will not breed with a member of her pack or family group, except of course with her lifelong mate. When a female wolf-dog I owned came into heat, none of the team could get near her. If they tried she would growl and snap at them, and sit down if they persisted. Instinct wouldn't allow her to mate with any dog she considered part of her family. The moment I put a strange wolf-dog with her, she accepted him.

One February, from my lookout point I saw a family of seven wolves trotting single-file across the flats. As I watched them through binoculars the wolf in the lead stopped and moved to the last wolf in line, a somewhat smaller animal, threatening it and obviously giving it some sort of a message. Then the leader resumed its place at the head of the line and trotted along for another few hundred yards. It stopped again and returned to the last wolf, threatening again. But the smaller wolf refused to take the hint and continued to tag along at the rear of the column.

Finally the lead animal went back and furiously pitched into the smaller wolf, killing it within a few minutes. Then the family continued on its way.

I examined the dead wolf and removed its skin, finding it to be a young female in heat. I'm reasonably sure that the animal that killed it was the mother wolf of the group. When a young female wolf comes in heat when it is about 21 months old, she is expected to leave the family and seek her mate elsewhere.

March 31, 1928: 10 below at 8 a.m. Twelve below at 7 p. m., clear, east wind. Saw 10 gray wolves one half mile from the cabin. Lots of caribou around now.

After about 1926 on almost any winter day I could climb one of the high ridges near my cabin and with binoculars spot a band of wolves. From December through spring, feeding caribou were scattered across the hills and flats. Almost every night wolves killed one or more of them within a few miles of my main cabin. After they kill, and are full of meat, wolves trot off to lie down for a snooze on a good lookout point. Ravens relish wolf kill leftovers, and the coming and going of these big black flapping birds often helped me to locate wolf kills.

January 22, 1931. 24 below all day. Clear, calm. Wolves howling and caribou all over the hills.

Occasionally during the day a bunch of wolves crossed the big flat where there were scattered caribou, and sometimes they even chased these caribou. When wolves chase caribou during the day, it's usually just for fun. Most kills are made at night. Sometimes a young, foolish wolf will chase caribou in the daytime, but he's usually wasting his time. Caribou are faster than wolves. Even if a wolf sneaks to within 30 feet or a caribou, if the deer sees him when he makes his final dash, the wolf will pop his teeth in the place the caribou just vacated.

One three-mile by nine-mile flat I often watched not far from my main cabin lay between Savage River and Middle River. One March day from high on a ridge I watched a pack of six wolves make a rare daytime hunt there. The wolves must have been hungry, for when they are hungry they will kill any time they can. I first spotted the wolves about two miles away as they trotted single file off of a high knoll, heading across the flat, heads and tails down, looking less than ambitious. Half way across the flat they passed downwind of a lone caribou cow. Six sniffing heads came up, and six wolves swerved to head through low willows toward the caribou. When close to the caribou, a big black wolf lay down while the other five were transformed into shadowy, stalking, cats.

As its companions sneaked off, the black wolf issued a low, musical howl and boldly walked toward the cow. She raised her head and stared at him. This was what he wanted. He trotted back and forth, howling, keeping her attention as he gradually worked closer. When the caribou seemed on the verge of fleeing, the wolf backed off a bit. The nervous cow seemed fascinated. Once the wolf ran a short distance toward the caribou then stopped and retreated before the caribou panicked; the big predator made no real effort to give chase.

With my binoculars it was all I could do to occasionally spot any of the five wolves as they expertly slipped through grass and willow clumps, keeping to low ground, smoothly working their way behind the cow. They formed a rough semi-circle around the caribou and gradually closed in.

On their bellies, heads and tails low, they crawled and scooted ever closer. Occasionally a wolf raised up to peek at the cow, but she was so enamored with the howling black wolf in front of her that she didn't notice.

Finally one of the wolves got within about 30 feet of the cow and made his dash. She wheeled and started to run. But the other wolves rushed in, and she was surrounded. In moments she was smothered by the chopping fangs of all six of the efficient killers. The downed caribou was still struggling weakly when the wolves started ripping great chunks from her hams and gulping them down.

Normally a caribou can easily outrun a wolf. A straightforward chase of caribou on an open flat doesn't work, and wolves know it. That's why a sneaky, sly conquest like this has to be orchestrated.

When I walked out on that flat in cold weather I had great difficulty getting within gunshot distance of a caribou, for the deer are extremely wild in winter, especially with wolves around. The first caribou to spot me would run, spooking every other caribou in sight. I've seen that flat alive with running deer—all spooked by my presence. They usually ran toward hills and rough country where a healthy, adult caribou can easily outrun a wolf.

January 23, 1934: The sun hit the cabin at 10:50 a.m., left at 12:25. 54 below zero. Calm. At 3:30 p.m. I shot a monster gray wolf from the cabin door clear across the bar - over 250 yards. He is the largest wolf I have ever seen. Weighs 156 1/2 pounds, and is seal fat.

Wolves make their big caribou kills at night, and I could usually tell when there was going to be a big kill. One dark, quiet night in late March 1932, at about 11 o'clock as I was getting ready to go to bed, two packs of wolves were howling away on the big flat. I stepped outside to listen. It sounded as if there were three or four wolves in each bunch, and I guessed they were a mile or two apart. My sled dogs were all awake and uneasy; several perched on their houses looking in the direction of the howling. Tension bristled the air.

The wolves lapsed into quiet for some time, but just as I was dropping off to sleep, they renewed the howling. This time the wolves had merged in one place. They continued to howl for a long time.

I dropped off to sleep thinking, "They're singing me to sleep." I awoke perhaps an hour later. They were still howling. I knew now they had made a kill and I was hearing post-kill howling, a typical behavior I'd observed many times.

At daylight next morning I was out with binoculars and rifle. Ravens were flying and landing on the flat. I climbed to get a better look, and with binoculars I saw four wolf-killed caribou, all within 100 yards of each other. I went to inspect them and found the wolves had only eaten from the hams of three of the animals. The rest of the meat was untouched.

～

AUTHOR'S NOTE: *The following letters written by Frank Glaser in his own hand to Frank Dufresne, Executive Officer of the Alaska Game Commission, are from the Smithsonian Archives, RV 7174, Stanley Paul Young Papers, 1921–1965, Box 9, Folder 3. I have included Glaser's misspellings and sentence structure.*

Mr. Frank Dufresne   Healy Fork
Alaska Game Commission   March 19, 1932
Juneau, Alaska

Dear Friend:

I am a long time answering your last letter. About the bear hide will it be all right to just bundle it up and ship it with out a permit let me know and I will send it soon as I hear from you. I did not trap much this winter as fur is scarce and no price will give them a chance to increase and in a few years the price may be better.

I was thinking of going into guiding hunting parties again could I send to you at Juneau for a guides liccense please let me know. This has been a very tough winter on the mountain sheep the deep snow drove them out of the mountains on to the low rolling hills and the last mounth [month] the wolves and coyotes are killing them bye the hundreds. I found over 30 sheep that had been killed it seems that only the heart lungs and kidneys are being eaten the rest is left.

I shot a bitch wolf a few days agoe and she was fat most of the killing seems to be going on just north of the Park and I suppose in the Park to. This is the first time in eight years that I have seen the sheep leave the mountains and head for the flats they seem to feed on young poplar and willows as the ground feed is covered with hard snow and ice. Well Frank if you ever get over this way come and visit for the grayling fishing at my lower cabin is wounderfull.

Well, let me know about the bear hide and would you like a dark one or a light one like Mrs. Werner has.

Your friend,
Frank Glaser

Mr. Frank Dufresne   Healy Fork
                                                  Nov. 7-33

Dear Frank,
Your letter received and when I was over home I looked up the amount of wolves and coyotes I have shot and trapped and it is not many. 27 wolves 16 coyotes. At present their are no wolves here as the caribou are still north of here in the flats.

I made a trip into the Park around Yew Creek south of my upper cabin looking for coyotes but see no tracks. Mr. Harry Leik has given me permission to hunt wolves and coyotes in the Park anytime I want to. I have not taken advantage of it till this fall so if the caribou come here to winter I may get quite a few coyotes and wolves. If you ever get up this way you are all ways welcome at my place.
Frank Glaser

Mr. Frank Dufresne   Healy Forks
                                                  Dec. 26-34

Dear Frank,
Your letter of Dec. 2 received to day I just come in out of the hills. I am up Moody this winter right up in the home of the Ovis Dahli and also the home of the wolves. Their is a white female wolf up in that vicinity that is the cleverest wild animal I

have ever encountered in my 25 years of traping and hunting. She generaly has a bunch of about eight others with her they may be her pups they are all colors from coal black to brownish black and they sure do some killing why a market hunter in the old days could take lessons from this crew. They lay up in the high ridges in the day time. I have watched them with the glasses and tried to figure to come in on them from above the next morning but the next morning when I come from above and should get some shooting why here they are on another ridge about a mile away and generally the others run when I come in sight but the white one just takes it easy not a bit excited.

I had traps at all the places were [where] they urinate but in the first part of this month it rained here for a couple of days and then turned cold and that put them séts on the bum. I had several tell me about this white wolf she is not real white but very light gray and she looks more like a police dog big ears and the main thing she know man and his ability to shoot at long range. But I suppose if I get her I will feel sorry especily if I get her in a trap.

I don't mind shooting wolves but every time I find one in my traps I feel ashamed and can hardly get up nerve to shoot them they are the real gentleman of the predatory animal family.

Why Frank on Savage last winter I watched one wolf kill a big cow caribou and it was 58 below at the time he just run her down and finaly when she was tired and turned to fight he grabed her by the nose and throwed her then riped her throught [throat] open. I killed him about 25 minutes afterward and I thought why very few men could goe out when it was 58 below and with the best of gun get near enough to caribou to shoot them.

At present I have one big male skull of a wolf and will have more bye spring and when I get say four or five wolf and coyote skulls will box them up and ship them to you. I will give you my sincere opinion and say the wolves and coyotes are sure graduly doing away with the sheep and caribou the average trapper kills nothing but male caribou sheep and moose but the wolf and coyote long towards spring kills mostly females for they are heavy with young and don't last long when they are chased for hours they give out and turn to fight. I have seen coyotes kill sheep in the park and I did not dare to interfer because it was the Park if a wolf or coyote can find sheep away from any cliffs they are his that is their only salavation to get to the cliffs first. But this thing has been going on for centurys and when man first come to Alaska he found plenty of game. I suppose when their is not many caribou and sheep left then the wolves migrate or die off.

When the caribou come thro this fall they were not near as many as last fall they are gradually decreasing and the moose when their are no caribou around then the wolves kill moose the same as a man with a gun let a pack of seven or nine wolves get after a moose and he is done it may take them several hours but time means nothing to them. I found plenty of places on Savage were wolves killed moose but never any dead wolves that the moose killed like some of these writers tell. Well Frank when you read this you will think that bye spring the predatory animals will have all the game killed off but it is not so bad for the rabbits are coming back in this locality that will save many a sheep.

Yours truly,
Frank Glaser

Mr. Frank Dufresne,   Healy Fork
                                      Feb. 14-35

Dear Frank,
Your letter of Jan. 4 received glad to hear from yu. Well the white wolf of Healy river still lives so far as I know shortly after I had wrote to you the last time the wolves left up were [where] I was located and have not come back since. About the denning habits I know that most of the dens are located right up high in the sheep hills and the pups are born as early as the first of April from 5 to eleven to a litter. Many times I have watched a family in the fall when the old ones were taking the pups to a kill and the smallest family I have ever seen was seven—five pups and the two old ones. The average family seems to be about nine and they give the pups a fine education before the trapping season starts. You know that about nine tenths of the men trapping use traps that are to small and weak to hold a wolf so the result is

most every wolf before he is a year old gets in a small trap for a few minutes then either pulls out or breaks the chain and it is part of his education.

I have noticed that every year on certain ridges that wolves travel if I hook one in a trap and don't hold him the rest of the winter the wolves avoid that ridge they sure can reason. Now if a man went way up high in the sheep hills were the snow is always blowed away and made blind sets around lone clumps of grass he is more apt to catch a sheep in the trap first and it don't seem reasonable but I have never knowed a wolf or coyote to tackle one that was in a trap.

One winter on Savage I simply had to quit trapping for a while on account of caribou their were thousands of them on the hills and as I use mostly blind sets allways on bare ground every round I made I had from three to five caribou in my traps I was using no. 31 Kangroo traps with 7 in spread but the springs are not half as strong as a number 4 newhouse they will hold a wolf if he is caught bye two toes but a good many times wolves get caught above the toes across the pad and the first lunge they make they pull their foot out of the trap.

Of all the caribou I have ever caught in 31 traps I had to kill just one when I come up to them they would give a lunge away from me and fall down then I would pounce on them and remove the trap rub their foot awhile all the time they lay real still then I would jump up quick and away they would goe none the worst for their experience. But while they were in the trap they dug the ground up and spoiled the place for to make another set.

You know Frank I have listened to fellows telling about big bands of wolves now the most I have ever seen in one band was 27 and that was in mating time in Feb. I went after them and shot two. About them tackling any one I could not say for were ever [wherever] I have seen plenty of wolves there was lots caribou. And all the wolves I ever caught or shot were in good shape some real fat even in the coldest part of the winter. But it stands to reason when game is real scarce and wolves are starving they will tackle anything but this part of Alaska is not in that stage yet for their are still lots of sheep and caribou left. If say most all the real trappers had wolf traps say 14 or even 4 newhouse traps many more wolves would be caught but the average trapper now days can hardly afford to buy that kind of traps he has a hard time trying to make a bare living at the price fur is at present.

Frank Glaser.

❧

Often in winter on moonlight nights before I went to bed I scanned the ridges around my cabin with binoculars and usually could see several bunches of 25 or 30 caribou. Undisturbed, these deer might feed in one general area for a week. Perhaps I'd watch a bunch in the same place for several days. At daylight I'd look again with the glasses. If a group of caribou I had been watching for a few days was gone I would often go and investigate. Frequently I'd find that wolves had attacked, driving the survivors away. If the wolves had been successful the evidence was there in the form of caribou carcasses.

Caribou don't see well in the dark; wolves do.

I remember one mild December night, with the temperature hovering near zero. Snow was falling. About 10 o'clock I was reading, my favorite evening recreation, when suddenly my sled dogs hit the ends of their chains, roaring and growling. I slipped my parka on and with flashlight went out and looked around. I could see nothing, but in the nearby timber I heard brush crackling.

Next morning at daylight I found fresh tracks in the snow. They printed out an easily-read story. Three wolves had chased a caribou down off the ridge. The caribou had run within 20 feet of my dogs' houses but the wolves detoured around them. The terrified caribou fled into the nearby forest, where it had slammed into a tree and fell. Wolf tracks went *around* the trees. When the caribou hit the first tree, a wolf grabbed it. There on the snow I found blood and a piece of caribou hide big as my hand.

The caribou escaped, and ran on. But soon it had hit another tree, again falling down. This time at least two of the wolves pounced. Bloody tracks of a staggering caribou trailed another hundred feet or so, to where the wolves finally brought it down.

The three wolves had devoured almost all of that caribou, leaving the remnants about 300 yards from my cabin.

I often found places where wolves had killed eight, ten or a dozen caribou during a night kill. Usually all the dead caribou were fairly close together, perhaps within a few hundred yards of each other. Again, sign in the snow the next day told the savage tale. Wolves had encircled a bunch of caribou, spooking them. Spooked caribou in a herd have a tendency to crowd away from the edge of the herd and move toward the center, trampling one another, tripping and stumbling in the dark while wolves swiftly kill as many as they want simply by running up close and slashing.

I've watched reindeer herds on moonlit nights when I drove a dog team near them. Sometimes they panic at the sight, sound, or smell of the dogs. If bedded down they leap to their feet. They may climb over one another in their efforts to get away from the dogs so they can move closer to the center of the herd.

I've seen reindeer pile up two or three deep in such melees. I've seen fawns killed and adults severely injured in these desperately frantic getaway attempts. It has always seemed strange to me that these animals don't scatter when attacked by predators. Reindeer and caribou are essentially the same animal, and I believe their reaction to danger enables wolves to make their big kills at night.

Some nature writers claim that wolves cripple their prey by cutting their hamstring to make their kill. I've watched wolves kill caribou dozens of times . I've found many hundreds of dead caribou and reindeer killed by wolves. Only once have I seen a caribou that had been hamstrung. It had apparently escaped after what I assume was a wolf had cut a hamstring in one leg just above the hock. The caribou was dragging its leg, and I shot it to put it out of its misery, using the meat for dog food.

In killing a caribou, a wolf usually runs beside it biting it in the flank. It can slash a five or six-inch-long gash that looks like a knife-cut. One good slash and the caribou's paunch falls out. The caribou drags himself a short distance, steps and walks on the paunch and his attached entrails, and falls over within a few hundred feet. Death comes soon.

"Balance of nature" idealists (there is no such thing as the balance of nature; there *is* a see-saw of nature) love to claim that wolves take mainly the sick, halt and lame, and they are beneficial to the health of their prey species. I don't see it that way. Caribou cows heavy with calf—arguably the most valuable to the species— are more vulnerable to wolves than barren cows. Caribou calves, the future of the species, are even more vulnerable. And then there are the old bulls, important for breeding.

In the Alaska Range the caribou rut ends in late October. By mid-December the antlers of the adult caribou bulls are shed. These old bulls are very thin at this time, almost walking skeletons. In late December, January, and into February they are easy prey for wolves. I have often found seven or eight skinny old bull caribou in one place where wolves killed them, with only a little meat eaten out of a few of the hindquarters. Often it seems as if it is the fun of killing that entices the wolves. The wolves weren't really hungry; they simply killed because the tired old skinny bulls were vulnerable, easy prey.

In extreme cold, when a caribou runs at full speed for any distance, its tongue hangs way out, wagging back and forth at every bound. When a wolf manages to catch up to a caribou when its tongue dangles, it may leap and grab the tongue. One quick bite and the tongue is gone. The caribou hemorrhages, and eventually dies. Several times as I watched winter chases I observed a wolf biting a caribou's tongue off, then ignoring that caribou to chase another. Seemingly, the predator realized that the tongueless caribou was done for.

Wolves are cannibalistic. Occasionally a local pack kills an intruder wolf. When food isn't plentiful, and sometimes even if it is, the dead wolf is gobbled. One winter I was walking up the Dry Delta River in the Alaska Range and saw many caribou in the nearby timber. Ravens were flying up and down over a spot ahead and I investigated. I found two or three different colors of wolf hair; gray, light gray, and black. Scouting around for a few hundred feet, I located the remnants of at least three wolves. Their skulls had been cracked open and their brains eaten. In fact, just about everything had been eaten but the animals' feet. As near as I could reconstruct, nine or ten wolves got into a big fight. The three killed in the battle were eaten by the others. It seemed odd to me, because there were so many caribou near.

Wolves don't welcome strangers into their territories, or social groups. Sometimes wolf-fights result in the death of one or more wolves, sometimes not.

In June, 1940 I was assigned by the U.S. Fish and Wildlife Service to study wolves in Mount McKinley National Park, and I spent several weeks watching six adult wolves and a litter of young pups at a den. One day the six adults were sleeping near the den when a strange big gray wolf arrived on a nearby ridge and trotted toward them. When he was about a hundred yards away one of the six, a female, ran to meet him. The other five quickly joined her, running full speed. When the first wolf reached the gray stranger she struck it with her shoulder, knocking it sprawling. Then all six wolves, growling fiercely, grabbed the stranger from different sides. There was no snapping and letting go. They stretched him out and banged him up and down on the ground. After a few moments, they released him and stood watching.

The stranger got up and hobbled off several hundred yards and bedded down. Though I watched that den for some time afterward, I never saw the strange gray wolf in the vicinity again.

I guess the message was, "This is *our* territory. We don't want you hangin' around here Mr. Gray."

The speed of big game animals, even within the same species, varies greatly. Some wolves are much faster than others. I saw a good example of this during my McKinley Park wolf studies. One day, park ranger Harold Herning and I were eating lunch on a little hill overlooking a fork in the Teklanika River. In the V of the fork 350 or so caribou, mostly cows, yearlings, and calves were congregated.

The wolf family we had been observing, led by a small black female, trotted up the river, and upon smelling the caribou, dashed over the bank toward them. The caribou fled.

The little black female was much faster than the other wolves, and soon left them behind. Some 40 or 50 two and three-week-old calves bunched up and dropped behind the main body of caribou, and the black wolf was soon among them.

She grabbed a calf by the middle of the back, reared up, shook it, flung it aside, and continued the chase. She bowled over the next calf with her shoulder. Before it could get up, she grasped its back, shook it three or four times, and dropped it. She knocked over a third calf, grabbed it, and shook it. The fourth calf she seized happened to be on soft ground where a wolf is clumsy. She hit the calf with her shoulder, knocking it down, but at the same time she stumbled and rolled end over end. The calf was first to its feet, and as it started to flee again, it accidentally bumped into the just-recovering wolf, knocking her flat.

That angered the wolf. After half a dozen jumps she caught the calf by the back and raised it high in the air, shaking it. Then she slammed the calf down, putting both front paws on it, and biting out large chunks of flesh which she tossed aside as fast as she could.

The wolves didn't eat any of those calves. Each of the dead calves suffered bites through the backbone and into the lungs and heart.

In November 1926 at Savage River I found a six-month-old black male wolf in one of my #31 kangaroo traps—a smooth-jawed trap that usually won't hold a wolf. Occasionally, however, this trap obtains a good hold above the foot of a wolf, as it did in this case.

The freshly caught wolf, which resembled a big handsome German shepherd dog, was uninjured. He boldly stared back at me and I had to admire him for his nerve. I decided to take him home alive.

I was carrying a birch stick I used to tap trapped foxes on the nose to knock them out. I tried to tap the wolf with it, but he was too fast for me, dodging each time I swung. I simply couldn't hit him on the nose where I wanted to. I went down the side of the ridge to a patch of willows and cut a short willow stick.

When I returned, the wolf came out to the end of the trap chain. He was angry, wanting to bite me. With my left hand I held the short willow stick out. It clamped its teeth on the stick, and while it was chewing, I cracked him a light tap across the nose to knock him out. I tied his jaws shut, and tied his legs. I put him on my packboard and carried him home.

I put a collar on him and chained him to a dog house, then straddled him while I untied him. As soon as his jaws were free I jumped clear, fearing his teeth. I needn't have worried; the instant he was released the wolf plunged into the dog house.

At first he refused to come out of the house during the day, but at night he emerged to drink the water and eat the food I left. But for some time, the moment I would appear he would dive out of sight.

He soon stopped being aggressive toward me. In a few days I could pull him out of his house and handle him without worrying about being bitten. But when he was about a year and a half old he became cranky and I had to watch him carefully.

When my wolf was two years old he weighed 145 pounds, very large for a wolf. I had quite a time weighing him on a beam scale. I had to tie his jaws and legs to immobilize him so I could put him into a tarpaulin I hung from the scale.

When I went to town I couldn't leave the wolf untended at my Savage River cabin, so I harnessed and hooked him to my dog sled with the rest of my team. I always waited until the last moment to hook him in the wheel position immediately next to the sled where I was close and could keep an eye on him. He didn't pull much. The only time he ever really pulled was when a caribou appeared in front of the team. Otherwise he went along with his head and tail down, not showing much interest.

I didn't try to force him to pull, and I was satisfied simply to be able to handle him. I had plans for that wolf.

The Wolf Dogs

In February 1927 I tied my captive black wolf so he could reach Nellie, my female malemute. She had tried to make friends with him almost from the first day I brought him home. Soon she was obviously carrying pups, and I was eager for them to arrive, for I wanted a team of wolf-dogs.

Five pups arrived in late March. The four males, in varying shades of gray, became Buster, Wolf, Kobuk, and Denali. The female, black with white throat and chest, I named Queen, which soon became Queenie. The pups were fat, warm, squirmy and lively and did not appear different from pure malemute pups I often raised. The difference showed up when they got older.

I bred the captive wolf to Nellie again the following year, and another litter arrived in March 1927. When Queenie was two, I bred her to a beautiful big half-wolf/malemute belonging to Bill Green, another trapper. In May 1929 she had 13 pups; ten females and three males. I kept the three males, naming them Kenai, Yukon, and Wolf.

November 17, 1927: Nellie got in a trap and I had to shoot her. She was the best little dog I ever had.

I kept the best pups from various litters. From 1926 until 1937 when I left Savage River, I had from seven to eleven wolf-dogs. Most were half wolf, some were three-quarters wolf, and a few were one-quarter wolf. Animals I selected from the various lit-

Frank Glaser with Queenie (right) and Buster, littermates, circa 1938.
Both were half wolf, and were part of Glaser's sled dog team.

FRANK GLASER

ters made fine sled and pack dogs, much better than pure malemute or husky dogs. They had more endurance, and tougher feet.

A sled dog's feet are critical. Usually, they are the first thing to
give out. Running on ice, snow balling between the toes, or ice
crystals on rivers and lakes can all give a dog sore feet. My wolf-
dogs could travel day after day under conditions that would have
produced sore feet with other dogs and they never seemed to
notice it.

Like most sled dogs they were chained to their houses most
of the time. The main exercise they got was during winter when
they were hooked to a sled, and they always enjoyed that, pulling with real enthusiasm.

I started to train my wolf-dogs in the summer and fall when
they were four and five months old (the litters, wolf-like, were
born between late March and early May). I soon realized these
animals had the intelligence of a wolf plus the tractability of a
dog. They were also far more sensitive than most of the malemutes or huskies I had owned. I was fortunate, for not all wolf/
dog crosses produce animals with desirable traits.

I have seen vicious, intractable wolf/dog crosses I wouldn't have
kept five minutes. There couldn't be a meaner, or more savage dog
than a half or three quarter wolf-dog raised or handled wrong. A
trapper I knew casually in interior Alaska was once attacked by
three wolf-dogs in his team. He told me he had to yank the gee
pole out of his sled and beat them to death. I suspect he brought
the problem on himself; he was pretty rough on his dogs.

I believe much of my success came from the way I handled
my wolf-dogs. I was firm with them, but not cruel. When I punished a dog by voice, switch, or otherwise it knew it had the
punishment coming and there was no resentment. An angry word
from me was often enough; those animals hated to have me upset
with them.

For the ten years or so before I acquired wolf-dogs, I owned
sled dogs and had driven a number of dog teams belonging to
others. Owning a team of malemutes or huskies requires a major
commitment of time, energy, patience, and emotion. Owning a
team of wolf-dogs called for an even greater commitment, for
there were few people I felt comfortable in leaving them with. I

never allowed anyone else to drive those sensitive, intelligent animals. They had to be controlled carefully, and couldn't be treated like ordinary sled dogs. Except for my occasional trips to town when I left them with trusted friends or knowledgeable dog handlers, I had to tend them 24 hours a day, 365 days a year. In a way they were my family. I spent more time with them than I ever did with another person until I was married at the age of 52.

My wolf-dogs viewed me as their leader, much as they would view the leader of a wild pack. I had to dominate them so they would obey and remain loyal, yet not be cowed. In the eleven years I owned, bred, and drove wolf-dogs, Kenai, one of Queenie's pups who sometimes seemed more wolf than dog, was the only one that ever repeatedly challenged me. Kenai was three-quarters-wolf, and it showed in his size, appearance, and unfortunately, sometimes in his behavior. More on Kenai later.

Queenie, the black female half-wolf from the first litter of half-wolf dogs, was the quickest to learn what I wanted. She was also more affectionate with me than the others, although aloof with strangers. I made her my leader, and it was a decision I never regretted. She loved to have me pet and handle her, and I frequently allowed her to come into my cabin. In winter when her coat was heavy she couldn't stand the heat very long, but she would stay until she was panting and obviously uncomfortable.

The first thing I taught the wolf dogs was to come when I called them by name. Next, they learned what the harness and sled were for when I hitched them to an empty sled on bare ground. Both of these steps were simple and they learned them quickly.

The next step, to teach them to lie down and remain steady when I was hooking them up, required hours of patient training. I tied the sled to a tree. Then I harnessed Queenie and hooked her in the lead position on the towline, telling her to lie down. She caught on quickly. I would harness the others one at a time while they were still at their doghouses, turn them loose, and call them to their position on the towline. I would make each lie down in turn, and wait while I repeated the process with the others.

When the entire team was hooked to the towline and lying down, I would go into the cabin as I would in winter to warm my hands and to put on my parka and mittens. During the summer/fall training, I stood in the cabin and peeked out to see how they were behaving. Every wolf-dog would be quivering, ears up, watching the cabin, waiting for me, eager to go.

Often when I left the cabin during my training, several of the animals would be tempted into standing. "Down," I would order, patiently pushing them down. Then I'd go back to the cabin. Sometimes I worked with them that way for an hour or more, without releasing them to run. Sometimes I removed their harnesses and called them to their houses and chained them up for a time. Then I'd do it all over again.

By winter I could leave them lying in place without having to snub the sled. They would anxiously wait while I went into the cabin for my parka and mittens, or anything I wanted to put in the sled. They were like coiled springs, hardly able to contain themselves. They might lie quivering for half an hour, but they wouldn't move. At my "all right," they were away like a shot, leaping into action and speeding down the trail.

In some matters I don't know whether my wolf-dogs were particularly intelligent, or were simply exhibiting wolf behavior. One September seven of my four-month-old wolf-dog pups running loose near my cabin encountered a porcupine. They trotted back to the cabin, seeking my help. Four had a few quills in their noses, three had no quills. One, the most aggressive male, had quills in his mouth where he had grabbed the porky.

I yanked the quills out and tied them up. Next day I took the dog that had had the mouth full of quills and searched out a porcupine. I pretended to hit the porky with a stick, and I egged the young wolf-dog on. "Sic 'im, boy, sic 'em," I urged.

He had apparently learned his lesson, for he wouldn't get closer than three feet from the quill-rattling porky. Most dogs don't learn from a porcupine encounter; in fact, after being quilled, some dogs grow to hate a porky, and will tackle one whenever they can, with sad results.

Over a 40-year period I handled more than 500 dead wolves in Alaska. Only one of that number had porcupine quills in him, and I believe that wolf was rabid. Did my wolf-dogs learn from their porcupine encounter, or did their wolf blood tell them to leave the porky alone? I don't know. I do know that when those seven pups found the porcupine, it was the only time any of my wolf-dogs acquired quills.

My dogs weren't vicious with me or other people, although they did tend to be one-man animals. Queenie especially disliked to be petted by anyone but me. She was friendly with people as long as they didn't put their hands on her. Even then she never tried to bite. When she was loose she would stand behind me when other people were near. If anyone tried to touch her, she walked a short distance then stood and looked at them.

All my wolf-dogs had the peculiar odor typical of wolves. Many times I rubbed my hands through the fur of a fresh wolf skin and smelled it. I like the smell, although some people don't. It's different from the smell of a dog.

When the dogs at the town of Healy, where I usually shopped, smelled my team, they would tuck their tails between their legs and disappear after about one whiff. Eventually the mere sight of my team arriving in town caused loose dogs to vanish.

When my wolf-dogs occasionally fought among themselves they tried to kill one another. From the time they were pups, though, I worked to convince them not to fight. When a pup started a fight I gave it just enough of a switching to sting. As adults most of my wolf-dogs weighed 120 to 130 pounds. Kenai, the biggest, weighed 155. To break up fights when they were adults I used a padded leather blackjack filled with about a pound of lead shot. When a dog started a fight I'd tap him across the nose and knock him down. If he growled at me or showed any more inclination to fight, I'd knock him down again.

That broke most of them of fighting. These animals were so powerful and their wolf-like teeth so sharp they could have easily killed one another. Usually a fight started when a dog tangled his harness when running or pulling, and he'd blame the dog running beside him and light into him.

Queenie never fought because she knew I didn't want her to. If a dog tried to pick a fight with her she simply turned away.

My wolf-dogs made a superb dog team, with unusual abilities and traits. Every March and April when temperatures rose to around zero and the snow was deep and crusted, I often visited several distant trappers. Those were some of my happiest days.

There is no more beautiful place in the world than the Alaska Range country when the sky is blue and the air calm and mild. The snowy peaks looked like ice cream cones. As I traveled I would see caribou and moose, and tracks of other animals. I'd use a light sled and carry food for just the dogs and me, as well as a rifle, axe, sleeping bag, tarp and extra ropes and harnesses, so that the sled moved easily even with me riding. Some of my friends lived 60 or 70 miles from Savage River and the wolf-dogs could travel that distance easily in a day; I could have turned them around and returned home without stopping, they were that tough.

As my wolf-dogs matured and knew what I expected from them they became easier for me to handle. Queenie, as leader, exercised a lot of control. When I had them lying down while in harness she would snarl at any dog that became restless and he'd usually get the message.

Like dogs, wolf-dogs communicate their mood by the position of ears, tail, and body. I could tell at a glance when one was unhappy and usually could figure out what was bothering it. Maybe a harness would be chafing, or the animal didn't feel well. And, like dogs, they communicated by voice. I could tell what kind of an animal was near the cabin by their bark. If they saw or smelled a man approaching the cabin, a rare event, their bark was distinctive. Once two men built a cabin in McKinley Park about three miles from my cabin. When the wind came from that direction, the dogs either heard or scented the men and their bark told me about it.

When caribou crossed upwind of the cabin the wolf-dogs announced it with another, distinctive bark. If I needed meat I would grab my rifle when they barked their "caribou" bark. When wolves came within scenting distance, they looked toward me and the cabin and wagged their tails, barked, then howled a little, behavior they exhibited only when wolves were near.

Sometimes when I noticed the dogs standing on their houses sniffing and looking upriver I'd walk 200 yards up a hill behind the cabin to where I had a clear view for about three miles. Invariably I'd spot a grizzly, a moose or a caribou.

I fed the wolf-dogs dried salmon much of the time as well as caribou and moose. Wolf-like, those dogs could hold a caribou bone in their paws and feed it into one side of its mouth and chew off little pieces. They could crack the heaviest of moose and caribou bones to get at the marrow, a feat impossible for the ordinary sled dog. The wolf-like shearing action of their strong teeth was considerably different from that of dogs.

Occasionally when short of meat or fish, I made my wolf-dogs a big batch of hotcakes. I usually saved two or three five-gallon cans of grizzly bear fat every fall, which I rendered into oil. I'd dunk four or five big hotcakes for each dog into the bear grease. I would then release all the dogs and call, "Hotcakes today, boys!" They would crowd into the cabin and line up like a bunch of eager kids. I'd hand each dog its hotcakes, and it would carry them back to its doghouse to eat. Then I'd snap their chains on them again.

In June 1927, when my first bunch of wolf-dogs was a little over a year old, I was walking between my cabins on a bar of the Savage River. Three of the dogs, including Buster, ran loose and I led the others on chains.

Here and there on the bar I noticed fresh foot-deep holes where grizzlies had dug up pea vine roots. The bears follow the roots down, digging with their big claws and eating the roots as they dig.

As I broke out of the willows into a clearing, about 150 feet ahead was the rear end of a sow grizzly bear sticking out of a hole where she was digging a pea vine root. Her nearly grown cubs were 30 or 40 feet beyond her, also digging.

Buster rushed at the old sow. She heard him coming and whirled to meet him. She sat on her haunches, jaws wide open, one of her ivory-clawed paws sticking out. Buster actually ran into her. She reached down and scooped him up with her paw and started to grab him with her jaws.

I dropped the chains of the other dogs, lifted my rifle, and fired at the bear. She either let go, or Buster broke loose or both, probably. She was just about to shove him into her mouth and one bite could have killed him.

I hated to kill her, but I had to in order to save the dog. He had never before attacked a bear and he never did it again. Usually my wolf-dogs ran around a bear, feinting, and retreating when threatened, often howling while at this game and sounding very much like wolves. In this manner they often chased grizzlies away from the cabin until bear and dogs were out of sight. They always returned in an hour or two, happily wagging their tails and unhurt. Wolf-like, they had no fear of bears. Buster just got carried away that time.

✍

MY CAPTIVE MALE breeding wolf and the resulting wolf-dogs gained me a reputation as a wolf expert. I learned through experience and I suppose that somewhat qualified me. At any rate it brought me a certain celebrity, and in one case, a $50 bill.

In the summer of 1927 while at Fairbanks I encountered Theodore Van Bibber, who owned a boarding kennel for sled dogs at the edge of town. "I have a problem, Frank," he told me, "and I think you can help me."

His "problem" was a female wolf he was holding in a big corral. "I've been offered $200 for her. But I can't handle her," he explained. "I've spent days trying to get a collar and chain on her, but she won't let me near. I'll give you $50 if you can get a collar and chain on her."

That was a challenge I liked.

Van Bibber acquired the wolf, a handsome, gray three-year-old, a couple of months earlier from Newton, a trader on the Tanana River. Newton got her from Indians when she was a pup.

I went into the corral with her but as long as Van Bibber was there the wolf ran to the farthest corner where it nervously paced. Clearly, she was afraid of him.

"Do you have any pups?" I asked. "A little dog puppy, say three or four months old will do."

I selected a pup from one of the litters he had, and sat in the center of the wolf's corral petting it. Van Bibber kept opening the gate and peeking in. This caused the nervous wolf to run to the farthest corner, where she would growl and snarl, her mane standing on end.

"You'll have to stay away," I told him. "I can't do anything with you here."

I spent the afternoon with the wolf and the pup. From time to time I turned the pup loose and it would run to her. She smelled of it, and after a bit responded when the pup wanted to play. The pup kept jumping up and putting its paws on her and she seemed to like that.

I retrieved the pup, and again sat petting it. And I continually talked to the wolf. From time to time I howled like a wolf, which seemed to interest her. Several times she followed the pup almost to me. From time to time I walked around the corral continually talking to her and occasionally howling. She circled me, around and around wanting to play with the pup, and I could tell she was curious about me.

She'd run one way, and then the other gradually working herself closer to me. Finally she tip-toed near to smell the pup and I touched her on the neck. She leaped back stiff-legged, and her mane came up. By evening I had had my hands on her two or three times.

I returned the next morning and took a chain and had a choke collar in each coat pocket. I figured if I could slip a choke collar on her I could then snap the chain on it. I again spent much time petting the pup, and the wolf became tamer by the hour.

Twice that day I had a choke collar almost slipped over her head but she leaped back each time.

The next day when the pup and I arrived she was clearly pleased. She came close almost immediately and I allowed the pup to play with her for a time before taking it to the center of the corral where I sat petting it. I kept a choke collar handy.

The wolf came close to sniff and lick the pup and remained still long enough for me to slip a choke collar over her head. She leaped back but within minutes came close again. Snapping the chain into the choke collar was simple.

When she came up against the chain she reared back and pulled, but I held her, trying to soothe her. She ran around and around me, growling and making a big fuss, but didn't attempt to bite. I put a stout leather collar on her without any difficulty.

Van Bibber made his sale and I got my $50.

The buyers of that wolf were John and Robert McComb, students at the University of Alaska. They sold it to Shorty Russick, in Quebec, who bred her with an Irish wolfhound. He used the resulting pups as racing sled dogs.

Many Alaska sled dog handlers have bred dogs with wolves. It seems to work well only with a male wolf and a female dog. Female wolves are high-strung and often they will not breed with a dog. When they do, they may be so nervous they kill the pups. I am aware of only one successful female wolf/male dog cross and that was the female that went to Quebec after I caught her for Van Bibber.

≋

THE FIRST CAPTIVE WOLF I ever saw belonged to Demone Wheeler, a Californian who spent his summers in Alaska. I was in Chitina in 1920 when Wheeler and his wife arrived there one day on the Copper River Railroad. They had arranged to drive from there over the Valdez Trail to Fairbanks with Billy Fraim. Billy had his Model T Ford loaded, with Wheeler's full grown male wolf sitting in the back seat when he called me over to meet Wheeler and see the wolf.

Wheeler's wolf, acquired in Montana, was very gentle, resembling a big police dog. Eventually Wheeler moved to Ruby on the Yukon River, where he crossed his wolf with a female part-wolf belonging to the Dago Kid who had fishwheels and crews catching and drying salmon for dog food.

The three-quarter-wolf dogs from this cross were used in teams along the Yukon River for many years. In 1923, when Olaus and Adolph Murie made an extended dog-team trip into the Koyukuk country on U.S. Biological Survey work, they used a couple of the Wheeler/Dago Kid wolf-dog crosses. Olaus later told me they worked well.

≋

EARLY ON, my wolf-dogs insisted on chasing caribou while in harness. When hot after caribou, they bawled at the tops of their voices dragging the sled with me on it wherever the caribou went. Too often that was high into the sheep hills. At times those powerful dogs dragged the upset sled with me clinging to it and cussing them for a mile or more through brush, across creeks, and over the tundra before I could stop them. My winter clothing was often torn, and I sustained a lot of scratches and bruises. I also spent a lot of time repairing dog sleds.

I decided to break them of this bad habit. At the time I worked Queenie and Buster as double leaders, running them side-by-side. One winter day when many caribou were on the flats not far from the cabin, I harnessed the dogs and snapped a lariat rope between knots in the neckline between Queenie and Buster. I tied the other end of the lariat to the bow on the back of the sled.

I headed the dogs down a trail we often traveled until half a dozen running caribou appeared. That electrified the dogs. All eyes latched onto the fleeing caribou and every animal made huge leaps in pursuit, all yipping and growling with excitement. We left the smooth trail and the sled leaped, plunging over cut banks, and ricocheting across the bumpy ground. I hung on for dear life, not daring to use the jerk line on that rough ground for fear of killing myself or a dog or two. We finally came to a big flat where it smoothed out a bit and there was a couple of feet of snow.

I hit the brake a couple of times and yelled, "Whoa, whoa, dammit." They knew the meaning of "whoa" but as usual when pursuing caribou paid no attention. I wrapped the jerk line around my wrist a couple of times and with a last "whoa," leaped from the sled.

Queenie and Buster's weight, combined, was about 250 pounds. They yanked my 155 pounds a good 10 feet through the air. Snow flew as I bounced, skidded, and rolled to a dazed stop. Queenie and Buster were somersaulted backward into the rest of the team, which rolled into a huge squirming, growling ball. The sled rammed into the pile.

When I had them straightened out and I had recovered somewhat, I hunted up another bunch of caribou. The dogs ran lickety split after them. This time when I yelled "whoa," I hauled back on the jerkline while standing on the sled—I'd had enough of being yanked through the air. Again the leaders were pulled over backward into a confused melee and again the team was rammed by the sled.

After that when I yelled, "whoa," the wolf-dogs slowed, whether or not they were shagging caribou, warily eyeing me over their shoulders. I made no more involuntary trips into the high sheep hills. Whenever they started to get a little hard to stop, I'd rig the jerkline. Occasionally on the first trips in fall or early winter I had to use it again, but as intelligent as those dogs were, the mere sight of it was usually enough to get them back under control.

Even when they responded to "whoa," it took all my strength and agility to keep my sled upright over much of the country I traveled with those dogs. At the edge of one 4,000-foot-high ridge a hundred-yard-long snow drift usually formed on my winter trail. I often found that drift broken off, leaving a 10-foot wall. I never knew in advance its state, for it kept changing. I often stopped the dogs and walked ahead to look it over before going on. If it was chopped off too abruptly, I'd swing the dogs down on the side of the steep ridge to go around it. The sled would upset almost every time and roll over and over. I used a big swivel on my towline for just that reason. I always kept my load tied down with a tarpaulin over it so I wouldn't lose anything when the sled rolled. As the sled rolled, I'd hang on, and it would go over maybe six or seven times. The dogs would keep right on going.

Often when the dogs were running, my sled would bounce from snow drifts to fly three or four sled lengths before touching down again. Especially when first starting out, when they ran as hard as they could, it was sometimes all I could do to keep the leaping sled upright and to stay with it.

Mrs. Green, the Healy railroad depot agent's wife, once said to me, "I've often told my husband that we don't have to worry about you, Mr. Glaser. If you should break a leg or something out on the trapline, you could sit in your sled and your nice doggies would bring you to town!"

Little did she know.

My wolf-dogs taught me much about wolves and their ways. Living with and working with those animals gave me great pleasure and satisfaction, and though many years have passed since the last of them, the memories they left me are still fresh and bright.

A Few Mosquito Bites

DURING THE 12 YEARS I LIVED ALONE in the Savage River wilderness I was constantly aware that if I became injured or ill I was on my own. My close neighbors were bears, caribou, moose and other wild animals, but no people. Mrs. Green's suggestion that I "..could sit in the sled and let my nice doggies bring me to Healy," was, of course, nonsense. I was always careful not to fall when I was on my trapline or traveling in the mountains. I used an axe with great care. I guarded against fire at my cabins. I handled my traps with special care; most were small and light enough so I could open them with my hands, although a few required a special clamp to open. I was careful in handling my guns. I was cautious on river and lake ice. In short, I was always aware that I could not expect help if I got hurt or became seriously ill.

But I couldn't guard against everything.

In late May of 1932 I needed some babiche (rawhide) to repair one of my dog sleds. I soaked a moosehide in water, rolled it up, and left it in a warm place so the hair would slip. After a few days when it was slimy and smelled pretty strong, I scraped the hair off, then nailed one end of the hide to a tree so I could cut strips from it.

Using a sharp knife, I walked backward as I cut nice long straight strips from the big hide. A few mosquitoes kept biting me in the neck. I noticed a little blood on my fingernails where

I'd scratched mosquito bites, but I paid no attention to it. I didn't think about the slime on my hands from the moosehide. It was only a few mosquito bites, a common minor annoyance. That night my neck started to swell. The glands under my jaws and in my armpits began to swell. I felt awful and the swelling increased. For days my condition worsened. Finally my jaw was so swollen I couldn't eat. My neck ballooned to about twice its normal size. I couldn't even hold water down.

After nearly two weeks of this I was desperate. I cut deeply into the back of my swollen neck with a razor. It was terribly painful, but I kept cutting. When I felt I had cut deep enough I stopped. By then I was bleeding heavily.

My large bottle of iodine, on hand for eight or nine years, had thickened to a syrup-like consistency. I dumped some of this on my hand and rubbed it into the cuts. I immediately tasted iodine. In about ten minutes the cabin began to whirl around and around and I passed out and fell to the floor. A doctor later told me that the concentrated iodine was a strong poison.

When I came to I realized I had to go for help. Unfortunately, it was breakup time and water was running bank-full in many creeks, while other creeks were still covered by ice with water running on top of the ice. Worst of all, Savage River, which I had to cross first, was high. To compound my difficulties I had seven big wolf-dogs I had to take with me.

I turned all the dogs loose, which I rarely did, for I always worried about them fighting. I left my rifle, which was almost like leaving my right arm, but I was so weak I couldn't have carried it. With my wolf-dogs accompanying me I was in no danger from grizzly bears. I cut a strong cane to help me walk, and to use if any of the dogs started a fight.

It was early in the morning when I slogged upstream on Savage River until I found a place with the least depth of water on top of the ice. I waded up to my waist, skidding on the slick ice, fighting to stay upright, the frigid water taking my breath away. After that came the 18-mile walk to Healy and the nightmare of crossing streams that were bank-high with water. On some of the streams I had to walk upstream for a mile or two to find a safe crossing. As I walked, I had to lie down frequently, and because of my swollen, sore neck I could only lie face down.

My wolf-dogs realized something was wrong. There was no fighting, and during my frequent rests they all gathered around me whining, wanting to help. None strayed far from my side. Their behavior touched me.

With frequent rests on tundra moss, I walked all day and all night. On one mountain I slowly climbed nearly 2,000 feet; I'd go a short way then I'd lie down and rest and when I could, I'd go at it again.

I must have been a sight as I staggered into Healy, wet and bedraggled, with a grossly swollen neck, surrounded by my pack of seven big wolf-dogs quietly walking around me.

John Colvin, a trapper friend, tied up my wolf-dogs, promising to take good care of them. Luckily a coal train was ready to pull out for Fairbanks. The conductor, a good friend, put me in his bunk in the caboose, then gave me two Anacin tablets, the first medicine of that kind I had ever had. The pain stopped and I went to sleep not waking until we arrived at Fairbanks.

My conductor friend helped me walk the short distance to Fairbanks' St. Joseph's hospital. There Doctor Aubrey Carter consulted with two other doctors before he operated on my neck to clean out and drain the poison. Just before giving me ether, one of the Catholic sisters asked, "What is your religion?"

I was so sick that I wanted to get it over with. "Sister," I said, " I have no religion right now. Just let me have the ether and get this over with." She insisted on an answer, but I repeated, "I have no religion right now." One big sniff of ether and I saw a black, spinning funnel. My last thought was, "Well, I'll get away from all those questions, anyway."

I awoke five hours later. Dr. Carter told me that the poison had been nearing my spinal cord and it probably would have killed me in another day or two.

I slept most of that day and night and awoke the next morning hungry as a spring bear. When a sister brought breakfast I wolfed it down.

"Had enough?" she asked.

"I could eat more," I told her. She brought me another breakfast, and I ate all of that. It was the first food I had eaten in more than a week.

Four days later I left the hospital feeling fine.

"What do I owe you, Doc?" I asked Carter.

"I'll make a deal with you," he offered. "If you'll promise to take me hunting next fall out at your place, we'll call it even."

That suited me fine.

He came to Savage River that fall and I helped him kill a nice bull moose and a couple of big bull caribou. He was very good company.

Alone I survived charging grizzlies, dangerous climbs, violent rides on a bucking dog sled, terrible mountain blizzards and months of deep cold.

But a few mosquito bites and a rotten moosehide almost killed me.

15
Queenie

I ALMOST KILLED QUEENIE, my favorite wolf-dog, when she was newborn.

In March 1927 I drove my dog team, with my captive wolf, to Healy. My leader was Nellie, the malemute bred by the wolf. I chained the wolf and the dogs to dog houses behind the Healy hotel where I was staying. In a day or two the temperature dropped to 40 degrees below zero and I became concerned about Nellie. Her pups were nearly due, and I didn't want her to have them outdoors in the deep cold. I put her in the unheated dog barn near the hotel.

Next morning, March 24, John Colvin, a trapper friend, and I went to feed and check on her. She was licking her first pup dry when we arrived. Steam was rising from the still-wet, wriggling baby. It was probably 25 below in the dog barn.

"Let's take her to my cabin," John suggested. I put the pup, a male, inside my parka to keep it warm and led Nellie to Colvin's house where he put an old mattress down for her in a room where there was a stove. She seemed grateful, and when I gave her the pup I had carried, she licked it some more. Over the next hour three other males arrived. Then came a black pup. After she licked it dry, I picked it up, and saw that it was a female. I didn't want any females, for they are a nuisance in a dog team when they come into season, and I decided to kill it.

"Maybe she won't have any more pups, Frank. Better save it," Colvin suggested.

That changed my mind. I let Nellie keep her black pup and named it Queen, later calling her Queenie. Colvin was right in that she was the last pup of the litter.

Half-wolf, Queenie weighed 125 pounds when full-grown. She was all black except for a white chin and white chest patch. The white revealed the dog in her; without them she could easily have passed for a full-blooded wolf. She had the prick ears, the face, the huge tough feet, the long bushy tail, the heavy ruff, and the dense coat of a wolf.

I trained Queenie and the other pups when they were four and five months old. With the others she quickly learned to pull an empty sled on dry summer grass. In October when she was eight months old I harnessed her in the lead with Nellie, her mother. Nellie was a good leader, but she had seen eight or nine winters and was old for a sled dog.

After only two trips, Queenie understood gee (turn right) and haw (left). And she caught on very quickly in other ways. I've never known another dog with her intelligence. By the following year I put her alone in the lead and by then she was a better leader than her mother. Sometimes I ran her brother Buster with her as a double leader but I usually went back to using Queenie alone. A couple of years after that I put Kenai, one of Queenie's pups, beside her in the lead.

Queenie developed into the finest lead dog I have ever seen. After two years of driving Queenie I rarely had to give her the gee or haw command, for she responded to arm signals. She continually looked back at me. If I held out my right arm, she would take the trail to the right; if I held out my left arm she took the trail to the left. She would even leave a broken trail with the arm signal. We might be zipping along on one of our old sled trails when I would hold out one arm or the other and she'd immediately leave the trail. She would keep swinging to the right or left until I called, "that's good," then she'd go straight until I gave her another signal.

Over the twelve years of her life, Queenie and I shared a lot of adventures. Once she helped me with a wounded grizzly. Each summer I caught up to 50 or 60 pounds of grayling at a time and packed them home to dry for dog food. One August a grizzly bear repeatedly smashed my fish drying racks and ate and scattered the drying grayling.

This went on for about three weeks. The bear would skip a day or two, then return after I repaired the racks and had hung a fresh batch of fish on them. The racks were near my cabin, and I worried that while I was gone the bear might kill some of the dogs, which were all chained to their houses.

One morning when I figured it was time for the bear to hit my racks again I waited for him. He arrived, but I made a bad shot and wounded him. He plunged into the thick brush. Chasing a wounded grizzly in the brush is asking for trouble, so I circled outside the patch of brush and found where the bear had gone in, but I couldn't find where he had come out.

I returned to the cabin and turned Queenie loose. She quickly found the bear's trail and followed it into the brush. I heard the bear growl and then Queenie howled. The bear ran from her, and I hurried to intercept him.

But the bear circled as Queenie harassed him, crashing through the brush growling, Queenie following and howling. She sounded just like a wolf. She didn't attack the bear, just chased and howled, chased and howled.

After half an hour, she managed to run the bear out of the brush and I finished him off. After he was down she grabbed the dead bear by a hind leg and yanked and growled and wooled him as if she had killed him all by herself. She grinned, wagged her tail, and pranced about proudly.

Another minor adventure started one evening near dark when I was watching a couple of cross foxes at play on a sandstone bluff just above my cabin. They showed up clearly in my binoculars and I was enjoying seeing them chase each other up and down the steep slope. Suddenly, the foxes fled from something they had seen.

I swung the binoculars down from the foxes and saw three wolves trotting down a bar of Savage River. One of the wolves broke off and chased the foxes. Suddenly, the other two wolves were less than 100 yards from my cabin.

I dashed to the cabin for my rifle. Though it was nearly dark, I saw one of the wolves with my naked eye, and he appeared big and clear in my rifle scope. I fired and the wolf dropped. The wolf that had chased the foxes was loping off of the bluff and I centered the scope on him and fired. He rolled 50 or 60 feet off of the bluff, then got up and ran off. I missed a shot at the third wolf.

October 1, 1928: A band of gray wolves come close to the cabin. It was pretty dark but I killed the old bitch and hit one other.

I turned Queenie loose to go with me to collect the dead wolf. It was full dark when I picked the animal up by the hind legs and hoisted it to my shoulder. It's head just cleared the ground and I started for the cabin where I could hang it up and skin it. Suddenly it floundered around and I heard teeth snap. I thought that Queenie had grabbed the wolf and was pulling on it. I dropped the animal and whirled around and saw that Queenie wasn't anywhere near. The wolf was on the ground, its teeth locked in my pants, shaking his head. Queenie had been running toward me, but she shied off, startled by the moving wolf.

The wolf turned my pants loose and sat up. Foolishly I had left my rifle at the cabin. I leaped to a nearby pile of driftwood, pried a spruce pole loose, and bammed the wolf over the head with it. About then Queenie pitched into the wolf and ripped its throat open. I think she thought I was threatened. My bullet had just creased the wolf's skull.

I praised Queenie for helping me and she pranced about grinning and wagging her tail, pleased with herself.

October 2, 1928. Found a big dog wolf dead about 200 yards from where I hit him last night. Twelve above at 6 a.m.

SUMMERS, when there wasn't much to be done on my traplines, I often traveled across country exploring for a week or two at a time, taking the wolf-dogs with me, each dog carrying a pack. It was hell the first year, for I had to lead most of the dogs on chains. They clustered tightly around me, bumped into one another, and often got cranky and fought one another. They wanted to chase every caribou they saw. Loose dogs with packs that chase game either get hung up in brush or trees, or they return without packs, or with empty packs.

I allowed one or two dogs to run loose, while I led the others. When the loose dogs chased caribou, I used a willow switch to punish them when they returned, pretending I was going to murder them. It took a long time and a lot of patience to teach all those dogs to ignore caribou but eventually they learned. Queenie caught on quicker than the others, because she always wanted to please me. After two trips that first summer, Queenie would stand and watch as a caribou ran off.

Queenie possessed real intelligence. One day when it was about 50 below zero, so cold I shouldn't have been going anywhere, I decided to go to town and get my mail and a few things I needed. I hadn't been to Healy for about a month.

I hooked the team up as usual and left them lying, waiting while I went into the cabin to get warm. While harnessing dogs during extreme cold I wore light wool gloves because mittens are too awkward. On this day my hands became pretty cold, so it took some time in the cabin for me to get them warm.

When I was ready, I put on my fur parka, left the cabin, and was about four feet from the sled when a caribou jumped down a cut bank on the other side of the river and ran out on the river ice. At sight of the running caribou the dogs leaped up and ran down the trail, growling as they always did as they headed out. I made a dive for the sled and missed, landing flat on my belly. The dogs swooped over a cut bank and on up the river trail. I reached the river in time to see them going around the first bend 200 yards away on a dead run, every dog in place.

I ran toward the bend, but at 50 below zero one doesn't run very far and I had to slow down. I had just reached the bend when I saw the team returning, every dog still in place. The only change was the upset sled.

As they went by me I grabbed the sled, pulled it upright, and called to Queenie, "Come gee." I grinned as she swung back onto the trail, head high, ears pricked, tail wagging, and headed for town. I was sure proud of those dogs.

Their tracks in the fresh snow told me what had happened.

The caribou had disappeared in the timber, and they had apparently forgotten about it. I was in the habit of talking to the dogs when we started out. Normally as we left the cabin they growled and half-barked at every jump and were so lively I'd caution, "Easy, boys, easy," for a mile or so. They always ran as hard as they could for the first five minutes or so.

Queenie immediately realized that I wasn't on the sled, but she didn't turn in the narrow part of the river where the team might have tangled. Instead, she waited until they came to a wide area on the river to circle and return for me.

On another occasion I was a few miles from Healy, headed for town. The team was on a dead run, going downhill on smooth, hard wind-blown snow. The experimental farm of the University of Alaska had some Yaks in a fenced area a few miles from Healy. I was gawking at the Yaks, standing with one hand on the sled's bow, paying no attention to the dogs or the trail. The dogs followed a sharp turn, and I was thrown off. I hit hard and rolled over and over in the snow. By the time I picked myself up the team was a hundred yards away, still at a dead run. I saw Queenie throw her head up and look around. As I stood and watched, she turned a big circle and came right back. When she came by me she slowed down and I swung back on the sled and we went on down the trail.

After that, when the team got away from me I didn't worry; I knew that Queenie would return for me and she always did. That is unusual behavior for a sled dog.

Queenie didn't like to have strangers pet her. Her hair wouldn't come up on end but she'd stand and look at me with her big brown eyes, her ears drooping. She knew she couldn't move when harnessed with the team, so she stood and took it. The moment the stranger walked away, her ears would come back up, and she'd be happy again.

Although Queenie avoided strangers, she liked small children. In 1934 I went to Seattle to visit my father and I took Queenie and Buster, her brother, with me. I valued those two dogs too highly to leave them with anyone for the length of time I planned to be gone. At my father's home in Seattle I built a pen and doghouses for them, and chained them inside the pen.

*Queenie, Frank
Glaser's favorite wolf-
dog. Half-wolf,
Queenie weighed
about 125 pounds, and
Glaser claimed she was
the smartest dog he
ever owned. He used
her as a leader in his
wolf-dog team, and
during snow-free
months she performed
as a pack dog.*

FRANK GLASER

One evening I took their pans into the house to get their food, leaving the gate open. When I returned I found a little girl hanging onto Queenie's ears, trying to tug her out of her house. "C'mon out of there, you big studabaker," the kid, about four, was shrieking.

My heart almost stopped. I ran to the kid and picked her up, thinking, "That dog is half wolf! One bite and that kid's dead."

But when I put the kid down, Queenie ran to her with her tail wagging and licked her face. Queenie loved that little girl! I never

again left the gate open but the girl often visited when I tended to the dogs and she and Queenie became friends. Sometimes the child would climb on Queenie's back and ride her around the pen. Queenie seemed to get as much fun out of it as did the little girl. The big wolf-dog was always very gentle with her young friend.

Although she rarely encountered children in Alaska, ever after that she was attracted by them and seemed especially fond of the very young ones.

Queenie became an expert at catching snowshoe hares. As a

young dog she learned it was fruitless to chase them, although all the other dogs would chase a rabbit on sight and run until they were exhausted. Queenie would slip out into the brush and wait until a rabbit came near then she would leap on it. She ate every rabbit she caught.

She also loved to eat ptarmigan and spruce hens. Twice while I lived at Savage River the spruce hen cycle was high, and the birds were everywhere. They liked to roost in two big spruce trees behind my cabin. Queenie would growl until I came out of the cabin and she would look up into the trees, showing me the birds. Sometimes I'd turn her loose, and with a .22 rifle I'd pop off a bunch. She'd pounce on the birds as they dropped. All she left were a few feathers, the head, and legs. When abundant, spruce hens are often tame. I've killed up to 60 of them in a day.

With Queenie as leader, I never worried about losing the trail. She usually knew where we were going and somehow she knew where we were at all times. The 18-mile-long trail from my main cabin to Healy where I got my mail and supplies crossed ridges up to 4,000 feet elevation. Timberline is at about 2,000 feet so these ridges are open and exposed—right up against the high mountains of the Alaska Range. Many times my wolf-dogs covered that 18 miles in two hours flat.

Often while I was traveling across these ridges on a calm day with the temperature at 30 or 40 below zero, without warning a 50-or-60-mile-an-hour local wind would suddenly whip off the high mountains. Snow would fill the air so that I could scarcely see Queenie at the head of the team, and there would be a steady roar from the wild wind. Often I had difficulty clinging to the bouncing sled. Several times the wind hit so hard it turned the sled over. As the wind arrived, the temperature warmed to 20 or 30 below, sometimes warmer.

Despite high wind and lack of visibility, Queenie never lost the trail. Sometimes she had to face the wind, and I've seen her and the team crawl into a 60-mile-an-hour wind. When the dogs stopped, I knew their eyes were frozen together from fine snow on their eyelashes. When this happened they would lie down and wipe at their eyes with their paws.

I would crawl up the towline to Queenie and with bare hands

clear the ice from her eyes, then do the same for the other dogs. Then we'd go on. Each fall I drove stakes along the route to guide me during blizzards but with Queenie in the lead I didn't really need the stakes.

She was a master at picking the best route for the team when we traveled in rough country. When she couldn't see ahead she would run a few steps on her hind legs to get a good look, searching for the best route. She might do that two or three times before deciding which way to go.

Wolf-like, she ran a straight line between points. I often marveled at the absolutely perfect line we left on fresh snow when on a new route. On river ice, most dog teams follow the bank along one side of a river. Unless given a haw or gee command, they parallel the curves, or points. But Queenie, without a word from me, trotted an absolutely straight course from point to point, barring windfalls or other barriers she might have to go around.

A few miles out of Healy my trail crossed a lake that was about a quarter of a mile across. Once I was about a hundred feet from shore when I looked back and saw the ice breaking up behind the sled. I learned later that it had been open water the previous day. Queenie realized the ice was thin and dangerous at the same time I did. Without a word or signal from me, she swung toward the nearest shore and ran faster as I crawled up in the sled to spread the weight. Every one of the nine dogs in my team that day weighed well over 100 pounds. If we'd broken through, it would have been disastrous.

Queenie disliked some people, probably taking her cue from me. One was Hobo Bill, who lived near Healy. I usually avoided him because he was always dirty and he was an unpleasant man who frequently got into disputes with others. He once came to visit me at a cabin I was staying at in Healy. I didn't invite him in but stood in front of the cabin to talk. Queenie was tied nearby. Hobo Bill had quarreled with another trapper and he started to tell me about it. He stood close, excitedly waving his arms and talking loudly. Queenie bounded out of her doghouse and lunged toward him. Only the chain stopped her. She thought old Hobo Bill was threatening me.

Every time Hobo Bill raised his arms or spoke loudly, she

backed up to get slack and hit the end of her chain, trying to break loose.

He finally noticed her behavior and turned to look at her. She stared back at him, hair on end, growling like a wolf.

"If she got loose I believe she'd try to kill me," he said, shocked.

"Yes, I believe she would," I agreed. "And I have half a notion to turn her loose."

He gave me a strange look, turned pale, and left. He never returned.

In 1937 I left Savage River to go to work for the U.S. Biological Survey. I boarded all my dogs out but Queenie and Buster, keeping them at my cabin in Fairbanks when I was there.

On one of my first assignments with Queenie and Buster as pack dogs I walked from Eagle to Circle Hot Springs, following a caribou herd.

August 9, 1937: Left Dome Creek at 7:20 a. m. Had traveled just three miles when Queenie collapsed. Camped for the day. Dog was in bad shape in the evening, not being able to raise her hindquarters.

I believe Queenie picked up a poison bait left out by a trapper. She almost died from it and afterwards she never really recovered full use of her front legs. The poison also adversely affected the muscles that allowed her to curl up in sleep, an important heat-conserving ability for an outdoor dog in the North.

Queenie recovered enough to continue the journey, but she was never the same afterward. She died at Fairbanks in January 1939 at the age of 12 while I was away on a field trip. I never knew another dog that could compare with her.

AUTHOR'S NOTE: The December 1994 issue of *Alaska* Magazine carried a profile that I wrote on Frank Glaser. Queenie and Buster were mentioned. Arnold J. Elieff, of Sequim, Washington, read the article and wrote me the following about Queenie and Buster:

Reading about Queenie and Buster, Glaser's "dogs," brought back a poignant memory. In 1938–39 I lived at Fairbanks with Dick Acheson and Paul Huebner in a cabin that Glaser owned. No rent, just take care of his wolf-dogs Queenie and Buster.

These two animals looked more like wolves than dogs. Both had very long legs and huge pads. Queenie wasn't over-friendly— she was evidently a one-person animal. She was old and inactive, and she often simply stared at us. She didn't bark or howl. She was coal black except for white patches on her chin and chest. Buster was somewhat larger and had brown and gray fur. He was a pacer, and frequently walked back and forth on his chain.

I was cautious when I fed them; we always shortened Buster's chain before we put his food down because if we put it directly in front of him he became overly-possessive.

I enrolled at the University of Alaska. Dick worked at Waechter Brothers Meat Market and obtained bones and trimmings for the wolf-dogs. We fed them a cooked cornmeal and tallow (suet) mixture along with the meat scraps.

In late December Queenie started feeling bad and lost her appetite, so we moved her into the warm cabin with us at night. She could hardly stand up. Paul worried constantly about her deteriorating condition. We consulted with several dog team owners who said it was just old age. There was no veterinarian in Fairbanks.

On January 11, a bright sunny day, Paul helped Queenie from the cabin to her kennel where he chained her. He then went into town to the Co-op Drugstore to talk with the pharmacist, hoping to find something that could help her.

Returning home, he found Frank Glaser standing over a dead Queenie, still chained to her kennel. It must have been a tense moment, and Glaser did not spare Paul in his comments about how he thought Queenie had been neglected and what he thought we had done wrong.

That evening I went to the Nordale Hotel and tried to tell Mr. Glaser that it was not Paul's fault that his dog had died; we had given both wolf-dogs the best of care. My words were to no avail—he told us to get out of his cabin immediately. He was very upset.

16

Kenai

KENAI WAS ONE OF A LITTER of 13 my lead dog, Queenie, whelped in March 1928. His father was a great gray half-wolf sled dog and Queenie was half wolf. Every one of that litter of ten females and three males was gray. I kept the males, calling them Kobuk, Wolf and Kenai, all good Alaskan names. Kenai, the biggest of the three was the boss from the start. When full grown, he tipped the scales at 155, a good 20 pounds more than the biggest of any of my other dogs.

A person gets attached to dogs too easily, even to sled dogs that aren't pets. If I had known the trouble Kenai would cause me over the next five years I'd have killed him the moment he was born. During those five years I swore at the end of each season that I would not start another winter with him in the team. Kenai was nothing but trouble. If it wasn't a fight he started, it was something else. Once he almost drowned me. Yet I became attached to him and didn't have the heart to get rid of him.

He was difficult to understand. He was at once a clown, a hard luck dog, a working fool in harness, a foolish friendly mutt, a wonderful leader, a killer in a fight. He looked like a wolf, fought like a wolf, ate like a wolf. He wasn't all dog, and he wasn't all wolf. He was a strange mixture, and sometimes he changed from dog to wolf and back to wolf with bewildering frequency.

Kenai, the troublemaker. Three-quarters wolf, this dog weighed 155 pounds at maturity, and Glaser used him as a leader in his team of wolf-dogs. He kept him for five years, but he was so much trouble that Glaser gave him to Mount McKinley National Park for breeding purposes. After a ranger beat him, Kenai attacked the man, and had to be destroyed.

Kenai was one of the most powerful dogs I've ever seen. He had big feet and legs as thick as a big man's wrist. His tusks were longer than those of any wolf I ever killed. He could hold the frozen rib of a big bull moose with his front feet and feed it into the side of his mouth, chopping it off into little pieces. He broke caribou leg bones to get the marrow as easily as I can peel an orange; caribou bones are the hardest and toughest of any of Alaska's big game. An ordinary dog can't break caribou bones, although wolves can.

With his great weight and strength and his love of pulling, he could almost pull a loaded sled by himself. He was also a great pack dog although I never loaded him with more than about 30 pounds. Once in a while in the summer I killed meat some distance from my cabin. To get it home I'd take three or four of the wolf-dogs and their packsacks, bone the meat out and let them carry it. A few times in cool weather I loaded Kenai with 50 pounds or so for a short pack. I never liked to put a heavy pack on a dog. I've seen a lot of dogs ruined by making them pack over-heavy loads.

Kenai loved a good fight, and no ordinary dog could stand up to him. In 1931 he killed two big malemutes in Fairbanks in almost less time than it takes to tell about it. He didn't start the fight but he sure finished it. I had started to guide nonresident hunters, and was organizing a hunt for a couple of clients and had left my dogs at Ed Day's dog ranch at the edge of Fairbanks where he boarded sled dogs. I had just reached town after tying them in Ed's yard when Ed caught up with me and told me Kenai had broken loose. The dog's leather collar had rotted without my noticing it, and he had lunged a few times on his chain, breaking the collar and taking off. He refused to come to Day.

Soon after, I found the big dog trotting back and forth across the street, head and ears up, sniffing here and there and leaving his sign at every tree, post and corner.

"C'mon Kenai," I called, snapping my fingers. He ran to me and made it clear that he had been looking for me and was glad to find me so quickly. I started back toward Day's with him trotting at heel.

We passed a log cabin where two big malemutes were tied.

They lunged at their chains and barked at Kenai. He was ready to take them on but I spoke sharply to him and kept walking. He followed, but reluctantly. Suddenly the running wire holding both malemutes broke and they bounded across the little yard and hurdled a low fence.

I looked around in time to see them both dive at Kenai. Kenai staggered but didn't go down, then he turned and went to work. I was hunting for a club to break the fight up, but I tried to watch the fight at the same time.

Kenai was a foot-fighter—that is, he always bowed his neck, holding his head low and to one side, allowing the other dog to clamp down where his heavy wolf ruff protected him, and then he went for a foot. As soon as one of the malemutes had a grip on his neck, Kenai reached down, grabbed a front foot and started breaking bones. No dog can stand that. The instant the big malemute let go and tried to pull his foot free, Kenai released him, and as the dog fell backward, Kenai pounced. He slashed the malemute's belly open and yanked his guts out.

The second dog suddenly decided he had very urgent business on the other side of town and he lit out sprinting. He didn't get two hundred yards before Kenai caught him. His insides were on the ground and he was kicking his last by the time I got there. Both of those dogs weighed close to a hundred pounds.

I had to admire Kenai for his independence but cussed him for it too. He took his responsibility as a leader too seriously at times and felt that when things went wrong it was up to him to straighten them out. I often used a double lead, and ran Queenie, his mother, beside him. Sometimes when his harness tangled or something else went wrong on the trail he would reach over and grab poor Queenie by the scruff of the neck, pick her up, and carry her along. She weighed 125 pounds. Kenai accomplished this without so much as breaking stride. Queenie would cry, and of course I would yell at him. If we were moving too fast I couldn't do much but stop and straighten him out. If possible I kept moving and ran up alongside and cracked him across the nose with the padded blackjack I always carried.

I worked Buster, Queenie's brother, behind Kenai. On a steep slope, Buster growled and puffed and made a big fuss about how hard he was pulling. That always burned Kenai up. I don't know how many times Kenai quit pulling, whirled, and clamped down on Buster's nose. And it always seemed to happen when we were less than a sled length or so from the top of the slope. The rest of the dogs had to stop then, of course, and the sled would slip back. I would try to hold it with the brake, but the front end usually came around sideways. The whole works, tangled dog team, sled, me and all, would start downhill. I would grab Kenai and tap his nose with the blackjack until he turned Buster loose and quieted down. Then I had the job of straightening the team out, turning the sled, and getting started uphill again. After we started again Kenai would break his darned neck pulling to get up the hill.

When Kenai stopped suddenly, Buster sometimes bumped into him. That too was usually good for a fight.

It was my habit in the evenings when I came in off the trapline (which I covered afoot) to turn about two of the dogs loose at a time. When I turned Kenai loose, I usually let Queenie, his mother, or Kobuk, his brother, loose at the same time. They would run around the cabin, playing. They had the snow packed down in a huge circle, and chased one another having a good run. After half an hour or so I'd tie them up and loose another couple of dogs.

If I ever made the mistake of turning Buster and Kenai loose at the same time, however, it wouldn't be any time before Kenai would run at Buster, hit him with his shoulder and try to knock him over and grab him, precipitating a big fight. Buster was a great fighter too and could defend himself. But Kenai was so big and powerful I always worried that he'd kill Buster.

Kenai was smart. When I hooked the team up I carried my blackjack fastened to my wrist with a loop. When he smelled it he wouldn't start any fights that day. But if I forgot and stuck the blackjack under the tarp where I could reach it in a hurry, Kenai was likely to pitch into one of the other dogs at any time, apparently just for the hell of it.

Sometimes I'd work the dogs every day for a month or more without a fight. Occasionally I forgot to take the blackjack, and it seemed he sensed that, for on those occasions, old Kenai would rip into one or more of the others, and then I'd have a lot of trouble stopping the fight.

Kenai was more wolf-like than the other dogs in that he wasn't much to make noise. Buster, Queenie, Kobuk, Wolf—all the others—were dog-like, in that they often barked, growled, howled, or whined. Not Kenai. Of course when wolves howled, he howled back. If I killed a wolf near the cabin I often turned Kenai loose with one or more of the other dogs, and he'd be the first to reach the dead wolf. He would go to the rear of the wolf and sink his teeth into it. He always carefully avoided the front end. He would drag a dead wolf around and shake it and wool it for several minutes or until he was satisfied the animal was truly dead.

Kenai was a clown, too. I remember well the fall when he was two. As soon as there was enough snow I drove into Healy for supplies. I always drove down the main street—in fact the only street—in Healy, directly to the hotel. When I came into sight loose dogs always disappeared behind buildings.

I was amused at the team that day as we came pouring down the hill and into town. A stray dog running ahead of them ducked out of sight, and they were all looking for something else to chase, heads and ears up, and bounding into the air with every other jump. If they ever got away from me when in that mood they'd quickly kill any dog they caught.

Just before we came to the Baker place, Mrs. Baker opened the front door and let out her tiny Boston Bull, weighing about seven pounds. That thing danced into the street in front of those eight bounding wolf-dogs, screaming, "Yipyipyipyipyipyip!"

I was scared to death. I *knew* that dog was a goner and stood on the brake, yelling, "Whoa, boys, whoa there."

They stopped, and then my eyes just about popped. Kenai, in the lead with Queenie, lay down and sniffed of that little pooch as it came up to him. As he sniffed, the little fool ran in and grabbed one of Kenai's front legs and started to chew on it. I expected to see Kenai bite the idiot in two right there. Instead, what did that 155-pound clown do? He cringed! Then he started to cry and whimper!

The rest of the dogs, most of which had felt Kenai's teeth at one time or other, seemed as amazed as I was and looked around at me uneasily as if to ask what was going on. I ran and picked the tiny dog up, and the damned thing tried to bite *me*! Mrs. Baker came running out into the street and I gladly handed it to her, mumbling something about, "My gosh, they'd kill that little thing. One bite and that would be all!" She gave me a strange look and took her pet back into the house.

After that, whenever I was in town and had the dogs tied behind the hotel near the Baker place, Kenai watched for that little Boston Bull. When it came into sight he coaxed it to him, and the little thing would run up, growl, then dive in and start chewing on one of Kenai's big legs. Kenai would act surprised and reel back then scoot into his doghouse, crying as if he were being killed. It was a game with him.

And then there was the time Kenai dumped a case of canned milk into Savage River. One fall, after I had spent the summer at Healy, I put packs on Kenai and Buster and hiked to my trapping cabin at Savage River in order to kill my winter's meat. Kenai carried 24 cans of Carnation milk; Buster packed spuds. When we got to Savage River I dropped my pack, put Buster's on the ground and started to unfasten Kenai's pack. Just then a big white-necked bull caribou trotted stiff-legged out of the willows on the other side of the river, then stopped and stood looking at us. I was after meat, and there it was, right next to the cabin. I snatched up the rifle and held for his neck.

Wham! went the rifle, followed immediately like a peculiar echo by *kerplunk* as Kenai, pack and all plunged into the water and started toward the caribou. The bull went to his knees at my shot, but he bounded up immediately and leaped over the bank into the river and started upstream.

Buster used his head and ran upstream along the bank, then swam out to sock his teeth into the caribou's nose. I watched as he held the bull's nose under water and drifted past me. I couldn't shoot because Buster was right beside the caribou. By the time the two were a couple of hundred feet downstream, Buster had drowned the caribou, for it had stopped struggling. The dog and caribou drifted ashore, and Buster kept mauling the caribou and chewing its throat. I called and he reluctantly left the bull where it had stranded on a gravel bar.

In the meantime Kenai, with the heavy pack on, had a terrible time. He never reached the caribou, for he had all he could do to keep from drowning. He kicked up an awful fuss, lunging, jumping and growling.

I was about to jump in after the darned fool when he hit a shallow place and struggled ashore. The big waterproofed dog pack must have had 10 gallons of water in it and—I thought—the canned milk. Both pouches dragged, and Kenai's belly almost touched the ground as he walked, splayfooted, toward me. He must have been carrying more than 60 pounds.

I dumped the pack and found nothing but water. Kenai's ears drooped and he looked so woebegone it was hard for me to keep from laughing but I knew better than to laugh at Kenai. Instead I patted his head and said, "Good job, boy. You've done fine!"

That darned dog had packed milk 18 miles only to dump it in the river right at the cabin. I never found a single can of it.

He was the most sensitive dog I've ever known. If I was angry with him or even pretended to be and spoke sharply, his hair would immediately stand on end. He would walk away from me stiff-legged, looking at me over his shoulder. Several times after I talked roughly to him when he was loose and I turned my back, he ran and hit the back of my knees with his shoulder, knocking me flat. I rolled over and jumped up each time and laughed at him. He cringed then; Kenai hated to be laughed at.

One early September after returning from a day in the hills I turned Kenai and Kobuk loose and they started to play around in the grass. I had set my rifle against the front of the cabin and was watching the two dogs when a bull moose arose out of the high grass about 50 yards from the cabin. It had obviously bedded down there while I was gone.

The two loose dogs saw him the same instant I did. I grabbed my rifle and shot. The moose dropped to his knees but got up and ran into the timber before I could shoot again. The two dogs rushed after him.

I crawled into the thicket and within 100 yards found the moose with his back to me with the two dogs worrying him. Kobuk would bite him on the rear end, he'd turn his head to look around, and Kenai would jump up and bite his nose. The moose's ears were pinned back and he was kicking like a mule. I knew if I didn't do something quickly he'd kill or injure one or both dogs. There was little room to maneuver in the brush.

As the moose spun around I shot him in the neck. He dropped, dead. Instantly, the two wolf-dogs started to cut into him to eat— one on his belly, the other on the front end.

I walked up to the moose and said, "Good job, boys." But Kenai would have none of it. Dining on the moose's belly, he turned on me snarling, bristling up and jumping to his feet. He thought he had killed the moose and he wasn't going to let me have it. Then I started to laugh and that kind of shamed him I guess. After that he turned into a dog again. With Kenai, the wolf was never far from the surface.

After he was a year old and fully grown, some mornings I'd leave my cabin and he would be at the end of his chain like the rest of the dogs to greet me. Then, suddenly, he seemed to turn into a wolf right before my eyes. He would squat and stare at me with his wolf eyes, his tail dropping to the ground, his mane standing on end. He would growl, and back toward his house and dive into it as I walked to him. That bothered me. I thought something was wrong with him. I would grab the chain and yank his head out of the doghouse, which really took some yanking. Then I would grab both ears and pull, with him growling and snapping at me every bit of the way. He was always careful, though, not to bite me.

I would rub him behind the ears and try to get friendly with him but no, the instant I let go, he would dive back into the doghouse and lay there peeking at me as if he had never seen me before. The wolf I kept for breeding purposes wasn't a bit wilder than Kenai at such times. I don't know if he just pretended not to know me, or actually didn't, when he behaved that way. I think it was just a good act because he pulled that stunt most often after I had punished him, but not always.

On other days Kenai would be all dog. He would jump up and put both feet on my shoulders with his head beside mine, happy and friendly as he could be. I never could figure him out and never knew what to expect from him next.

November 1, 1931: Back at cabin after stay in Healy. Had a hell of a time to cross the river. Six above. Cloudy, calm.

Kenai almost drowned me once. It was late October when Savage River had frozen over enough to cross with the dog team. I hooked up and went to Healy for some grub and mail. When I returned the next day I found that the ice had run, even though the temperature was 20 degrees below zero. There was nothing but slush ice where I had crossed the previous day. Normally the channel where I crossed is narrow, but ice had jammed below, damming the river. As far as I could see up and downstream there was nothing but slush ice. I had eggs, spuds, onions and a few oranges on the sled that would freeze if I didn't get them to the cabin. I didn't know how I was going to get the dogs and myself across, much less the grub.

I unhooked the dogs, leaving their harnesses on, and started upstream looking for a place to cross. Queenie was usually very good on ice but it wasn't her day. She decided to cross the slush ice to the cabin.

"Queenie, come back here," I yelled as she started.

Usually she minded well, but either she didn't hear me or she had to keep going to stay on top of the half-frozen slush. She ran 50 or 60 feet and broke through. That shouldn't have been so bad, for she was a strong swimmer. Ordinarily she could have fought her way ashore, but she tried to paw herself back on the ice, and in so doing she shoved one front foot through her work collar.

That pulled her head under. She struggled, but every time she pulled with her front legs her head went under. She was spinning, her head under water, her tail whipping back and forth in the air.

I ran toward her, even though I knew I would break through. I was wearing a caribou fur parka and heavy winter clothes. I traveled about 15 feet before I broke through. The water was eight or ten feet deep. Cold clamped on my chest like a vice as I frantically pawed my way toward Queenie. Then I realized all the dogs were in the water with me, and big Kenai was next to me. I threw an arm over him and felt his powerful muscles bunch and work at that slush. Right then I was mighty glad to have Kenai around.

I reached Queenie, pulled her against me and yanked her foot out of the collar. Her head came up, she blew water and chunks of ice, coughed and started swimming toward the shore from which we had started. I had followed her a short ways when a dog behind me put both paws on my shoulders shoving me under. Submerged, struggling and gasping, I swallowed what seemed like gallons of water and pounds of ice. I thought I was a goner. When I came up and glanced around, guess who? Kenai, acting true to form. By golly, it looked like he was waiting to shove me down again. I continued to swim, crawl and fight the ice and freezing water, bound up by that big parka. I was seriously beginning to wonder if I would make it to shore.

When I got to where the water was normally shallow I relaxed and reached for bottom. I went clear under again, and as I came up, gasping, that damned dog shoved me down again. He simply walked over me. I got another big dose of ice and water before surfacing. This time I was angry enough to wring Kenai's neck. He had turned and was waiting for me when I came up and I slugged him with a right to the jaw. He stayed away from me for the rest of that icy swim. I finally broke my way ashore. I was numb and completely winded when I crawled up on the snow.

I stood and reached for my snoose box to get a chew before my hands got too cold. It was gone, no doubt floating downriver. All I found in my pocket was a handful of ice. I was numb, but it struck me that I was unusually heavy. It was more than the soaked caribou skin parka. I was wearing a pair of loose-fitting, choke bore Filson pants, laced pretty tightly on the bottom. I'll bet I had 50 pounds of slush ice inside them. They bulged out all the way around.

I was on the wrong side of the river from my cabin near exhaustion and in bad shape. My hands were numb, with water freezing on them. With that big load of ice in my pants, I clattered like a sack full of broken glass every time I moved.

I had to act quickly. I ran toward a narrow place in the river a quarter mile downstream where I thought there should be open water. I didn't dare tackle the slush again, knowing I could never make it. I must have been a weird sight trying to run, water freezing on me, and ice clattering in my pants with every jump.

I found a spot where anchor ice lay on each side of the river with open water in the center. All eight dogs and I walked out on the ice until, about 10 feet from shore, a big cake broke off, tilted, and dumped us all into the water. I had no trouble swimming across, but I nearly drowned getting out on the other side. Every time I put my elbows on the edge of the thin ice it broke off. I reached for bottom and dipped clear under—it was much deeper than normal. Time and again I tried to pull myself up on the ice and it kept breaking and I kept going under. By then I was getting terribly weak. To top it all off, the dogs could get their front feet on the ice but couldn't get any further, so they struggled in the water, pawing and crying for me to help them.

I broke a channel and finally managed to crawl out, then yanked the dogs out and pushed them behind me. Old trouble-maker, Kenai, came along last. Just as I was ready to grab him, he decided to swim back to the other side of the river. I was in a mood to leave him, but knew he would probably drown if I did, so I kneeled on the ice and coaxed him back. It took a lot of coaxing. When he finally came to me, I jerked him out. Then I trotted the quarter of a mile to the cabin, ice still clattering around inside my pants.

In fifteen minutes the dogs and I were crowding each other for space around a roaring stove. Later I dropped a tree across a narrow place in the river a mile or so downstream and carried my fresh grub across.

Things like that made me decide every year that I was going to get rid of Kenai.

Several times in summer I turned him loose, took a .22 rifle and went for a walk in the woods, each time planning to return without him. Then I would shoot a spruce hen and that potlicker would run and retrieve it for me. I'd have quite a time prying it out of his jaws, and it would be pretty well chewed, but he would give it to me. I would look at him and he would wag his tail and prance around, just a big, happy-go-lucky mutt having a good time. I never had the heart to shoot him.

Kenai got crazy spells every once in a while and conjured up all kinds of mix-ups. Then he would go along for months without giving me the least bit of trouble. I never beat or whipped him although there were times when I was sorely tempted. The only time I used the blackjack was when he started a fight, picked up Queenie, or some other such thing. Then I had to be right on the spot in order to protect the lives of the other dogs. He was just too powerful a fighter for me to take a chance.

I kept Kenai five years. Sometimes I got my mail at McKinley Park, a few miles from my cabin on Savage River. Park Superintendent Harry Liek, who came out to say hello every time I drove by Park Headquarters, was completely taken by Kenai.

Kenai liked to be petted, and he knew Liek would pet him when he could. That darned dog was a show-off too, because when I left after talking with Liek, he would throw his weight into his collar savagely, and growl enthusiastically. He was faster than the other dogs and it looked like he was doing all the work.

Liek thought Kenai was wonderful. He *was* a beautiful animal, there was no question about that. After a couple of years Liek tried to buy him for use in the Park. He had some very fine female malemutes and thought Kenai would make a good sire for their pups. Liek also though he would make a wonderful show dog for park visitors to see.

Time and again I told him, "You're wrong, Liek, dead wrong. Kenai's just a lot of trouble. The guy who gets him will be sorry. I wouldn't sell that dog to my worst enemy." I couldn't convince him.

By the spring of 1934 I had had enough. I had tried every trick I knew to straighten Kenai out, but it was hopeless. As fond as I was of him, he caused me more trouble than he was worth. I told Liek that I would *give* Kenai to him if he would promise never to work him. I thought he would be all right for breeding purposes, and he would make a fine dog for the tourists to see and photograph. Liek agreed to take him on those terms. As a final warning I told him that if in an emergency he had to use him in a team, to be sure and put him in the lead; he wouldn't work in any other position.

I heard the rest of Kenai's story from Chief Ranger Louis Corbley. One day a new ranger, transferred to McKinley Park from Yellowstone Park, decided to harness the park dogs into a team to get some mushing experience. He had been told not to use Kenai.

Disregarding instructions, he dragged Kenai from the pen and snapped him into the wheel position just in front of the sled. In harnessing my dogs, I always turned them loose and called them to the sled, so the green ranger's first move probably upset Kenai. When he turned his back on the dogs to walk to the sled, Kenai tore into the dog beside him. The inexperienced ranger rushed up with a big club and beat Kenai on the head and the body until Kenai was dazed and almost unconscious. He then dragged him back into the corral.

Next day the ranger decided he would break Kenai of fighting. With a dog harness in hand he went to Kenai's 15 x 20 corral and stepped inside. He then made the mistake of turning his back on Kenai to latch the gate. All that saved his life was the big fur parka he wore, with the hood up. Kenai remembered the beating he had been given and who gave it to him—it was the only beating he ever received.

Corbley ran to try to stop the ranger but he was too late. He saw Kenai lunge and put both feet on the man's shoulders and grab the back of his neck. He rode the man down, snapping and trying to chew through the heavy parka. The ranger groveled, screaming for help, trying to keep from being turned over by the angry wolf-dog. Kenai would have killed him if Corbley hadn't rushed in with a club and knocked Kenai out.

Kenai never gave me that kind of trouble. He deserved any punishment I ever gave him, and he knew it. A beating though, is something a wolf-dog can't stand.

Kenai had to be destroyed.

I'm glad I didn't have to do it.

Ghost Grizzly

DURING MY YEARS AT SAVAGE RIVER I had numerous encounters with grizzly bears. Most came when a bear or bears found a moose or caribou I had killed and cached. I always carried a loaded rifle when I returned to meat I had left, ready to defend myself as Alaskan hunters must still do. Grizzlies are possessive of meat they find, and will occasionally attack an unwary hunter who returns to a kill unarmed. When bears claimed my meat, I usually shrugged and forgot it. Meat that has been scattered, chewed on, or buried usually isn't worth trying to recover.

Game meat, mostly caribou and moose, fed me and often fed my wolf-dogs, and both of these grand deer were abundant at Savage River. Moose numbers increased during my time there, while caribou numbers decreased. With the amount of game I killed it was fairly common for me to have to cache meat and to return for it later. It was meat that I had cached that finally brought about a showdown between me and the big bear that I half humorously called the "ghost grizzly."

I often traveled the seven miles between my main cabin on Savage River and my Fish Creek cabin. In summer I walked that distance along bars of the Savage river, usually with my wolf-dogs. Because of the abundance of bears, moose, and caribou, I led them on chains. Several times with the dogs I unknowingly walked between a grizzly sow and her cubs. Each time the old ladies stood up on their hind legs to look me over, then dropped to all fours and ran off, calling their cubs as they ran.

Even though most grizzlies will flee from a man, I didn't trust them and always carried my .30-06 Remington Express. It saved my neck a number of times.

In those years bear tracks were almost everywhere in the Savage River country and they were especially common along the river bars I traveled. I usually didn't pay much attention to them. However, the enormous tracks of one bear caught my eye. Their wide spacing and his long stride told me they were made by an awfully big bear. His left front track always toed in a bit more than any of the others. He wasn't a cripple, but he seemed to step differently with that foot.

Commencing in 1925 I saw those tracks each spring and fall for many years, and came to know that bear's habits. He apparently denned each winter in Mount McKinley National Park. The boundary of the park was only a couple of miles south of my main cabin. Usually in late April he left the high country and passed between my cabins, heading north. He would be gone all summer and come fall I would again see his tracks heading back toward the park.

Sometimes a grizzly can be clever. I'm not certain whether this one was very clever or very timid; perhaps both. He avoided my cabins, and, although I watched for him in his comings and goings, I saw him only twice in nine years.

There was something truly ghostlike about him. He seemed to get by me no matter how hard I watched. Several times I followed his huge fresh tracks for a few miles, but he moved too swiftly and too far for me to catch sight of him.

Nine years is a long time to hunt a bear and toward the last of that time he seemed almost supernatural in his ability to keep out of my sight. Other trappers told me they had seen his tracks but as far as I could learn, no one else ever saw him. That isn't surprising, because the region he summered in was almost uninhabited.

I first saw him in late April, three years after I first came upon his tracks. He was apparently alone and feeding on cranberries that had wintered over on the hills above my lower cabin. I had seen his tracks on the trail between my cabins the previous day, and was looking for him. The moment I put my binoculars on him I knew it could be no other bear, as he was much larger than the average grizzly of that area. Too, he was dark, almost black; most grizzlies in that region are the straw-or cream-colored Toklat type.

I grabbed my rifle and hurried up a steep ridge toward him. I was nearly to the top when suddenly, around the side of the hill, came a galloping grizzly. In moments it was practically on top of me. I realized it was the wrong color and the size wasn't right, but it was a bear, and I had bear on my mind, so I shot. It plowed its nose into the ground, then rolled downhill to pile up against a little bunch of willows. When I got to it I found it was a large sow. I knew I had shot the wrong bear and I ran around the point from where she had come, looking for the big one.

I found his tracks where he had been running after her. Bears breed in the spring, and I assume that's what he had on his mind. His tracks were half again the size of the sow's. Then I found where, apparently at the sound of my shot, he had torn up the ground as he had wheeled and hot-footed it down the hill and into a little stream. He had really plowed a trail down that steep slope. Clearly, my shot had spooked him off.

I didn't see the big bear again for more than six years.

His tracks seemed to get bigger each year. I watched for him but somehow never hit it right. Sometimes he went through early, sometimes late but he always passed through on the same route. I missed seeing his tracks only two or three falls or springs in nine years.

Nowadays we know that grizzlies may live for 30 years or more, for Alaska's game biologists have learned how to determine a bear's age by cutting a thinly sliced section of a tooth and, with special light under a microscope, count growth rings. I didn't know anything about this, of course, but I did encounter some bears that appeared to be very old.

One grizzly in particular seemed to be ancient. In September 1932 I killed a bull moose on a bench about two miles below my main cabin. While butchering it I noticed a cream-colored grizzly feeding on blueberries about a mile away across Savage River. I made a trip home with moose meat that day, and next morning when I returned for more meat, the bear was still in the same place, apparently still feeding on blueberries. I didn't think much of it, but that afternoon when I made another trip the bear was still there. Likewise on the third day.

Something had to be wrong with that bear; there weren't that many blueberries in that spot. I walked over to him, approaching from downwind, keeping out of sight. He was facing away from me, and I sneaked to within 20 yards. Then I stood and walked even closer, right out in the open.

He heard me, for he stood up on his hind legs, *but he looked in the opposite direction from which I was approaching.* As he stood I saw that something was wrong with his face. I put a bullet under one ear and he dropped dead.

His face was full of porcupine quills, and he was blind. He had few teeth and those that he did have were worn almost to the gums. His mouth was full of quills and I found an old scar on his back that might have been made by a bullet. I think he had been blind most of the summer. Thin and in terrible shape, that bear was suffering. And surely he was very old.

I admired his long ivory-colored claws. Older grizzlies seem to have light-colored claws, while young bears' claws are darker. I sat on him sharpening my knife, getting ready to peel his hide. Just then I saw moose antlers coming up from Savage River. The antlers gradually came into sight, then the head, and finally the entire moose appeared. I sat perfectly still. The moose was going to pass near and downwind.

Never will I forget the behavior of that moose when he hit the combined scent of me and that old grizzly. It was almost as if it had been hit with a club. It reeled back a good six feet, almost falling over backward. It snorted, whirled, then high-tailed it back toward the river.

I finally killed the ghost grizzly, but he almost got me first.

In September, nine years from the time I became aware of the huge bear, I saw a big bull moose go into a patch of spruce timber about a mile from my main cabin. It was time for me to get in some meat, so I slipped over and shot him. I didn't want to pack all that meat home, and there was no snow on the ground to run the dog sled on.

I built a ladder of spruce poles, then sawed off three trees a good 10 feet above ground. I nailed poles between the trees and built a triangular pole platform where I put the meat. I piled spruce boughs on the meat, and then put the moose hide over that for protection against weather and ravens. I didn't want anything attracted to the cache, so I pulled the head of the moose up out of reach, and I piled moss and brush over the gut pile.

I couldn't see the cache from my cabin, but I could from a nearby ridge that I frequently traveled, and I watched it off and on for over a month. Weather was cool, and the meat was in good shape on the several occasions I walked over to check on it and take a chunk home. It was high enough so that I felt sure that a grizzly couldn't reach it.

About mid-October a foot of snow lay on the ground and the temperature dropped to 20 below zero. It was a good time to haul the moose meat home, so I hooked up my team of wolf-dogs. I had 11 dogs that fall and they hadn't worked much. They were full of pep, so I left my rifle home, knowing I would have all I could do to hang on to the empty bouncing sled with those powerful, eager, leaping dogs. Nothing was farther from my mind than a grizzly bear on that cold day. All bears should have been denned up by then.

I got a rude jolt as I called the dogs to a stop at the edge of the timber and saw familiar bear tracks in the snow. They were made by the big bear whose tracks I had seen fall and spring for nine years.

The dogs wanted to follow the trail into the timber but I snapped a quick, "Come gee" at Queenie and she whirled and headed back down the trail toward my cabin.

At the cabin I unharnessed and tied the dogs, took my rifle and a pocketful of shells and walked back to the cache. I can trace a lot of my troubles with grizzly bears in those years to using the wrong kind of ammunition. This day was no exception. The only cartridges I had were 220-grain round nose solids. I had bought three boxes of them the previous year, planning to use them on foxes. They had been made for African game, and mushroomed only when they struck something very solid. They were ideal for foxes because they didn't tear the hides.

Poles from the cache were scattered, and the moose hide was lying near, frozen and crumpled. About 20 feet from the cache trees the bear had built a mound of brush and snow that looked like a big beaver house. A hind leg of the moose stuck out of one end and the antlers were visible on the other.

Two-foot-wide, hard-packed bear trails spider-webbed all directions. There was snow on the ground, of course, and a little frost had formed the previous night. Many of the tracks were fresh.

I found later that the bear had cached meat from my moose here and there all through the timber. He probably patrolled day and night to keep foxes and wolverines away from it.

I removed my right mitten so I could get my finger on the trigger and shoot quickly, and kept the hand warm by shoving it inside my parka. With rifle ready, I slowly and carefully walked toward the bear's cache. It was impossible to walk quietly, for snow crunched at every step. I frequently stopped to listen and look, but heard only a lonesome wind sighing in the spruces.

I squatted and took my time looking things over, trying to decide what to do.

It was a poor place to tangle with a big bear. The spruce patch was on a sidehill on ground that was damp in summer, so it was full of head-high willows. When freeze-up came that fall it caught the willows with green leaves still hanging, and they had frozen in place. Snow had piled up on them and on the spruce trees which were bushy clear to the ground. In addition, here and there were three and four-foot deep potholes. It was impossible to see more than 30 or 40 feet in any direction.

After squatting by the big mound for several minutes, I started to walk away slowly and quietly, thinking I had better get out. It wasn't a safe place to tangle with a grizzly. He figured he owned that moose, and the meat probably wasn't worth salvaging. I decided to let him have it.

I had tiptoed about ten feet when I heard the bear snort.

The hair on the back of my neck up-ended and I whirled to see, 30 or 40 feet away, one of the biggest interior Alaska grizzly bears I have ever seen. He was uphill from me on his hind legs, his little pig eyes glittering, his nose sniffing, ivory-clawed front paws hanging. He had been lying behind his brush and meat pile and had heard me, of course. Perhaps he thought I was another bear after his meat.

A great rumbling came from his chest. He looked more like 20 feet tall than the actual 12 or so that he must have stood.

"One shot," I told myself. I had forgotten the kind of ammunition I was using. I raised the rifle and lined it up on his neck. That old Remington Express had a lot of trigger creep and I had just taken up the slack when the bear decided he didn't like my looks and turned to leave. The gun fired just as he turned. I simply couldn't help firing: I would have stopped if I could.

When that solid copper slug struck him he roared and started toward me. I slammed another shell home and fired again when he was about 15 feet away. That turned him, and he started off through the thick willows. I fired another shot, into his side this time. That turned him toward me again. He was thrashing about and roaring in the brush, and I was scared half to death.

I kept shooting. My life depended upon it. Another shot into his body turned him again, and he plowed downhill through the willows. I didn't want to lose him in the brush, knowing that it would take all of my nerve to follow him into the thick stuff if he went out of sight. I ran after him, firing whenever I caught a glimpse of his black hide. I refilled the Remington's magazine and followed him a couple of hundred yards.

Then I lost him in the brush. I stood still trying to follow his progress by the crashing of brush and by his roars and growls. When I came to a clearing where I could see 60 or 70 feet in all directions I sat down and chewed a wad of snoose. My nerves needed taming.

After I quit shaking and could think more clearly I started on the trail. Instead of following right on it, I crisscrossed, working parallel to it for a ways, then crossing and following on the other side. I was afraid the bear was lying in ambush.

Blood was clear on the snow and the trail was easy to follow. He had gone downhill, and after I had followed for half a mile or so, I was in a sheltered valley. Every step crunched loudly. When I stood still the silence was so heavy I could almost feel it.

I avoided the brush and kept in the open, walking slowly, rifle always halfway to my shoulder. After half an hour I was pretty jumpy. Twice I almost shot at red squirrels when they suddenly scolded and scampered off.

I stepped around a big bushy spruce tree and almost bumped into him; he was about 15 feet away. The moment I came into sight he growled and started toward me, still strong, his movements sure and swift. My sights were on the base of his neck as I fired. He dropped and I circled and walked to within ten feet of him to put another bullet into the back of his head.

It was over.

I estimated his weight at 1,000 pounds. Next day I had to make two trips with my 12-foot freight sled when I hauled his meat home for dog food. He was hog fat and I pulled a full gunny sack of leaf lard from his abdomen. I cut four-inch-thick strips of fat from his loin. The dark silver-tipped hide squared (average of greatest length and greatest width) 8 feet, 9 inches, huge for an interior grizzly.

I sent the hide to my dad in Seattle and he had it made into a rug. He once put it on display at an outdoor show, and the mayor of Seattle, a man named Smith, offered him $400 for it. I told my dad he'd better keep it, and he did. He still had it when he died.

It was my ghost grizzly all right, for I never saw those big tracks heading cross-country again.

I missed him.

Moose and Caribou

ONE FINE FALL DAY in the early 1930s I left my cabin and quietly picked my way up a game trail toward the top of a low ridge. I planned to call up a big bull moose and shoot my winter's meat. The spruce trees on the side hill were dense, and the brush was higher than my head. There were plenty of moose around, and I half expected to bump into one before I reached the top of the ridge. Suddenly, through the brush about 30 yards above me on the steep slope, I saw the back side of a large set of moose antlers. They were the yellow-white of a newly cleaned rack, but I couldn't see anything else of the animal.

Quietly I stepped to a high spot. By standing on my toes I could see where the antlers came together, but I still couldn't see the animal. He was asleep, apparently, facing directly away from me, his head flat on the ground.

On tiptoe, I managed to put the picket of the scope on the spot where the antlers came together, and then touched a shot off. The antlers didn't move. There was no sound. I threw another load into the chamber and waited, wondering. In dying, an animal the size of a moose generally goes through a death struggle.

I waited as long as I could stand it, then decided to move closer and get a better look, so I started quietly zigzagging up the hill. When I was about 40 feet from him, I had a good view and started to raise the rifle to shoot again. As I did, that old bull leaped to his feet, spun around, and charged down the hill toward me, fast. He didn't have to come my way; he could have gone in any other direction.

He was as quick as a cat, and about as fierce-looking a thing as I've ever seen. He seemed all of ten feet tall and about the size of a locomotive. My rifle was half-way to my shoulder when he started toward me, so I pointed instinctively and pulled the trigger.

I worked the bolt as fast as I could and fired again from half-way to my shoulder, but this time I tipped the barrel higher. He was about ten feet above me, charging, head low, when I fired again. He collapsed at the shot, and as he slid by me his front feet skidded from under him and knocked me sprawling. When I shakily picked myself up, he was in his death struggle.

My first shot hadn't touched him. The second, as he started toward me, hit about six inches above his nose; and the last shot, the one that saved me from being steam-rollered, had taken him between the eyes.

While that was an unusual incident, it does demonstrate that a bull moose can be dangerous. Usually, when a bull hears, sees, or smells a man, he scrams as fast as his legs can carry him. That bull was out to get me.

Although a bull ordinarily won't attack a man, it's a different story with a cow with newborn calves. I'd much rather run into a couple of grizzly bears than an angry cow moose.

I used to walk the seven miles between my two cabins. In the spring the easiest traveling was on dry gravel sloughs that adjoin the river. Most of the cow moose in the region seem to gather along those sloughs to have their calves. At least a dozen times I have walked around a bushy spruce tree and found myself face to face with a cow moose and a freshly-born calf. The cow invariably would take one look, and mane on end and ears back, start for me, her ugly head shaking back and forth. They're horrible-looking at that time of year anyway, because they're shedding. The cow would get close, rear on her hind legs, and strike out with her front hoofs.

Seeing the calves, I didn't want to shoot, and I never had to kill a cow, but it was close a number of times. Twice I had to dodge from directly beneath cows' hoofs. If I hadn't jumped, those angry mothers would have flattened me.

Frequently, when they're young, calves will walk right up to you. They're appealing, but dangerous—I'd a lot rather fool with grizzly cubs. After several weeks, the lady moose loses a lot of the protective instinct, and will usually leave when someone approaches. But when the calves are fresh-born, *look out.*

Moose hunting is fun. Taking care of a moose after it is shot isn't—it's the hardest kind of work.

Between 1915 and 1924, my market hunting years, when a dollar was worth something, I raked in a nice chunk of money when I brought in, say, 800 pounds of moose meat at two-bits a pound. Killing and selling more than 60 moose taught me a lot about both moose and business.

I've heard a lot of fantastic talk about moose weighing a ton or more, but if they grow that big I never saw one. Curious about the weight lost by moose when dressed, one day I took a pair of accurate beam scales with me and weighed a very big bull.

Front quarters weighed 236 pounds each. Hindquarters weighed 182 and 190 pounds, making a total of 844 pounds. The head, with its 60-inch-spread antlers, weighed 115 pounds. The hide weighed 120 pounds. I sacked the entrails and weighed them at 300 pounds, making 1,379 pounds in all without blood. Blood in a moose weighs at least 25 pounds. Live weight of that big bull was at least 1,400 pounds.

Since my market-hunting days I have killed about 25 bulls, bringing my lifetime total to about 85 moose. In living near them and killing that many I've learned a few interesting things about this largest member of the North American deer family.

Starting around the first of September it's fairly simple to call up a big bull. Old bulls, the breeding animals, respond to a call more easily as the season progresses, and after September 15 there's nothing to it. Young bulls, however, don't pay much attention to calling.

A call I use, imitating adult bulls, is fairly easily described. I pronounce "eeeeeerrrrrooooooOOOOOOOOPP," somewhat like "Europe," using a birchbark horn about a foot long, six inches in diameter at the bell, and about 2½ inches at the small end. The outside of the bark is on the inside of the horn. For some reason the sound is different when the outside of the bark is turned in; I think the loose bark and fibers give resonance to the call. I hold my fingers over my nose, giving the sound kind of a grunting quality. Start the "eeeee" part at a low pitch, and end with "ooooOOOOOOPP" in a very abrupt rise in pitch.

Usually I give that call three or four times, wait a few minutes, then give a cow call, which is a little harder to describe. It goes "EEEeee," starting at a high pitch, descending, and ending with a combination cough and sneeze. It can't be spelled.

If it is calm, either of these two calls will reach any moose within a two-mile radius. Their hearing is twice as acute as a man's. A young bull calls occasionally in the fall, sounding somewhat like a cow, but his call doesn't carry far.

For years I made the mistake of remaining quiet when a bull got close to me as I called, expecting him to come closer. Now I get much better results by making as much racket as I can. I clatter pieces of caribou or moose antlers together, strike a willow bush with a heavy stick, or chop at a dead tree with an axe. The more noise of the right kind the better. Silence makes a bull suspicious. It will circle to get your wind, and be gone before you see him. A moose's eyesight is only fair, but his sense of smell and hearing are tops.

I like to make a small blind 10 or 12 feet up in a tree near a lake where moose feed. If I don't get a bull to come on the first day I call, I do the second or third. It's foolish to stomp all over the country when they'll come right to you.

I get tired of people telling me they killed a moose with such a "gamey" flavor they couldn't eat it. It's "gamey" all right. Anyone who hunts moose should know something about their breeding cycle.

In Alaska about September 15 is the beginning of the season I call "walking time" for moose. Breeding bulls at least three years old start traveling and looking. Though not breeding then, they travel for miles. Through a 45X telescope mounted on a stand at my trapping cabin, I've seen bulls 10 miles away dashing into every patch of trees or brush they can find in search of cows.

Walking time lasts from the middle of September until breeding starts about the last week of the month. I have been within 25 yards of cows when a bull reaches them during this period. The bull runs to a cow and starts licking her body all over. Soon the cow urinates. Immediately the bull stops licking and starts to swallow her urine. I have found two or three gallons of cow urine and little else in the stomach of a breeding bull. Naturally, urine flavors the meat strongly. The liver swells and becomes light-brown, and almost like a honeycomb. I've offered such livers to my sled dogs, and they wouldn't eat it. I didn't blame them. "Gamey" flavor! I call it spoiled meat. If you try to cook it, the unpleasant odor will drive you out of the house.

Two-year-old bulls killed as late as October first are as fine eating as prime beef, but I won't even consider shooting a full-grown bull after mid-September.

During walking time the two-year-old younger bulls may follow the old boys as they travel. The big fellows hook willows and spruce trees they pass, all the time grunting and fussing loudly. Every time they turn and look cross-eyed at one of the young bulls—"students" I call 'em—the youngster reels back and acts as if he is about to be hit. Nevertheless they persist in following the old "masters" around, seeming to want to know what's going on, but seldom engaging in breeding, something the older bulls won't allow.

In good moose country many small potholes are usually well tracked up by moose (both cow and bull tracks are pointed, differing mainly in that the bull's are usually larger). Some potholes may be three or four feet across and a couple of feet deep. In early September, during the build-up to breeding season, cows urinate in one of these pits with the bull following and doing likewise. Then the bull gets down on his knees and tries to rub his neck in the urine-saturated earth, often hooking it up with his antlers and throwing it over his body. I've witnessed such performances many times from close range.

When cows are ready to breed, they call persistently, hour after hour. If two bulls answer a call at the same time, a terrific fight is apt to break out. I once saw a clash between a very large and a medium-size bull. They heaved and pushed at each other for a while, then stood facing one another a few feet apart, resting. The younger, medium-sized bull managed to keep out of the big one's way part of the time, but the big fellow kept after him. Antlers slammed together with a loud clattering, accompanied by grunting, roaring, and snorting.

Finally the big bull smashed the younger one head-on, pushing him backward so fast the smaller fellow toppled. As he staggered to his feet, the big bull slammed into his side, almost picking him up, giving him the bum's rush sideways and pushing over a row of two and three-inch fire-killed spruce like so many match sticks. After about 60 feet of this punishment the smaller moose managed to recover both his equilibrium and his discretion and he prudently high-tailed it.

Experienced moose hunters make sure they kill only what they can handle. Backpacking moose meat can be tough. I never killed a moose far from the Valdez Trail unless I had a horse with me to pack it out. Many an inexperienced moose hunter has killed a big old bull too far from his camp, truck, or car. A lot of meat has spoiled simply because there was too much to backpack out.

An important rule; never kill a moose in water. One late June day soon after I started market hunting one of the Road Commission workers went with me on a hunt. Wearing head nets, we sat at the edge of a lake in a cloud of mosquitoes. When a small bull moose wandered along the edge of the lake within easy range, I lifted my head net so I could see better to shoot.

"Just a minute," said my companion. "Let me fix you for the skeeters." He then smeared a handful of citronella over my face. The stuff rolled into my eyes, and I thought he'd burned them out. I lost all interest in the moose, and shoved my face into the cool moss. My friend shot the animal, and when my eyes cleared, all I could see of the moose was one side of his antlers and about six inches of his belly floating above the surface of the lake. Dressing that animal was a terrible job. The hot meat got wet, and I had a tough job keeping it from spoiling. I had to work hard and fast to get it to the Road Commission camp and a cooler.

Another time, I shot a young bull at the edge of the only deep hole in a small stream. My neck shot hit a few inches low, and the animal stumbled into the water before I could shoot again. I dragged him to a riffle where he grounded in about two feet of water. Though I butchered and skinned him right there and hung the meat immediately, it spoiled. Hot meat and cold water don't mix; the meat almost invariably sours.

One fine day early in September, needing meat for winter I glanced out the door of my cabin and saw a nice bull moose standing on a hill about 250 yards away. He was in the right place at the right time, looking toward the cabin, but not alarmed. I aimed at his head. Down he went.

I had taken only a few steps toward him when I looked up and saw him standing there again. Dropping to my belly and getting a good prone position, I fired once more. Again he dropped. When I got there I found two big bulls, one lying with his head and antlers on the rear end of the other. Cleaning them and taking care of all that meat was a whale of a job.

Dressing a moose can be burdensome and intimidating for the inexperienced. A few tricks I've learned make the job easier. One man can handle the biggest moose that ever lived if he knows how. After bleeding a kill, I tie a rope to a hind leg, pull it back and up as far as I can, and tie the other end of the rope to a tree or bush. This holds the moose on its back, belly up, where I can work on it. Then I peel a strip of hide four or five inches wide from the brisket to the junction of the hind legs. This makes it easier to open the animal and remove the viscera.

After slitting from the brisket to the crotch, taking care not to cut into the stomach, I reach in and cut everything free of the body, behind the kidneys and around the diaphragm. Then, at the flank, I cut right down to the backbone, and remove the flank material on one side, creating a huge opening out of which to roll the viscera. Next I cut the animal in two crossways, and then into convenient size pieces, depending on how I'm going to take the moose home. Sometimes I leave the hide on, sometimes I remove it. Removing it cools the meat faster; leaving it on results in cleaner meat at home. This depends on temperature and the likelihood of rain wetting the meat.

I've killed moose with a wide variety of rifles, from a .22 Hi-Power Savage, to a .405 Winchester. They're not hard to kill if you place your shots right. But if you hit wrong, a moose can take a lot of punishment. A prominent national gun editor once wrote that he didn't think it possible to kill a moose instantly with a single shot. That's silly. I've killed many with one shot. A good neck or brain shot will almost invariably stop cold the biggest of bulls.

A body hit is usually slow in stopping a moose, and a frightened, lung-shot moose may run 100 yards or more before dropping.

In the years I guided non-resident hunters seeking Alaskan big game trophies I learned that the spread of a moose's antlers (important to trophy hunters) is easy to determine when viewed from behind, and if possible, from slightly above. It's difficult to judge antler spread from the front or side. A good Alaskan bull should have a spread of at last 60 inches.

~

ALASKA'S OTHER SPECTACULAR DEER is the caribou, which has completely different habits. Moose have a home range, may move from summer to winter range, but they don't wander. Caribou are forever moving; their home is where they stand. They may migrate hundreds of miles between summer and winter range for years, then suddenly alter their migration route and not appear for decades in an area they were numerous in yesterday. I watched caribou year-round during my years at Savage River, and I learned something new about this spectacular wanderer every year.

Much of the meat I ate and fed to my wolf-dogs at Savage River was caribou, and I learned to take it when I could: one day the animals would be abundant around my cabin, perhaps the next there wouldn't be a caribou in sight.

One early September I collected a good part of my winter caribou meat in one quick hunt. Caribou meat is best in late August and early September when mature bulls' backs are layered with up to four inches of fat. On this day the hills were dressed in red and yellow, and early snow powdering the slopes announced the coming winter.

Climbing at daylight, I reached a lookout point 400 yards from my Savage River cabin and near an ancient, foot-deep caribou trail winding down from a high ridge. I glassed until noon without seeing a single caribou. A few moose were scattered on surrounding ridges and flats, and I idly studied them when not checking for caribou. Then, after a quick lunch at the cabin, I again climbed to the lookout. It was then I saw in the distance the flash of a white neck on a big bull caribou traversing the old caribou trail. I soon saw another bull with him, then another.

Swiftly, I climbed the rest of the way to the lookout and stationed myself behind a gnarled churn-butt spruce, its lower branches hugging the ground.

Through my binoculars I soon saw seven big bull caribou single-filing toward me, their heads moving slowly, drooping as if overburdened by their huge yellow antlers. Occasionally, as they traveled, they paused to nip at bunches of grass.

I waited until they were about 30 yards away, then poked my .30-06 through the branches of the tree and centered on the lead bull's neck. At the shot he dropped without a twitch. Quickly I swung the rifle to the rearmost bull, triggering another neck shot. Hair flew as the bullet hit, and the bull hit the ground so hard he bounced.

The shots riveted the other five caribou. They stood confused, staring in perplexity at their downed leader, and at the one in the rear. Three more quick shots toppled three more bulls. Jamming two additional shells into the gun I fired twice more. Seven neck shots, seven dead caribou. My winter meat supply was assured.

It was two months before I saw another caribou, but after that they poured across the hills in endless streams. Hundreds wintered all around my trapline.

January 31, 1931: Caribou herds by the thousands.

Caribou are unpredictable in their reactions, unpredictable in their movements, and unpredictably and constantly restless. Sometimes as you shoot they'll stand around wondering what it's all about. Other times they're off at the crack of a gun, sliding swiftly across the tundra with their smooth gait. One day they'll be in the country by the thousands; next day they are all gone.

September 23, 1930: Not a damn caribou in the country.

For years on end a caribou herd will move into a region punctually until you think you know their schedule. Then suddenly, for no apparent reason, they don't arrive anywhere near that time or at all: they might not be seen in that area again for years.

Caribou have deer traits as well as traits unique to themselves. They have the largest antlers proportionate to body size of any North American deer. A large bull may stand four feet at the shoulders, and his antlers may extend four feet or more from the top of his head. Unlike other North American deer, female caribou grow antlers. And, as in other deer, antlers are shed annually.

Herd behavior at breeding time, September 20 to mid-October, is spectacular. I've often crawled into the midst of a big herd at breeding time and found them so preoccupied they ignored my scent. It was easy to traverse a deep gully or tunnel through thick brush into their midst to get an inside view.

Big bulls are bent on collecting cows. Other bulls challenge to take them away. It's then that butting, sparring and antler-clashing occurs. Even at the peak of rutting, bulls quit fighting after a couple of clatters and a push or two. It is as if after strenuous bouts of straining, twisting and slamming they say to themselves, "Oh, to hell with it."

In behavior similar to that of moose, early in breeding season a caribou bull, excited and nervous, curries a cow with his tongue until she begins to urinate. Then the bull stops licking and swallows as much of the stream as he can. Sometimes a gallon or more accumulates in the bull's stomach. This, of course, flavors the meat.

At breeding time the meat of old bulls is smelly, strong, and inedible. It's so bad even hungry sled dogs won't touch it. Occasionally a novice hunter drops one of these bulls and later complain that the meat is "gamey." When one handles this meat, the odor permeates the hands so strongly the smell can't be scrubbed off with soap.

The first two weeks of October is a time of fierce and competitive breeding activity in the herd. At the peak, I have often watched their excited behavior. A cow might be standing around feeding and behaving normally. Suddenly she will toss up her head, look wildly about, and light out, running full speed. Her running galvinates nearby bulls and they take out after her. The tundra is wet then, and the animals, caught in this passionate annual ritual that preserves the herd, send spray flying all directions as they dash around crazily. I've seen as many as 20 bulls pursuing one cow, a stirring wilderness spectacle.

The cow coquettishly circles with the bulls panting behind her. Then she dashes back into the herd, coming to an abrupt stop, usually near a bull rolling his eyes and hooking at a little tree to show the world what a he-man he is.

Breeding usually takes place then, but the cow must be willing. I have seldom seen a bull chase and actually catch a cow.

When the rut ends, the old bulls indulge in a peculiar act. When I first saw bulls running from the herd in the fall of 1924 I couldn't figure it out. Watching with binoculars from my Savage River cabin I was surprised to see around 20 old bulls dashing at full speed away from the herd. There were no cows in front of them and no wolves—or anything else—chasing them. Occasionally, the fleeing bulls slowed and looked back toward the herd, then they started running again. As the last days of the breeding season came, other bulls joined the outward stampede. Some ran, some walked away from the herd. What was going on?

It finally dawned on me. The sudden exodus, dictated by instinct, was a natural sign that fun and games (breeding) was over, and there was no valid reason now for the bulls to stick around the cows. That's all it was. The rut was over.

One fall I arrived back at my cabin early in September. As I tied the dogs I noticed eight or nine bull caribou about 300 yards away on the hill behind my cabin. I had been gone for some time and badly needed meat. I took my Sedgely Springfield .30-06 and stuck a new box of shells in my pocket then slipped through the brush toward the caribou.

Crawling within 40 yards of the sleeping animals I aimed at a bull's head and squeezed the trigger. All that happened was a snap. The rifle didn't fire. I lifted the bolt to cock the rifle and snapped again. And again. In fact I lay there and ran that entire box of new shells through that rifle without a single one firing.

Apparently my Springfield had a weak spring. On some brands of ammunition it sometimes required several attempts to get a cartridge to fire. I assumed that some brands of ammunition had harder primers than others.

I sneaked away, figuring to get other shells from my cabin and return. As I stepped around the corner of the cabin I saw, about 25 feet away, a fat bull caribou. He was looking at the dogs. Then he turned his head and looked at me. There was no way he would remain while I went into the cabin for other shells, so I slipped into the chamber one of the shells I had already run through the rifle.

Again it refused to fire. I stood there cocking that bolt and pulling the trigger on that bull about 15 times. Nothing. Then, on the 16th try, surprisingly, the gun fired. The caribou dropped, and I had meat conveniently within 30 feet of my screened meathouse.

January 22, 1931: Wolves howling, and caribou all over the hills. 24 below all day. Clear and calm.

When it's 40 below or colder, I could clearly hear the sounds of a herd of caribou on the big flat a mile or so from my cabin. Their digging, grunting, and fighting to get under the snow for something to eat was a persistent, low, mutter. A cloud of fog hangs above a bunched caribou herd in deep cold.

Bickering caribou are common in winter. Old bulls drop their antlers by December. Antlers of young bulls are shed next. Cows retain antlers until after they drop their calves in late May or early June. In winter, a bald-headed old bull may paw through snow for three feet or so to find feed, only to have an old cow jab him away with her antlers to take over the hole.

September 6, 1931: Clear, froze last night. Freezing at 8 p.m. tonight. See two big bull caribou and lots of small ones. Grizzly eat a caribou I had cached.

September 14, 1931: Most of the caribou have gone north.

Caribou are swift afoot though they don't look it. A healthy caribou can easily outrun a wolf. In 1922 while riding with Roy Lund on the "racetrack" near Rapids we saw a caribou cow and calf suddenly leap onto the road ahead of us and race down the road, frightened by the noisy Ford. Roy sped up to 40 miles an hour and we were still the same distance behind the two fleet caribou. We yelled and cheered, and Roy kept honking the horn. This brought extra speed from the caribou. Even when Roy got us up to 45 miles an hour we were still 15 or 20 feet behind the fleeing animals. They kept their speed up for more than 400 yards before leaping off the road. That's faster than wolves can run. However, in extreme cold, caribou can't run that fast for any distance. When the mercury plunges, most animals tire quickly, and after a few hundred yards, the caribous' tongues emerge and wag as fatigue sets in. This plays right into a wolf's jaws. Frequently, in biting cold a wolf will speed alongside a tired, tongue-lolling caribou and leap and nip the tongue off. I've seen this occur several times and I've often found dead caribou with their tongues neatly snipped by razor-sharp wolf teeth.

But wolves don't have all the advantage. They cannot compete with caribou when running on glare ice. The deers' chisel-like dew claws penetrate and grip, as ice chips fly, while wolves skid and slide hopelessly. Mastery of the ice gives caribou a tremendous advantage in some wilderness chases.

September 23, 1931. Saw seven caribou, a grizzly, and a red fox. Snowed until noon.

Old bulls don't eat during breeding season, living off their fat. During the rut a caribou's neck swells. Immediately after breeding season the neck must itch because an old bull will vigorously rub his neck against trees. I've seen them with most of their neck hair worn away from scratching and rubbing.

In November and December, breeding bulls are so thin and depleted their backbone shows. Through December and January these old bulls, now antlerless, continue to be emaciated and in poor shape. It is now when they are most vulnerable to wolves—a time when they have little energy for running and no antlers for defending themselves.

March 13, 1934: I saw two bunches of caribou on the hills today. Found tracks of a band of wolves that followed my trail for a ways.

Unlike other deer, caribou do not see well at night. One dark September evening I was atop a high ridge headed back to my cabin. I blundered into a big caribou herd bedded down for the night. Behind me I could see hundreds of caribou antlers silhouetted against the western sky. About then I sprawled across the back of a caribou. It leaped to its feet, tossing me about eight feet. Then it bolted, grunting in alarm.

Instantly, the entire herd was running and milling, knocking one another over with loud thuds, grunting, and clashing antlers. I scurried to the nearby edge of the ridge where it dropped off steeply. Feeling ahead with my hands, I traveled below that protecting rim for half a mile before I was clear of the milling caribou.

Near the end of June or early July, when their calves are a month or so old, caribou often move into high country near glaciers or old snowdrifts, driven there by parasitic bot flies. This large orange and black bee-like fly, awing in July and August, lays eggs on a caribou's hair. When the eggs hatch, the larvae bore through the skin and migrate to the caribou's back, where they bore a hole through the hide for breathing. They live here through the winter and drop to the ground in June or later, and quickly develop into an adult. By July the adult again seeks a caribou to lay its eggs. The old snowdrifts on the high ridges of sheep country and glaciers sought by caribou at this time are usually too cool for the flies..

During botfly season caribou that haven't escaped to cool mountain areas dash madly about trying to escape the big insects. Young caribou seem to suffer most, and I've seen hundreds of bots in the backs of yearlings. For every bot, there is a hole in the hide of the caribou, and almost any caribou will have 50 to 100 bots. Older caribou have learned to get in the shadow of a cutbank, or behind a bushy spruce tree. Botflies don't seem to fly much except on bright sunshiny days and they don't bother animals in the shade. I think that's why caribou take to the woods in late July, through August and even into early September.

Sometimes caribou migrate in straggling bands, other times they'll crowd into a massive herd, like the one I saw near Healy in August, 1927. Fox traps I had ordered arrived at Healy while I was there, and I decided to start packing them to my Savage River cabin. I loaded Queenie and Buster's packs with about 25 pounds of traps, and put 50 pounds on my packboard and started out.

A week earlier I had walked the 18 miles from Savage River to Healy, and had seen only a few scattered bull caribou. Now, loaded with traps, three miles out of Healy I started seeing big bunches of caribou. Soon, I came to a solid mass of the animals literally flooding the mile-wide, nine-mile-long valley. As we met head-on they opened a lane about 100 feet wide for us. I led the dogs on chains. Those two wolf-dogs had seen me kill many caribou, and I was concerned about their response to that huge mass of animals. I need not have worried: the young wolf-dogs, usually eager to chase caribou, huddled close to me as we walked into the corridor that kept opening before us. I really didn't need to lead them on chains.

The lane closed behind us. The noise was like that made by a great herd of cattle. Cows continually grunted and calves bawled with their peculiar dog-like sound. Twigs and brush snapped, hoofs clicked, all creating a continuous low roar. I walked for nine miles surrounded by solid caribou. Strangely, I didn't see a single bull older than a three-year-old in that immense herd.

I was too fascinated to be frightened. Afterward, I wondered what my chances would have been if that herd had stampeded. When the dogs and I were in the open, the caribou showed no fear of us; opening a lane ahead of us and closing it behind as we walked.

But when I went through a patch of timber, the caribou ran in every direction. Caribou are always a little wilder in timber than out in the open. It seemed to me that every cow with a calf was more interested in keeping the calf safely beside her than anything else. I saw no tendency for the animals to stampede, despite my having two big wolf-dogs with me.

When I reached the top of the divide I cached the traps in the bushes. They were half way to my cabin, and I could eventually relay them the rest of the way.

I returned to Healy. The caribou had stopped traveling, and the valley was simply packed with them. They had been headed for the Nenana River, and would probably have crossed it near Healy. But a switch engine was working at Healy, and the wind was blowing from the noisy engine toward the herd and drifting black coal smoke among the animals. I think the noise of the engine plus the smoke stopped the herd. Some were feeding, others were lying down.

When I told people in Healy about the caribou, the town literally shut down. Stores closed, the roundhouse crew quit and the train crew side-tracked the engine. Everyone in town, some 25 or 30 people, walked out to see the spectacle. They didn't have far to go, for the animals had stopped only a mile and a half from town. One fellow brought a rifle, but after he had fired it a few times two men took it away from him. Everyone wanted to leave the herd undisturbed.

Those with cameras snapped pictures and people started trying to calculate how many caribou were in sight. As a group they soberly decided that there were at least two million. My guess was half a million. There were so many animals that counting was impossible.

Next morning I went to see the herd again. All the brush and grass was gouged from the ground and trampled flat. The stench of manure and urine was stifling. Wet ground had been trampled into mud. Now the animals were traveling again, streaming over the hills south and west of Healy like so many thousands of ants. It was one of the most spectacular wildlife scenes I ever witnessed.

Vinal, the Healy postmaster, went out there a few days after the main herd was gone and found many bunches of big, old white-necked bulls following the same route. He told me he shot two of them, and could have killed dozens if he'd wanted to.

In about four days that massive herd reached Broad Pass in the Alaska Range. Later I talked to train crews who told me the animals traveled along the railroad right of way at Broad Pass in such numbers that one of the trains was forced to stop for several hours to allow them to pass.

My Lady Judas

THE MOURNFUL HOWL of a wolf drifted up Savage river. Another joined it, then another, until a chorus of spine-tingling sound filled the air.

"Talk to 'em, Queenie," I encouraged my wolf-dog. She pointed her nose at the sky, and the seductive song of a lonely lady wolf sounded as she responded to the wild calls. Her wails sounded all wolf. She put her soul into it, then looked at me, wagging her tail.

The answer to her call soon floated back, seemingly close yet far away. It had an unearthly quality that lifted the hair on the backs of the other sled dogs tied nearby. Shivers ran up and down my own spine.

It was a bright March morning early in the 1930s. Wolves had overrun the country and they were killing many of the caribou from the herd that wintered on the north slope of the Alaska Range over the 35 miles between the Savage and Toklat Rivers.

I was waging war on the wolves, and Queenie was helping me. She loved to bait wolves in close with her calls, and she frequently lured them near enough to my cabin for me to shoot.

Queenie talked to that bunch of wolves off and on all day. She'd howl forlornly, and they'd answer with quavering cries. Several times they kept silent for an hour or more, and I'd think they'd gone, but eventually they resumed their long-range talk.

Their serenading came ever closer. I stayed near the cabin, watching with binoculars, my .30-06 loaded and a fistful of cartridges in my pocket.

Toward evening the wolves answered Queenie from very close, then shut up. She was extremely excited, and sat atop her house, ears pricked up and her eyes focused upriver. Once in a while she'd look around at me, wag her tail and grin.

I lay on my belly near a dog house, my rifle before me on the snow. Finally, a wolf trotted around the bend of the river 300 yards away. The river ice was about 200 yards wide, mostly from overflow, and the wolf ran right up the middle of it. I threw my fur cap down, fished some shells out of my pocket, and dropped them into it. Then I peeked at the wolf through my 3X scope.

As I watched, another wolf trotted into view, then another and a third. All eight of my male wolf-dogs were now on top of their houses moaning wolf talk. The visitors paid little attention to them, but every time Queenie called, one or more of the animals stopped and answered with a long, low, sweet howl.

Wolves kept trotting into sight, traveling single file, until I thought there'd be no end to them. They'd run a short way, stop, look back suspiciously, then catfoot closer. The lead wolf was within 50 yards of me before the last of the pack came around the bend. I counted 27 wolves strung out across that snow-covered bar and along the river ice.

I laid the post of the scope just below the withers of the *last* wolf, and squeezed a shot off. The animal, a small black, dropped on the ice. By the time I'd pulled the bolt and rammed in another shell at least 15 of the wolves had bunched up and were running away from the dead wolf and toward me. Two quick shots into the massed animals killed two and left another floundering on the ice, dragging its back legs toward the nearby willows. The remaining 23 scattered like dry leaves in a whirlwind, running frantically all directions, throwing snow, and scratching the hard ice as they sprinted.

Some headed directly for my wolf-dogs' houses, running low, their tails straight out behind them, mouths open, ears flat against their heads. Apparently they thought my dogs were wolves and figured it would be safe to be near them. The dogs loved it, and all of them screamed their approval at the tops of their voices.

I was starting to center the scope on a big black wolf 70 or 80 yards away when out of the corner of my eye I saw ears, close. I yanked the rifle around just as a wolf came over a cutbank not 10 feet away. There was nothing but wolf in the scope when I pulled the trigger; I just about blew him off the end of the gun barrel.

Then I spotted a gray wolf streaking for the willows 150 yards downriver. Centering on him, I fired and saw him plow his nose into crusted snow. Most of the animals were getting pretty well away from me by then, and I missed several shots. I'd burned up most of my cartridges, and the barrel on my rifle was sizzling hot.

I counted six dead wolves on the ice, then remembered the one that had dragged itself into the brush. When I got there I found it had crawled 20 feet and died. I'd killed seven.

That was March, wolf breeding season, a time when it wasn't unusual to see big wolf packs at Savage River.

Caribou were the wolves' main prey in the Savage River country but the big predators also killed many moose. A moose doesn't have much of a chance against a pack of wolves, unless it happens to be a big bull with antlers when there is no snow on the ground.

One fine April day I was at my cabin watching coyotes running sheep in the hills when a running cow moose showed up on the skyline, frequently looking behind her. Soon five wolves appeared on her trail.

Hoping I could save her, I grabbed my rifle and binoculars and hurried up the mountain behind my cabin to a lookout point. I watched the wolves chase the moose into a patch of spruce trees. When she burst out of it a few minutes later she was close enough that I could tell she was heavy with calf, and she was staggering from exhaustion. I was much too far away to help her, and all I could do was watch through my binoculars.

She finally stopped out in the open and turned to fight the wolves. As they closed in she tried to whirl and face each wolf as it attacked but she was too slow. The wolves jumped in and slashed then leaped back. She stood on her hind legs and struck with her front hoofs, and several times she ran four or five steps while erect trying to smash down one of the wolves. Her head swung back and forth, her ears were back, but she couldn't counter all the attacks. Whenever she lurched forward on her hind legs, one or two wolves tackled her from the rear. Eventually they swarmed over her and pulled her off her feet.

By the time I got there she was dead and the pack had gulped down about ten pounds of steaming flesh from her hindquarters. She was heavy with two unborn calves. Slashes from the wolf attack were all over her body, and big flaps of hide dangled here and there. Cuts on her shoulders looked as if she'd been ripped with a sharp knife. The wolves had heard me coming, and they had vanished.

The average Alaskan wolf weighs from 80 to 100 pounds, but sometimes a really big one turns up. I saw a 212-pound wolf put on a scale by the two Purdy brothers at Chicken, in the Fortymile country. They'd trapped it, and it was the biggest *dead* wolf I have ever seen. My captive black wolf was an unusually big wolf at 145 pounds.

Queenie called an unusually large wolf close to my cabin one bitter cold January day. For six weeks the thermometer hadn't been higher than 40 below zero, and often it seemed stuck at 50 or 60 below. One morning a wolf woke me with his howling. When it's that cold, sound carries well in the dense air. That wolf sounded as if he were right under my window. When I spotted him with my glasses he was on a hill about half a mile away, a big, handsome, gray fellow. I'd see steam go up from his breath, then a second or two later I'd hear his cry. My wolf-dogs answered, Queenie seemed especially eager to talk to him.

The rest of the dogs gave up after a bit, but Queenie sat atop her house and coaxed that wolf all day. There was no use in my going after him. He was in the open, and he'd have seen me the minute I started out. I watched him trot back and forth on the ridge, disappear, and show up on a nearby point where he could look down at the cabin. Then he'd howl and I'd see the steam rise a moment before I heard the sound.

From somewhere far to the south another wolf answered him for a while, and he kept looking in that direction. Then he'd look back toward Queenie when she howled. Whenever she was quiet for a long time, I'd tap on the window and urge her on, and she'd cut loose with another heart-rending howl. With that she'd look around at me, grin, and wag her tail.

Toward mid afternoon, Queenie was howling low and intimate-like, and from her behavior I could tell the wolf was close. I slipped out of the cabin with my rifle but it was too dark for me to see anything with the unaided eye. I looked through the rifle scope, and swung it back and forth. In a minute or so I saw what I thought was the wolf silhouetted against the snowy slope about 200 yards away. I lowered the rifle until the scope post disappeared on the wolf, let drive, and saw him collapse. I leaned the rifle against the cabin and walked over to him.

I made sure he was dead, remembering the live wolf I had once picked up, then started to hoist him to my shoulders. I picked up his hind legs, slid them across my neck, and yanked hard enough to pull his flanks even with my shoulders. Then I bent over, strained, and glanced back to see how he was coming. About a third of his length was still flat on the ice!

My dogs were yelling blue murder, anxious to see, smell and chew on the dead wolf. I dropped him and returned to the cabin and harnessed Queenie and Buster to a sled. When they got to the wolf they growled, hair on end, and both grabbed him by the rear end and dragged him a few feet, shaking their heads, and wooling him good.

By the time I got him into the cabin, not more than half an hour after I'd shot him, his feet and tongue were frozen solid. He tipped the pointer on my beam scale at 154 pounds. His skin, cased, was 8½ feet long, and 16 inches wide. A big wolf.

After skinning him I found five or six pounds of sheep meat and wads of sheep hair in his stomach. Next day, on the nearby ridge where I had first seen him, I found the remains of a three-year-old ram he had killed. He had eaten some of the sheep, and then had tried to call more wolves to the feast. That was his mistake; he hadn't figured on Queenie.

Wolves were so abundant in the Savage River country in the early 30s that sometimes I could successfully stalk them. One November morning in 1933 I was looking for fox sign on a big gravelly ridge back of my cabin. There was no snow on the ground, unusual for that time of year, and it was fairly warm, around zero. I happened to look north. Three miles off I saw something black on the side of the ridge about the top of the willow line. I focused my glasses and made out 20 wolves gathered around a kill. They started to fight, flared away, milled around then went back to eating. All but two were blacks.

There were some benches and drops between me and the wolves, so I lined myself up with a distant mountain and lit out in that direction. I lost sight of the pack, and didn't see it again until I poked my head over the edge of the bench above them. Was I surprised! It had taken me about two hours to get there, and as I neared the edge of the bench I got down and crawled the last few feet so I could peek over.

I figured the wolves might be 300 or 400 yards away, nevertheless, just in case, I stopped to check that my rifle was loaded. Then I carefully worked to the edge, took off my fur cap, slowly raised my head—and looked a gray wolf right in the face. She was about 10 feet away. I thought she stood with one foot raised, frozen, staring at me just like a pointer dog. Out of the corner of my eye I saw the others strung out across the hillside, 20 or 30 feet apart. They'd eaten their fill and had started up the bench to find a place to lie around where they could watch their kill, a big cow moose.

With my rifle across my arm pointed forward. I snapped a shot at that frozen wolf. She didn't stand there long and it all happened in an instant. That hurried shot missed; the wolf was so close I figured I didn't have to aim. She whirled and plunged into the willows, and as she did, I saw that one of her front legs was missing.

I scrambled into a sitting position, lined up on a big black running downhill, and fired. It swapped ends, and landed with a loud *whunk*. Next I put the sight on another black about 50 yards off and sent him rolling. He stopped, limp, against some willows. I missed a little wolf streaking away but a second shot caught it in mid stride. It skidded 20 feet before piling up against a low bank.

With their bellies full of fresh moose meat, the wolves were slow. I vaguely remember the rest of the shooting. I swung the gun on this wolf and that, the closest first. When they got a long way off, I'd take careful aim and shoot. Sometimes I'd see a geyser of grass spurt ahead of a wolf, and the animal would whirl broadside and stand still for an instant. If I didn't kill it on the second shot, it would run to where some others had ducked into the willows. The one farthest away, a gray, was diving for the willows just as I lined it up. The gun cracked, there was a *yipe*, and the willows closed over it.

When the shooting ended I had fired 21 shots and I could see eight dead wolves scattered across the tundra. Then I remembered the gray one that yipped.

I had a hard time finding the place, but after zigzagging at the edge of the willows I found and followed a blood trail. I had gone about 20 yards when I saw bushes moving ahead. The animal had remained there until I came along; now it was trying to get away. I hurried after it and he hurried off. Finally I lost sight of the movement and had to go back and pick up the blood trail.

Bit by bit I found where the wolf had run through the willows, exited on the other side and gone across a hummocky flat. I followed across the flat and up a hill. From the blood trail he left I was certain I had hit him solidly in the body and was surprised at how far he had traveled.

The trail led to a lone clump of willows on a high knoll, a dense patch with dead leaves still hanging not over 25 or 30 feet across. I didn't think the wolf would stop there but I was beginning to wonder. I walked toward the willows, my rifle forward and safety off. Just as I started to part the brush that big gray wolf, lips curled back and jaws agape, roared and lunged at me. I pulled the trigger. He dropped within a foot of my moccasins.

I dragged him into the open and found that my first shot had broken the bone and slashed an artery just above the hock on a hind leg. His teeth indicated he was young, whelped the previous spring. He weighed close to 100 pounds.

Why had he turned on me? I think he'd just given up. A young wolf doesn't have the guts of an adult. I believe an older wolf would have kept going until he died. This one wasn't lying in wait for me. He had just quit, facing his back trail, and I had blundered into him. He probably would have bitten me if I hadn't fired when I did.

That made nine wolves I killed out of that bunch. I dragged them together, built a fire, and spent the next nine hours skinning them. It was after midnight when I staggered toward home with that load of prime pelts worth $135 in bounty alone, never mind what I would get for the pelts. This was at a time when $10 a day was top wages.

A few months later, a ranger killed a three-legged female wolf in McKinley Park five miles from where I'd missed that first shot. Both the gray I shot at and the gray the ranger killed had the left front leg missing. (McKinley Park Rangers regularly shot wolves in the park until the early 1950s).

My wolf-dogs were always far more excited when I killed a wolf than when I killed a caribou or a moose. When I brought a fresh wolf hide in sometimes I'd lay it on the snow and the dogs would smell of it, roll on it and show every sign of excitement. And they were just one jump away from being wolves themselves.

I collected a $15 Territory of Alaska bounty for every wolf I killed in those years. I also sold the skins, which are valuable in Alaska for parka ruffs. In 1927 a good wolf skin brought up to $18 from a fur buyer, more sometimes from a local fur parka sewer.

I liked to think that for every wolf I shot or trapped, somewhere there were caribou, moose, or mountain sheep whose lives I had saved.

It always seemed strange to me that Queenie, a half-wolf, got so much enjoyment out of calling wolves to the cabin where I could shoot them. When one or more wolves that she had called were close she became very nervous. I'm sure she could smell them. Often, with wolves very close, she would look at me and wag her tail as if saying, "Here they come."

There was never a Judas like Queenie.

Hunting Wolves

ONE COLD CLEAR MARCH DAY I sat on a hillside a mile or so from my Savage River cabin watching a muskeg flat where several hundred scattered caribou were feeding. A quarter-mile below me a coal ledge jutted from the 15-foot-high river bank. A yellow seepage from the coal smeared the blue-white river ice. Five caribou stood licking at the stain.

As I looked for wolves, I idly glanced at the five caribou from time to time swinging my binoculars and scanning the snow-covered land. After about an hour I saw a lone gray wolf trotting across the flat. Soon three others single-filed down the river to my left. Then another appeared on my right, picking its way upstream.

The five wolves were converging on the caribou at the coal seep.

The wolf on the flat trotted to the edge of the bank above the unsuspecting caribou and peeked over at them. Then it backed off to lie down and wait. The group of three wolves left the creek and disappeared into the spruces below me. I lost track of the fifth wolf.

I then watched the five caribou. After about ten minutes a gray wolf streaked out of the timber and grabbed one of the cows by the flank. The remaining four caribou scattered as the frantic cow skidded and staggered, trying to shake off the clinging wolf. She tried to jump from the slick ice to the bank but immediately fell on her side floundering with the tenacious wolf's jaws still clamped firmly to her flank. Three other wolves appeared and swarmed over her, chopping and slashing.

Then, incredibly, she pulled free. All of the animals skidded on the slick ice, but the terrified cow made it to the bank with sharp hoofs giving her traction on the ice, humped her way to the top, and hooked her front legs over. The wolf on the bank met her head-on, sinking his teeth into her nose. He hung on as the two of them rolled and flopped down the steep slope to the river ice. A red stain spread across the white ice as the five wolves then killed the cow.

I waited, knowing they would eat their fill and go lie down for a sleep. They'd have heard me if I had tried to approach them while they were eating since the snow was crusted enough to make walking noisy. Fortunately, the slight breeze was in my favor, so they couldn't catch my scent.

Soon they were gorged on the hot meat. I watched them leave their kill, climb the riverbank and trot toward a low knoll in the middle of a flat. As they trotted their tails were over their backs, rolling around and around—a sure sign they had full bellies. When hungry, wolves carry their tails straight behind and down, almost dragging.

They reached the knoll and selected a spot to curl up in for a nap. I slipped into the snowshoes I'd been sitting on and took my time walking to a little willow-choked stream that passed close to where they were sleeping.

I was within 100 yards of them when I got into shooting position. I carefully centered the rifle scope on one of the sleeping animals and squeezed off a shot. He half rolled over as the .30-06 bullet hit, while the four other wolves leaped to their feet staring about wildly.

As if by signal all four ran directly toward me and the creek. It was the nearest cover and they wanted to be in that creek. I waited until they were about 50 yards away and fired at another wolf; he threw up a shower of powdery snow as he skidded and lay dead.

The others split, two to my right and one to my left, as they continued to dash toward the creek. I watched the two until they were in the clear streaking downstream, and fired three more times. At the third shot my 180-grain bullet slammed home and one of the two collapsed in mid-stride. By then the others were out of sight.

Three out of five—that gave me a feeling of accomplishment. It would also beef up my bank account. If I hadn't known those wolves would take a nap after eating, I would probably have barged down to the river as soon as they had made their kill and I doubt if I'd have had a chance to make a single shot.

On another cold March day, this time in 1932, I was awakened at daylight by a bunch of wolves howling not far from my cabin. I got up, ate a quick breakfast, dressed warmly, then with rifle and binoculars climbed to a lookout point where I could see the nearby big flat. Sitting on a snowshoe, I searched with binoculars and soon located nine wolves on the flat.

As I watched, the wolves all stood up, noses pointed into the air, a cloud of steam rising above each animal. Next I heard their spine-tingling, weird and beautiful howls. There's no other sound like it. Then the wolves laid down again.

I studied the area, trying to decide how I might get within rifle range of them. Pinto Creek, lined with willows and an occasional spruce, meandered across the flat about 400 yards beyond the wolves. Beyond Pinto Creek and about half a mile from the wolves about 500 caribou were scattered across the flat, digging through the snow, feeding. The wolves kept looking at the caribou, frequently howling.

Pinto Creek was my only chance. I decided that if I could get into the creek opposite the wolves I might be able to throw a shot or two beyond the wolves and maybe spook them toward me.

I lit out downhill toward a bend in Pinto, about a mile away. I ran, thinking only of the wolves, until I reached the bottom of the hill. Suddenly I realized I had left my rifle on the hill. I had been concentrating so hard on the wolves, planning my stalk, that I had forgotten it. I had to climb the hill again to retrieve it. While there I checked and saw that the wolves hadn't moved.

This time I reached Pinto Creek, where I had to put my snowshoes on. The snow was mostly crusted but here and there were soft places where I needed the shoes. I made a lot of noise as I hurried along, once in a while stepping on frozen hard snow that broke off with a loud *clunk*.

I reached the place nearest the wolves, near a lone spruce. The creek bank was about a hundred feet high, with a steep folded snowdrift on it. There I bent and removed my snowshoes. I was kneeling to pick them up when I looked down the creek and saw two black wolves, heads up, looking wildly about, tearing down the steep drift into the creek bottom. I quickly threw a glance behind and saw another wolf skidding down a drift about a hundred yards away.

The wolves, watching the caribou, had heard me coming down the creek and assumed I was a caribou. They went into action. Surprisingly, instead of charging en masse toward the supposed caribou, they had spread out. The three I saw were the flankers. I read sign later and found where the other six wolves had fanned out in a big arc between the flankers. They were just over the top of the bank, waiting for action to begin. It was a beautifully-executed maneuver. If I had been a caribou I wouldn't have had a chance.

But I wasn't a caribou.

I quickly shot at one of the running wolves halfway down the snowdrift ahead. My .30-06 slug relaxed him and he piled up at the bottom of the drift.

By then his companion had reached bottom, and as he hesitated I shot him in the body. He started trying to climb back up the snowdrift, but couldn't make it. He was obviously done for so I ignored him and whirled around to try for the wolf behind me.

He was scratching and clawing up the steep slope for all he was worth. I put the rifle scope on him at the last moment, and he collapsed over the rim as I fired.

I then climbed the bank. The snow was hard and slick. My moccasins skidded and slipped and I had to dig the gun butt in and lean on it to reach the top. I expected the other six wolves to be long gone. Instead, they had bunched together about 300 yards off, and were standing looking toward the creek, puzzled I guess. The three that had led the way to the creek had disappeared. They had heard the shots and hadn't figured it out.

The moment I came into sight they scattered, most of them running toward the nearby sheep hills. I started shooting, but wasn't very steady after climbing the creek bank, and they were at extreme range. I hit two. Both left small blood trails which I followed, but they were still going strong so I left off and returned to skin the three I had killed.

In March, 1936 I watched a family of nine wolves for more than a week, trying to learn something of their daily routine. They howled early each morning about daylight from the big flats near my cabin. Then they would single-file to the top of a mountain where they would howl a few more times then lie down to sleep. A huge gray acted as sentry as the others slept. During the morning he occasionally got up and walked around, looking.

Twice I tried to catch them on the mountaintop by sneaking through a nearby patch of spruce trees. Unfortunately, the range from the tree line and the mountaintop where they slept was too far for me to shoot. Both times, just as I stepped into the open, the big fellow spotted me and started howling. Then the entire pack left.

I followed them most of one day trying to get close enough for a shot. They saw me each time I neared, howling a few times and loping to another ridge top. I was wasting my time.

The weather was still and cold all that week. In very cold weather—30 to 40 below—an inch or so of frost may build up on crusted snow. Early one morning I heard the nine wolves howl on the nearby flat, then lost track of them. But when a gusty south wind came up I put on my parka and grabbed my rifle. Things were beginning to break my way.

When the wind blows after a long spell of quiet and cold, it can pick up the sugary frost and create a dimout with blowing ice crystals. As I left the cabin I saw that stuff flying on the sidehill between the timber and the place where the wolves had habitually slept the previous week. I couldn't be sure, but suspected they'd returned to their usual daytime beds.

Wind gusts staggered me from time to time as I climbed the mountain, almost blinding me. I could see ahead perhaps 40 yards as I climbed the west side of the ridge, reasoning the wolves would be on the north slope out of the wind.

When near the top, I crawled, but found nothing at the summit, so I started to crawl down the north side. Occasionally I raised up to look around. Finally I saw a wolf less than 25 feet away, lying with his tail over his face with wind whipping snow around him. One moment I'd see him, the next there'd be a white curtain between us.

During a lull I shot squarely into him. He rolled over, kicked a couple of times, and lay still. At the shot the other wolves ran every which way. Most of them had been lying farther down the mountain, and at the shot they headed for the top. A black wolf almost ran over me before realizing his mistake, and by then it was too late—I had him. Another ran past me and through a clear spot in the driving snow I snapped a shot at him and saw him collapse.

That made three out of nine, very satisfying, all because I had anticipated what those wolves would do.

The first wolf I had killed was the gray sentinel. When I skinned him I found at least 20 scars on his chest and neck, some old and calloused, some fresh. Some wolves habitually grab sleeping caribou by the face. I believe antler wounds, made by struggling caribou, accounted for the scarring on that wolf.

When I started trapping at Savage River in 1924, I concentrated on trapping foxes on top of windy, gravelly ridges, but I frequently trapped wolves too. Both wolves and foxes stepped into traps I set near clumps of transplanted grass.

Wolves like to travel ridges, well-beaten caribou and moose trails and river bars. They'll travel the same routes year after year. One November while on my trapline I saw seven wolves about a mile away trotting single file along the side of a mountain in open country. They hadn't seen me. They were traveling about as fast as a man can trot, and I knew if they kept that up I couldn't get near them. However, remembering the habits of wolves, I ducked out of their sight and ran to head them off. Every time those wolves came to a place to leave sign, all the males clustered around it and sprinkled. They didn't take long, of course, but what they did next took longer. After they'd trotted on, sometimes as much as several hundred feet, some of them returned to the spot for a repeat performance.

Because of this peculiar habit, I gained enough ground to reach a spot on a big open ridge about 300 yards from where I knew they usually crossed. Then I lay down to catch my breath.

I hadn't waited long when they trotted into sight. A 300-yard shot at a wolf, even with a scope-sighted .30-06, isn't easy. My first shot went over a gray fellow. Three of the bunch dashed away from where the slug struck and toward me. I hit one when he was about 200 yards out and watched him plow into the snow. Another veered into a gully and out of sight. The third kept straight on, ears pinned back, tail floating behind. He soon appeared on a low rise just in front of me, not 20 yards away. An easy shot.

I probably wouldn't have even tried to follow those wolves if I hadn't known how they waste time at their scent posts, and where they would probably cross the ridge.

February 8, 1934: Wolves were howling in three different places. Went after them but did not see them. Went down the river five miles. Overflow everywhere. Ice and water in every patch of timber, just like last winter. Ice over 25 feet thick in some places.

For 40 years I've gotten almost as much pleasure out of watching wildlife as I have out of hunting. In both cases, the knowledge that animals are creatures of habit has been a big help.

Many well-meaning people interested in wildlife believe wolves always take sick, crippled or otherwise misfit animals, thus benefiting the health of their prey species. A wolf takes what is available. He doesn't go out of his way to kill misfit animals. Wolves commonly kill stragglers. Some are weak animals, others aren't. A pregnant caribou or moose is more vulnerable to wolves than a barren cow. The same animal at another time of year might be able to run circles around the wolf, which is a relatively slow runner.

Young moose and caribou calves are especially vulnerable to wolf predation. These are not "sick" or "misfit" animals needing to be weeded from the population. It takes a large number of wolves to pull down a mature hard antlered bull moose in good condition, with good footing. But two or three wolves can finish off the biggest bull that ever lived if he's antlerless and bogged down in deep and crusted snow. Mature moose or caribou herd bulls without antlers and tired and weakened from a long, vigorous breeding season can be killed easily by wolves; they aren't "sick" or "misfit" either.

Once a wolf gets his teeth into its prey, severe damage takes place. A wolf's teeth work like shears, the upper teeth fitting on the outside of the lowers. A wolf's jaw muscles are extremely powerful.

Wolves slash, leaving cuts in a moose or caribou's hide resembling cuts made with a sharp knife. The soft flank or underbelly is the usual target. A long slash and the moose or caribou's innards fall out, the animal trips and walks on them as it tries to flee, and is soon dead.

Some humans are said to "wolf" food and the word is appropriate in that context. I have examined the contents of hundreds of wolf stomachs and have often found fist-size chunks of meat. Wolves feed weaned pups by regurgitating such chunks and I often found these pieces at wolf dens.

The wolf's cruelty is not exaggerated although that's viewing it from the human perspective. The wolf isn't *intentionally* cruel; he's just being a wolf.

One September day in 1935 I noticed a bull moose standing in Savage River near my cabin. The next day he was lying on the bank with his head on the ground. I went to see what was wrong with him. Although alive, he couldn't lift his head. Wolves had eaten 25 or 30 pounds of meat from one of his hind legs. When I had first seen him, the suffering animal had been standing in water trying to cool the feverish leg.

I ended his suffering with a shot into the brain then followed his trail back to see what had happened. Part of his backtrack ran across a sandy stretch of river bar where tracks were fairly clear. As best as I could tell, five wolves had run and pestered him until he became exhausted and fell. The wolves ate what they wanted then left, perhaps after hearing my dogs bark, or sensing my cabin.

Twice after that at Savage River I found live moose with meat torn from their hams by wolves. In both cases deep snow with a light crust supported the wolves but not the moose. It was no contest.

When hungry wolves kill they usually drink hot blood and then go for the hams. Sometimes they eat the tongue. When there are many wolves, they may consume an entire animal except for the skull and the very largest bones, and often even these are cracked open for the marrow.

When wolves eat off a freshly-killed caribou or moose, they swallow large chunks of meat. Commonly hair of the moose or caribou accompany the meat, so whenever I opened a wolf's stomach, I could identify the kind of meat eaten by the hairs.

At Savage River I was always careful to keep my .30-06 rifle sighted in. This paid off many times on long shots at wolves. One April morning I was in my main cabin when I heard a wolf howling. It sounded as if it was at some distance. Taking binoculars, I walked to the river bar and looked around. There on a hill sat a black wolf. I put the binoculars on it. It howled again, and it was looking toward the cabin.

Queenie had been howling a little and he was answering her. I returned to the cabin for my rifle and loaded it with some 172-grain boattail cartridges. I had found them to be very accurate, and they carried better than the 180-grain bullets I often used.

If I had tried to get closer, the wolf would have left, so I decided to try a long shot. With naked eye it looked like a mouse, just a black spot on the snow. I later stepped the distance off at 700 yards. I rested the rifle across a log, got into the sling, and lined up very carefully on that wolf. It sat facing me, and continued to howl from time to time. I put the sighting picket just above the top of his head. The air was still so I didn't have to consider windage.

I carefully squeezed off a shot, and after what seemed like some time, I heard the bullet smack into him with what sounded like a solid body hit. I watched through the rifle scope as he rolled downhill. To my astonishment he picked himself up and limped off into the brush.

I got some more rifle shells and my packboard, expecting to go find the wolf dead and pack it home to skin.

I followed a blood trail where I had hit the wolf. Within a few hundred yards I looked ahead and about 400 yards away something black was moving in the brush along the rim of a canyon. With binoculars I made out the wolf. As I watched, he stopped, head down. I could have shot then, and I should have, but I thought he was dying.

Then he was moving again. I shot, but missed. I marked the tree near where he had stood and walked to it. There I found six or eight pounds of caribou meat chunks he had vomited. There were plenty of snowdrifts in the brush and timber and I followed his blood trail across them.

He headed for a nearby high ridge where tracking was easy for the first two or three miles. But by the time he reached the ridgetop he had quit bleeding, and I was convinced I had lost him.

But I found I could track him there. On that ridge, the gravel is loose and round, from marble-size to the size of a hen's egg. It's brown on top, but when moved about it's white on the bottom. I could see where the wolf had turned that gravel over as he ran—just a white place here and there. He followed the ridgetop for a mile or so then went down the north side and into crusted snow I could walk on most of the time.

Now I could see his tracks more clearly. A drop of blood showed every few feet. His right front leg had been hit; he put all his weight on his left front leg, and at each step I could see where the left front foot was spread

I tracked him towards Middle River, heading northwest. Then he came to where a lot of caribou had been feeding. Among the caribou tracks were other wolf tracks, which slowed me. The caribou had been digging up and working in the snow. It took me a couple of hours to work out his trail there. But there's lots of daylight in April so I kept going.

At midday the snow had turned soft and I kept breaking through but I found where the wolf had broken through in a few places also. I got a line on where he seemed to be heading, and I'd trot along pretty fast for a ways, cross his trail and pick up his tracks again.

I was about eight miles from my cabin when I topped a bench and saw the wolf on a snowdrift about 200 yards away. He was flattened out, facing his back trail. He must have been lying there for six hours or more while I was tracking him. I had been carrying a hardnose cartridge in the barrel, thinking that if I came upon him close I didn't want to blow a big hole in him. As I worked the bolt and pulled that cartridge out of the barrel and replaced it with a boattail, he jumped to his feet and ran down a big snowdrift. .

I centered him in my rifle scope and fired. He collapsed, dead.

I skinned him right there, for the hide was prime and a good one. My early morning long-range shot had struck to one side of his chest and gone under the shoulder blade, separating the shoulder from the body without breaking anything. A big blood clot had formed. He might have recovered from the wound if I hadn't trailed him and finished him off.

The Neighborhood Killers

21

IN THE SUMMER OF 1928 a pair of wolves lived in an old fox den they had enlarged within a mile of my lower cabin. I often traveled between my cabins and kept all but one of the dogs on chains as I walked, usually allowing Queenie to run loose. That summer, every time I walked to the lower cabin Queenie found an animal the wolves had killed. Altogether she found five big bull caribou, a two-year-old bull moose, and a yearling moose. She would get wind of a kill and head for it and I would follow her. Without Queenie I wouldn't have found any of them. Each of those kills was in or near shallow water at the river's edge. There were probably more kills that Queenie and I didn't find.

The kills were all near a mineral game lick. The way I read sign, when caribou or moose were at the lick, the two wolves bushwhacked them. Antlers are in velvet in summer, tender, and not much use for defense. It didn't appear as if the moose or caribou had given the wolves any trouble. The two-year-old bull moose was still fresh when I found it and I took some of it home for dog food.

A couple of days after that I was on a lookout behind my lower cabin about three quarters of a mile from the moose remains. As I watched through binoculars, a cream-colored grizzly shuffled aimlessly across the tussocky tundra toward Savage River. Occasionally he stopped to dig and eat a root, or swallow a mouthful of blueberries. Several times he sat on his haunches like a gigantic ground squirrel, swiveling his nail-keg-size head back and forth, peering with small eyes, nose wrinkled and sniffing, then dropping to all fours and ambling on.

He came to the river and started across a gravel bar. Half way to the water he stopped, his head twisted to one side, his nose detecting the scent of rotting moose. He whirled and loped upwind, his bulky body moving surprisingly fast as he splashed through shallows, following his educated nose.

Reaching the dead moose, which was lying in shallow water, he mouthed it excitedly, waded around it a couple of times, then clamped his powerful jaws on a front leg, leaned backward, and splashily dragged the carcass to dry ground where he started to eat.

As I watched through binoculars, a black and a gray wolf appeared suddenly on the bar and stood watching him. The bear didn't notice the wolves until they started to close in with a mane-bristling, stiff-legged walk and circle him. He dropped to his haunches to face them.

The wolves walked as if tiptoeing on eggs, moving slowly, heads down, hair on end, tails straight out behind. Around and around they went, the bear twisting and trying to face both wolves at once. Finally when they got the bear between them, the black leaped in and slashed the bear's rear. As quick as a trap the grizzly whirled, bawling—I heard that bawling even from my distance—and rushed at the nimble wolf. The gray wolf dashed in then, snapping at the bear's heels. Bruin plowed to a quick stop, turned and swiped at the gray with a front paw. The wolf was too quick for the bear, and easily leaped out of reach.

The bear swiftly lumbered after it, but he hadn't gone 20 yards before the black wolf was again tormenting him from the rear. At one point the wolf actually leaped on the bear's broad back, slashing through his thick hide.

The grizzly skidded to a stop and reared over backward trying to reach his tormenter. For a moment he sat on his haunches, facing both wolves. The grizzly is generally the boss bully of the Alaska wilds and I got the impression that this bear was not only frustrated, but bewildered.

The panting wolves appeared to be grinning, as they continued to bait the bear, working silently and in perfect coordination. The bear kept roaring and growling and it became clear the wolves were working the bear away from their kill.

Soon the battling animals disappeared into the timber, but I could follow the fight by the roaring of the bear. I hoped they would appear again on a bar of Savage River below me, but they didn't. Occasionally, in breaks in the timber I saw flashes of the moving bear and running wolves. In about 20 minutes those wolves worked the bear into the timber a full mile away from their kill.

While tormenting the big yellow grizzly the wolves didn't make a sound, but when they were satisfied, they howled a low sweet musical song and trotted off. The bear slouched off across the tundra. That dead moose belonged to the wolves who weren't about to let any waddling loafer of a bear have it.

Those wolves must have lived close to me and my dogs for some time without me being aware of them. Several times that summer all of my dogs suddenly growled and made a fuss. I would come out of the cabin and look, and the dogs would be leaning on their chains looking at the three-foot-high redtop grass around the cabin. I couldn't see anything. But one day the dogs kept insisting there was something there, so I put the ladder up on my cache and climbed a few feet. Then I saw a gray wolf lying in the grass not far from the cabin.

I went for my rifle and climbed the ladder again, but of course by the time I got back the wolf was gone.

I went to Healy several times that summer. Each time I returned to find that some animal had dug all the dry grass out of the doghouses, and had packed the dogs' bones off. I later realized that it had to have been that pair of wolves.

Two or three times during summer evenings the dogs would look out on the bar of nearby Savage River and growl. I would look and see the back of a wolf loping along there. I never got a shot.

That fall, the gray and black wolf pair got into the habit of killing caribou on a nearby open flat. Early one mid-September morning I climbed a ridge overlooking the flat, hoping to get a shot at wolves. The flat was dotted with little bunches of up to 20 or so caribou as far as I could see across the nine-mile-long flat. I stayed high, searching with binoculars.

About nine that morning, a gray wolf walked out of the red-top grass, stretched, and looked around. He was about mile away and perhaps 800 feet below me. Then a black wolf appeared nearby, stretched, yawned and also looked around. They started to howl softly. They were the pair from the nearby den. The gray was the female, the black the male.

Soon they started after a caribou. It was hard for me to believe they were the pair that had killed all the big game I had found dead close to my cabin, for on this day they couldn't seem to connect.

Every time they tried to stalk one caribou, another would see them and give the alarm. The two wolves would belly down like cats and slide along flattened out, every now and then raising up and peeking ahead. When within 30 or 40 feet of a caribou, quick as a flash they'd dash at it, but the caribou had been forewarned every time and would bound away across the rough tundra almost like a rubber ball.

On such terrain, a caribou can easily outrun a wolf. The wolf trips and stumbles, while the caribou bounds along smoothly. After a failed stalk, those two made no effort to chase caribou, but sat and howled real low. Then they'd trot off single-file, looking for more caribou.

The country was full of snowshoe hares and every time the wolves went through a willow patch, rabbits ran out all around them. The wolves ignored the rabbits. Not once did I see them even turn their heads when rabbits were near.

Knowing they were hungry and had big pups to feed, I was fairly certain they'd hunt until they killed. I had a good idea where the den was and the flat where they hunted wasn't far from the den. There were two possibilities for me to get a shot. One was to wait until they killed and gorged themselves then try to stalk them as they slept. The other was to get closer to the caribou they were stalking and hope for a shot as they hunted.

There were the pups to think of, too. If I worked it right I might be able to get a crack at them. At that time of year wolf pups depend almost entirely on their parents for food. Usually, by September when the parents make a kill they'll either lead the half-grown pups to it, or they'll howl and call the pups to the kill. When pups are still very young, the adults return to the den and regurgitate food for them. These pups were beyond that stage.

All that day I walked back and forth on the ridge, staying back so they wouldn't wind me, yet trying to keep them in sight. Occasionally I struck a match to test the wind; it remained steady from the south, and I couldn't get any closer to the wolves without being scented.

The gray wolf took the lead in all their stalks. The wolves would get downwind of a caribou and she would get down like a cat and slide along with the black right behind her. Now and then the gray lifted her head to peek. I'd frequently lose sight of the wolves, but could tell where they were by the behavior of the caribou. One of a bunch of caribou would raise its head and stand and watch the wolves. When the wolves got too close, the caribou would run.

Several times, the wolves got within 30 or 40 feet of caribou. Quick as a flash, the gray would make a run, with the black right behind her. She missed catching caribou again and again. She would be just about ready to grab a caribou when it would bound away. The ground was mostly soft, and caribou can easily outrun a wolf in such footing.

Once the pair stalked a big white-necked bull caribou with hard-polished, rocking-chair-size antlers. He was on a little knoll, fighting with a willow bush. He'd waltz around, rub his antlers up and down the bush, then back off to rush and hook at it as if it were a rival. The wolves, flat on their bellies, squirmed closer and closer. The bull was too busy trying to impress himself to see them. When they were about 20 yards away the wolves got to their feet and *walked* toward the bull. As they neared him, the black wolf suddenly made a rush, but the puffed-up bull whirled and lowered his rack, ready for the attack.

The two wolves ran around him, howling, rushing and pestering him, trying to make him expose a flank. He simply whirled to face them, shaking that big rack in their faces. They finally howled a few time, turned and walked away, heads and tails down. The bull had bluffed them out. He went back to dueling with the willows, probably more impressed with himself than ever.

I still don't know why those two didn't kill that bull. I think they could have if they had persevered.

I kept trying to get into position for a shot, but they remained out of range. It was nearly five in the afternoon and I was ready to quit and go home. I figured they'd make their kill after dark; most wolf kills are made at night.

Then a cow caribou started down the ridge with a calf at her heels. The wolves quickly scented them. The caribou were following a line of willows running down to the flat, a perfect place for wolves to make a stalk. They ran and sneaked to the line of willows to lie in wait.

That was the break I hoped for. When the stalking wolves came to the lower end of the willows they were within 300 yards of me. As they went out of sight in the thick growth, I crawled to the willows, stopped in a little opening and sat down in a game trail. The wind was right. Neither the wolves nor the caribou saw me.

I watched the brush shaking as the wolves crawled through it. Soon the cow caribou also noticed the moving willows, and stood staring. Occasionally the gray wolf poked her head up to peek, making the cow nervous. She still didn't run. Closer and closer the wolves came. I could hear them sniffing, trying to use scent to keep track of the caribou's movements.

Suddenly the gray wolf stuck her head out of the grass about 20 feet from me. She practically filled my rifle scope's field of view and all I had to do was pull the trigger. As I fired she disappeared with a growl, then the grass started twitching where she thrashed about.

I jumped up to see where the black wolf was in time to see him leap over his mate and run along the game trail toward me. He didn't know where the shot had come from and he was so close when he saw me that it was too late for him to turn. I had him in the scope, but before I could shoot he scooted past me within 15 feet, ears pinned back, feet scratching for all they were worth. I let him run 50 yards into the open, then fired. He swapped ends, stone-dead. I looked up and saw the caribou cow and calf streaking to safety.

I skinned both animals mostly for the bounty, for the skins weren't worth much. Wolf skins don't prime up until well into the winter. The stomachs of both were empty. That was hard for me to believe because rabbits were abundant. Those two ignored rabbits all day in order to try to kill caribou.

There were still the pups to consider. I sat and started howling, trying to call them. Within five minutes I had an answer from where the two adults had come out of the grass that morning. A young wolf's howl ends with a dog-like bark. I kept calling, and soon saw five half-grown wolves through my glasses, trotting single file, heading straight for me. They weighed about 50 pounds each, all head, legs, and feet—and capable of eating a lot of caribou and moose.

I called them right up to me. When they were very close I shot one. The other four ran into some willows. I walked through the willows and one by one those big pups got up to run. They'd flatten out again, hiding. I found and shot each one. Seven wolves, seven bounties. Seven fewer wolves to kill Savage River moose and caribou.

The Wolverine

THE WOLVERINE IS WELL-DRESSED, sleek and handsome, but he smells bad. He's also cranky. He can't even get along with other wolverines, including his girl friend, and a mated pair fights constantly. Occasionally a wolverine gives a trapper grief by breaking into a cabin and raising havoc, and once in a while one robs a trapline. That's because he's hungry.

Nature made the wolverine a bandy-legged, relatively slow-moving critter. He's not fast enough to catch and kill big game, and he's lucky when he stumbles onto and kills a rabbit. Not that he can't kill most animals he's able to catch. He can and does, for he's probably as powerful an animal for his size as any in North America.

He's frustrated, I guess, because he's hungry much of the time. He'll eat anything he can find and when he finds something edible he eats as much of it as he can hold, hence the handle "glutton" has fixed on him. If he can't eat it all he'll foul what's left with strong, vile-smelling musk and urine. He'll even leave his droppings on food, probably figuring nothing else will touch it and he can return and finish it himself. He's right about that.

Like his cousins the weasel and mink, the wolverine is a bully, born with a chip on his shoulder. If whatever knocks it off has the cards stacked in its favor, say a grizzly or a wolf, the wolverine doesn't hesitate to turn and run. But if he can bluff his way through, he'll go as far as he can.

Once in a while conditions are right for a wolverine to raid a trapper's cabin and do a lot of damage. Actually it's unusual, but so many stories have been told of his destructiveness that most people take it for granted that all wolverines are hell-bent to rob traplines and tear cabins apart. It's not true. Wolverines steer clear of man.

However, the belief is so strong that in the early 1950s the Alaska legislature imposed a bounty on wolverine after a legislator from Nome convinced members that it would reduce the number of cabins damaged by wolverines. Fortunately, the legislature came to its senses and rescinded the wolverine bounty law after a couple of years.

On the rare occasion when a wolverine does wreck a cabin, however, the results can be spectacular. Take what happened to Perry "Doc" Drase, who had an excellent 60-mile trapline in the Nelchina country.

Doc's main cabin was well-built except for an ill-fitting piece of tin over the stove- pipe hole. He didn't have an outside cache, as do most Alaska trappers, so when he left to run his trapline, Doc always hung his furs from the ridgepole inside his main cabin.

One winter day near the end of the trapping season, Doc left to run his trapline, leaving a new lynx-skin sleeping robe lying across his bed and 62 prime marten skins hanging from the ridgepole. The marten were worth $35 to $100 each, and the lynx robe maybe $400.

He returned ten days later. As he mushed up to the cabin he noticed the stove- pipe lying in the snow. He thought the wind probably knocked it off. When he opened the door he couldn't believe his eyes. A great heap of finely shredded marten and lynx fur lay on the floor. Torn clothing was scattered everywhere. Every shelf had been cleaned off. Flour, sugar, beans, and other staples were spread across the floor. The whole mess had been fouled by strong, unpleasant-smelling wolverine secretions.

The wolverine had entered through the weak place by the stovepipe hole and left the same way.

When he told me the story, Doc had a sad look on his face. He was sick over it. A distinguished-looking, fatherly kind of a man, gray-haired and upright, we called him "Doc" because he always carried a medicine kit. If anyone got hurt he'd be right there with his bandages and tinctures. I always thought of him as kind and thoughtful.

The next time Doc ran his trapline, he told me, he hung a chunk of moose meat from a tree directly over a three-foot stump near his cabin, and set a trap on top the stump. He did a good job of setting that trap, covering it first with paper so it wouldn't freeze, then with snow, anchoring it firmly.

A wolverine was in the trap when he came back. Doc took great pleasure in killing and skinning it, but the value of its skin didn't come anywhere near replacing the $5,000 worth of furs the wolverine had destroyed. He continually fumed and fussed over what the wolverine had done to him.

Doc's experience illustrates how very destructive a wolverine can be, and how easy he is to trap, despite all the tales to the contrary. A trapper's anger at a wolverine because of damage it causes often lasts for years, helping to perpetuate the legends.

Men like Doc Drase often take it personally when a wolverine wrecks a cabin or steals fur from a trap, but their anger is wasted. The wolverine doesn't have any animosity; he's simply driven to extremes by a constant, gnawing hunger. He's got to eat, and he will swallow anything edible he can find. Why should he tear up a marten or lynx skin? Maybe for the meat he knows should be inside, and when he can't find it he flies into a rage.

I've read many stories about how cunning the wolverine is supposed to be and how he frequently drives trappers from their traplines. In these tales the wolverine usually robs the traps, then, when the trapper is out on the trapline, the clever animal enters his cabin and tears it up. The trapper finally either has to leave the country or he becomes so afraid of wolverines he goes crazy and commits suicide. This is all nonsense.

I trapped for more than 50 years, 40 of them in Alaska both as a private trapper and government wolf hunter. I've taken close to 150 wolverines and I've yet to come across one I'd say was smart.

The Savage River country is good wolverine country. When a wolverine found a fox in one of my traps, he'd grab it and pull until something gave. Usually I'd find an entire shoulder of the fox in the trap. Then the wolverine would carry the fox downhill, feed on it, and bury what it couldn't eat in the nearest snowdrift. When

I found where a wolverine had taken a fox from one of my traps, I'd follow his trail and set wolf traps around the fox's remains. When the wolverine returned, I had him. Nothing to it.

A caribou or moose head wired three feet off the ground in a tree, with a couple of traps underneath, is a sure-fire set for wolverine. They want that head so badly they think of nothing else and forget about traps.

Still another method I used that worked well was to catch wolverines at ground-squirrel holes. In the fall, after the ground froze, I'd poke sour grizzly-bear meat down squirrel holes, leaving a few pieces outside. Wolverines are great ridge-runners, always on the lookout for something wolves may have killed. They can smell sour bear meat from a long way off. Even if the ground was frozen in the squirrel holes, they'd dig into it and loosen dirt that would soon dry in the wind. Come trapping season, I'd throw more bear meat into the holes, then bury my traps in the fine, dry dirt the wolverines provided. I'd catch them every time.

The skunk-bear, as some call him, isn't all he is made out to be as a fighter, either. Don't get me wrong. A wolverine is nasty in a brawl, but some feats he's credited with, like making a grizzly bear back down and driving wolves from their kills, are pure hokum.

One winter day at Rapids I was giving the two Victoria Land Eskimo dogs I called Yukon and Red a run along the winding Valdez Trail when a wolverine ran out of a culvert. Both dogs lit out after it. At the time I believed stories I'd heard about what wolverines could do to dogs, so I ran after them hoping to help out.

Red caught up to the fleeing wolverine and Yukon was right behind. Without hesitation, Red reached over and took the neck of the bounding wolverine in his mouth, and Yukon grabbed his hind end.

I picked up a club and prepared to wade into the scrap, but I soon saw it wasn't really a scrap. Red and Yukon stretched that helpless animal between them and banged it up and down on the ground. It squirmed, turned in its roomy hide and slashed the air with its claws. Its mouth was wide open, but it couldn't make a sound, because Red had tight hold on his neck. Red finally got the whole neck in his mouth and bit hard. That was it. The only mark on the dogs was a small scratch on Red's nose.

Obviously, the wolverine was overmatched, but what I saw didn't jibe with the tales I'd heard about wolverines standing off entire sled dog teams, eventually killing two or three dogs and getting away scot-free. What a wolverine might do to an ordinary bird dog may be something else.

Wolves will kill wolverines when they get the chance and I think they do it for sport. I believe a lone wolf could kill a wolverine without any trouble.

One January day I sat on a ridge near Savage River scanning a big flat where a number of wolf-killed caribou lay, hoping to get a shot at a wolf. I spotted a wolverine chewing on a dead caribou. He would eat for a while, stand up, look around, run around the caribou in its nervous weasel-like way, and go back to eating.

Shortly, I spotted three wolves making the rounds of the dead caribou and watched them through my binoculars. When they were about 350 yards downwind of the wolverine they suddenly spread out. They got to within 50 yards of it before it stood up, looked at them for an instant, then lit out for the nearest timber. The wolves caught it in no time, one running on either side, the other following. All I saw was a rolling mass of fur and flying snow.

It wasn't much of a fight. The wolves got up, the wolverine didn't. The three wolves walked stiff-legged around the dead wolverine spattering him with little bursts of urine. One of the wolves was a female, but even she helped. I believe they were stimulated by the strong scent the wolverine had given out in the fight, but it may be they were showing their contempt. They finally scratched and threw snow over the wolverine, then trotted off.

Several times I've seen wolverines prepare for a fight. They stood like little bears and tried to box their foes. That won't stop a wolf or a bear. A wolf will just rush in and smother a wolverine. With a bear there's simply no contest. Wolverines, weighing from 20 to 35 pounds, are simply too small to challenge a bear.

I've watched wolverines run away from bears and I strongly suspect that between grizzlies and wolves the wolverine population takes a beating. The wolverine's only chance is to climb a tree and they'll head for timber whenever they're chased, but they are slow; bears are twice as fast.

One April when I was traveling with my dogs I saw a red and

a cross fox chasing a wolverine. I stopped to watch as the three gradually came closer. The foxes dived in and bit, then leaped back as the wolverine whirled to face them. Then the wolverine, which bounds along like a big, dark weasel, turned and bounded a few more yards. I shot the wolverine, and, after skinning him, I found four fox pups in his stomach. I checked a nearby fox den I knew about and found where the wolverine had dug for the pups.

The wolverine is almost unbelievably tough. Once when I went to pick up a sheep I had shot and cached in the mountains, I found a half-grown wolverine working around the carcass. He had rolled away the rocks I'd put inside the cleaned animal and dragged it about 20 feet. Imagine; that 20 pound wolverine moved a 125-pound (dressed weight) ram.

Wolverines habitually try to move dead animals. I once saw one trying to move a full-grown caribou. Another dragged a moose head I'd left on the Kenai Peninsula for more than half a mile, part of the way through thick alders.

I sneaked as close as I could to the one trying to steal my sheep. When he saw me, he ran off a little way, then stood up and looked back. He was sideways to me, and the bullet from my .250-3000 caught him in the middle, completing removing his innards. Maybe I should have shot him again, but I put down my rifle and went to the sheep, forgetting the wolverine as I tied the sheep to my packboard. I glanced up about ten minutes later to discover that he was still alive. I finished him off.

Bill Clark, an old-time trapper I knew who operated on the upper Chitina River, commonly caught quite a few wolverines every winter. He treated a wolverine as he did other animals in his traps by walking up to it and handing it a club to chew on, then whacking it across the nose with another club. This renders the animal unconscious. To finish the job, Bill kneeled on the animal's chest, stopping its heart.

One day, just as Bill was handing a wolverine a club to chew on, it pulled free of the trap and clamped its claws onto his thigh, then sank its teeth into Bill's leg. Bill had an awful time with that animal but he finally wrestled around with it, pried it loose, and choked it to death. He showed me the scars on his leg. Though Bill was a man of ordinary build and average strength, in his 60s at the time, he didn't think he'd done anything unusual in choking that wolverine. Like many trappers familiar with the animal, he had no fear of a wolverine.

I don't know how many times I have read that wolverine fur is used for parka ruffs because frost won't form on it. That's a silly fiction perpetuated by the ignorant. Wolverine fur frosts up just like any other fur.

In 1942 I was at a reindeer round-up at Theresa Creek on the Seward Peninsula, living in a tent with Henry Wyook, an Eskimo dog-team driver. It was March but the temperature dropped to 74 degrees below zero, the lowest I've ever seen. One night Henry and I went to bed when the temperature was 72 below. We kept our parkas and fur pants on when we crawled into our sleeping bags.

My parka had a wolverine face ruff, while Henry's sported a wolf face ruff. I awoke first next morning, sat up, and yelled at Henry. When Henry sat up he looked at me.

"Oh, Mr. Glaser, look at your parka ruff," he said. "It's all frost."

So was Henry's. But when I pulled at it the frost on the guard hairs of my ruff slipped off easily and no hairs came out. Every time Henry yanked on the frost on the guard hairs of his ruff, he broke off wolf hairs. About two winters of this and there's nothing left of a wolf ruff but underfur or wool. Not so with wolverine fur. Wolverine is rated 100 on the fur durability scale, along with the fur of otter (both land and sea), and it takes a lot to break or pull the guard hairs out. I own a wolverine parka ruff I've used steadily for 14 years and it's still good as new. But it frosts up just like any other fur when the temperature plummets below zero. Its beauty, the long guard hairs, and the ability to take the abuse of pulling frost from it, is the reason wolverine fur is prized and used on parka ruffs.

Wolverine tend to be solitary. The only time of the year I've ever seen or heard of two adult wolverines traveling together is April, apparently the mating season. I've actually seen four matings. Once, while walking up McGuire Creek, near my Black Rapids Roadhouse, in the distance I saw what I thought were two bears chasing one another. As I worked closer I saw they were wolverines and began watching them through my glasses.

They were pretty rough with each other and they made a lot of noise. A wolverine sounds off with a kind of hiss that carries quite a distance. The female raised an awful fuss, growling continually, and fighting off every advance. The male finally grabbed her by the top of the neck, shoved her head into the snow and had his way.

Even in good wolverine country these contrary little critters are seldom seen, for they're never really abundant, and they are night prowlers.

A wolverine is miserably hard to skin. It is necessary to cut all the way, for the skin won't peel when simply pulled. Also care must be taken around the anal glands. The brown liquid that comes from them smells like sour tobacco, only it's far, far stronger. That may be where the myth about a wolverine being able to whip a dog came from; a little squirt of that stuff in a dog's face may be enough to discourage fighting.

Wolverine, like wolves, seem to breed wild stories. One of my favorite wolverine yarns is about Ole, a long-time friend. He told me how, when he was freshly arrived in Alaska from Sweden, a wolverine forced him to postpone his wedding. Ole had come to the North to get into mining, but in winter he trapped for additional income. He had left his sweetheart in the old country and he was working desperately to earn enough money to send for her so they could be married.

After a couple of years of hard work, Ole figured that come spring when he sold his winter's furs he'd have enough dollars to finance his girl's trip to Alaska. He had a good pile of lynx and some marten skins, all caught the hard way, for Ole was primarily a miner; trapping didn't come easy for him..

One day he took off on his trapline, leaving his furs high in a cache. On his return he found nothing but small ribbons of fur scattered all over the snow, the work of a wolverine. This sent him into a rage. Even as he told me about it, many years after it happened, he pounded the table, his face got red and he shouted. He was determined to catch the so-and-so wolverine that had climbed into his cache and shredded his furs.

He brought in all of his traps and set them around the cache, and one night a wolverine stepped into one of them. Ole was in bed, but he heard the animal growling and fussing, so he went out with a club and pounded the animal on the head until he thought it was dead.

He carried it into the cabin and dropped it into the wood box, planning to skin it and stretch the hide in the morning. He'd shed his clothes and shoes and was getting ready to go back to bed when the wolverine leaped out of the box and ran under the table of his little trapping cabin. There it bared its teeth and growled at Ole.

Ole, in his bare feet and red longjohns, grabbed an axe and started after it. The table upset and the wolverine dived under the bed. Ole got a pole and poked at it. The wolverine couldn't stand the poking and came out hanging on to the pole with its teeth. Then Ole again grabbed his axe, and around and around they went, bare feet slapping the cold floor, blood flying, Swedish oaths blistering the air. Everything loose in the cabin ended on the floor, including much of Ole's grub. By the time the wolverine was dead the place was a wreck.

It was another full year before Ole made up for the loss of his furs so he could send to Sweden for his sweetheart.

Ole still hates wolverines.

I can't say I blame him.

Book Three

GOVERNMENT WOLF HUNTER, 1937–1955

Government Wolf Hunter

FUR PRICES DROPPED in the 1930s, and fox furs, especially, lost value. My income plunged. I had depended heavily on the sale of fox furs I trapped at Savage River, and suddenly they weren't even worth trapping. I had to find other ways of making money, so I turned to guiding trophy hunters for grizzly bears in spring, and for grizzlies, sheep, moose, and caribou in the fall. I sold a few of the rifles I had collected over the years. In the summer of 1935 I worked as a temporary park ranger in McKinley National Park.

My reduced income forced me to live more and more off the land. There was no longer money to maintain a year-round room at the Nordale Hotel in Fairbanks, or to buy every new rifle that came out.

I had maintained my connections with the U.S. Biological Survey since Dr. Nelson's visit at Rapids in 1921. Since helping the Murie brothers trap caribou in McKinley Park, over the years I had sent many hides and skulls of wolves, bears, foxes, and other mammals to the survey. In early 1937 I wrote to Juneau Territorial headquarters of the Biological Survey, applying for a job.

In 1927 a cooperative agreement aimed at controlling Alaska's wolves and coyotes was signed by the Bureau of Biological Survey and the Territory of Alaska. The Territorial Legislature appropriated $10,000 and the Survey contributed $2,000, to hire experts to trap predators and to instruct local trappers in trap-setting and scent-making. The program expanded over the years.

In early April, 1937, a telegram came to me at Healy from the Bureau of Biological Survey informing me I had been hired as an Agent Hunter, working for the Predator Control Branch under the cooperative program. My annual salary was to be $2,000. I was to hunt and trap wolves and coyotes, and teach trappers the best methods for taking these predators. My first assignment was to try to reduce wolf numbers in the central Alaska Range where they had decimated wintering caribou. I was to start immediately.

I was beginning a new career at the age of 48.

I hauled possessions I wanted to keep to Healy with the dog team and put them in storage, abandoning my Savage River cabins. On April 22, I left Savage River driving my wolf-dogs on my first federal wolf hunt. My sled was loaded with a tent, stove, food for me and the dogs, extra harness, a rifle, ammunition, extra clothes and other clutter. I headed west along the face of the Alaska Range, looking for wolves and wolf dens.

Spring arrived late in 1937 and the snow remained deep even into May. Days were warm, and the snow was melting with every little creek running beneath the snow. Water flowed over the snow in low places. In some deep drifts I could push a pole down seven or eight feet in slush. I was on snowshoes, of course.

When I reached the Toklat River (35 miles as the raven flies; 50 miles on the ground) I found a three-quarter-mile-wide overflow running about two feet deep atop the ice. I followed the riverbank upstream, avoiding the overflow. About ten miles upstream on the Toklat I found dry ice to travel on. An inch or so of fresh snow had fallen during the night and I soon ran onto a set of fresh wolf tracks.

I made camp and hunted wolves on foot. I managed to kill one wolf in that area, and went on to other river drainages. Snow was fast disappearing a week later when I headed back east, travelling at night when there was a crust. I reached Healy and the railroad with my sled skidding on slush and bare ground.

One incident during that hunt bothered me. I killed a gray female and a litter of young pups, but the black male escaped.

Afterward he came to my camp repeatedly over several days, no doubt searching for his mate. When he wasn't creeping up on my camp, he'd howl forlornly from a distant ridge. When I waited for him he didn't show up. But the minute I tried to get some sleep, he would creep close and the dogs would hit the ends of their chains and roar at him.

"How can a man break up a happy family as I've done?" I asked myself, feeling sorry for the black wolf. I had to remind myself that at their den I had found parts of two calf caribou and the remains of two Dall sheep lambs killed by the wolves. I realized that by November those cute little wolf puppies that I had destroyed would have been adults, and they would have been killing many moose and caribou. I thought of the times I had found bloody caribou remains on the flats near my cabin after a night of killing. I remembered the suffering of the three live moose I had seen with their hams partly eaten by wolves. I had seen mourning mother moose and caribou standing sadly over the remains of their young that wolves had killed. And I remembered the years when thousands of caribou had wintered near Savage River and how their numbers had dwindled as wolves had increased.

Wolf pups are born from about April 25 to mid-May, around the time cow caribou and moose are having calves and Dall sheep are having lambs. The easily caught and killed caribou, moose, and sheep babies makes it easier for the wolves to feed their pups. My job, I decided, would be to help tip the balance and allow more of these babies to survive. With their wise ways and large litters, there was no way that the few hunters, trappers, and predator agents then in the game lands of wilderness Alaska could ever wipe out Alaska's wolves; my goal would be to try to reduce their numbers.

At the end of that spring hunt I reported to the Biological Survey office in Fairbanks. With my wolf-dogs in a boarding kennel, I worked for a time hunting and trapping wolves along roads leading out of Fairbanks.

In July a wire arrived from the Juneau office asking if I could follow the Fortymile caribou herd that each fall migrated from Canada, near Eagle, an Alaskan village on the Yukon River, northwest toward Alaska's White Mountains. No one knew what route they followed. This was not a wolf-killing assignment, but a biological one, seeking information on the movements of a caribou herd numbering 100,000 or more.

I wired Juneau that I was on my way. I took Queenie and Buster as pack dogs, and arranged to ride with a trucker over the Steese Highway to Circle, a village on the Yukon River. There we boarded the steamboat *Yukon* and rode 150 miles upstream to Eagle, arriving August 3.

At Eagle, a few miles from the Canada-Alaska boundary, I learned that the caribou herd had not arrived. Thinking I might intercept them, I walked the old pack trail with the dogs toward the 100-mile-distant mining community of Chicken. Steep hills and heavy brush made traveling slow and difficult.

August 9, 1937: Left Dome Creek. Queenie collapsed. Camped for the day. Queenie was in bad shape in the evening. Unable to use her front legs . . .

We had traveled only about three miles from Dome Creek when Queenie was unable to stand on her front legs. Lying on her side and struggling to stand, she looked at me and whined. She had been packing about 15 pounds, a weight she often carried. I later learned that one of the local trappers had put out some poison in the area. Apparently, Queenie had eaten some of it.

I carried her half a mile to a place we could camp. There is no easy way to carry a 125-pound dog; I couldn't comfortably hold her over my shoulder, so I simply held her in my arms. I would carry her a couple of hundred yards, put her down and rest, then go another few hundred yards. Eleven-year-old Queenie's once-black muzzle was now gray. Still, she was strong and healthy and I was puzzled and upset by her collapse, for I knew nothing then about the trapper and his poison. We had been through much together, and I regarded her as family.

I made camp, and that night I spent hours massaging her back and legs. She lay, almost helpless, whining pitifully.

Next morning she was able to walk, but her legs were weak. I carried her pack and walked slowly. She managed to keep up for a few hours, but finally couldn't travel any farther. I wanted to reach Steele Creek for the night so I again carried Queenie, this time for several miles, until I found a place to camp. Again she whined, looking at me with her trusting brown eyes as if to apologize for letting me down.

August 10, 1937: Managed to get to Steele Creek. Packed Queenie part of the way.

I massaged her for many hours again that night and next morning she seemed better. Gradually over a period of a week or so she recovered use of her legs. She was never really strong again, and somehow the poison affected her ability to curl up, a necessity for a northern dog living outside in the bitter cold of winter.

We arrived at Chicken on August 13. A pilot for the Fairbanks-based Pollack Flying Service was there. "Seen any sign of the Fortymile caribou herds?" I asked him.

"Yeah, Frank. Yesterday I saw part of the herd about 30 miles northwest of here. They were heading toward the Yukon River," he answered.

That's all I needed to know.

I rested at Chicken for a few days (early miners had wanted to name the town Ptarmigan, but they couldn't agree on the spelling and compromised on Chicken) and walked back toward Eagle. When I reached American Summit, about 22 miles from Eagle, I saw the vanguard of the caribou herd, long strings of animals traveling toward me. They were headed roughly northwest.

August 15, 1937: Sunday. Walked from Franklin Creek to Steele Creek on the Fortymile River. 22 miles. See moose, caribou, bear, and wolf tracks in the trail. This is a hard trip. Lots of big brushy ridges to climb.

I walked to Eagle and re-outfitted, buying mostly dried food to last for my long trek. I weighed my pack at the Northern Commercial Company store in Eagle before I left there August 29, and was horrified when it tipped the scales at 87 pounds. That's a big load to carry any distance in the mountains. I carried a .30-06 rifle, and had waterproof packsacks for the dogs. I had no bedding, tarpaulin, or tent, planning to travel nights (which are still mostly light through August) and sleep days. Nor did I take any dog food; the dogs would have to live off the land. I had a map but no compass. A dozen black gnat flies and fishing line I carried provided me and the dogs with grayling from every stream I crossed.

I wore rubber-bottom leather-top shoepacks and summer

weight woolen clothing, including a Filson wool mackinaw jacket. At first, I had several pots and pans but eventually abandoned all but one, in which I boiled the grayling I caught, and meat from caribou I shot.

I returned to American Summit where I found the caribou migration going full blast. The dogs and I headed northwest, following the herd. On some nights, I saw thousands of animals; on others only a few widely scattered animals. They generally followed the high ridges, and I stayed up high with them. A big bunch would pass me, trotting along in their smooth way, then they'd slow or stop and bed down, or feed where food was especially good. I would catch up and maybe pass them, then we'd do it again.

Rainy nights sometimes made travel miserable; I had no raincoat, and when the brush was wet I got soaked. The work of carrying a heavy pack and climbing up and down steep ridges kept me warm. I usually waited until the sun was up, or at least until it was warmer during days, to find a bushy spruce tree under which I could spread my mosquito bar, tuck the sides in, and get a little sleep.

I heard wolves howling almost every night, but made no effort to hunt them. We encountered a dozen or so grizzlies, two of which were close. When those two got a whiff of me and the wolf dogs they left in peace. Buster and Queenie minded well, not attempting to chase the bears or caribou. Generally we detoured around bears we saw, avoiding trouble.

I stopped overnight with Ole Nord, who was mining at Barney Creek on the Seventymile River, 42 miles from Eagle. During the evening Ole told me that Charlie Yost was mining on Nugget Creek. "But you won't want to stay with him," he said. "His cabin's filthy."

I had known old Charlie Yost years before when I lived at Black Rapids Roadhouse and he was at Yost's Roadhouse, which he built shortly after the turn of the century. I couldn't imagine a man being so dirty I couldn't sleep in his cabin overnight so I decided to visit him anyway, for old times' sake.

Nugget Creek, where Charlie mined is a tributary of Washington Creek which flows into the Yukon River. When I arrived there it was pouring down rain. The dogs and I were soaked and tired after the 25-mile hike from Barney Creek. I saw Yost's cabin across the creek. A rusty cable was strung across the creek, with a board hung from a couple of pulleys, a tough way to cross. I put Queenie in front of me and Buster behind me. It was crowded on that board, and the three of us made a heavy load. I wondered if the old cable would support us.

The rope used for pulling oneself across was broken. I had to put my hands up on the rusty cable between pulleys and yank us across a foot at a time. When we got about half way, we were suspended 50 feet above the creek. It was then I saw Charlie, wearing a rubber raincoat, standing in the canyon below his cabin holding a hydraulic gun and blasting away at overburden to get to paydirt.

I tied the dogs outside his cabin. The door was wide open and I was astonished to see five big malemute dogs tied to a table inside. He had fed the dogs caribou meat that morning, and chunks of meat with the hide still on, as well as a plentiful supply of caribou hair and piles of dog droppings littered the dirt floor. Flies buzzed busily about the mess.

The table the dogs were tied to consisted of posts sunk into the ground, with boards nailed on top. When I walked in, Charlie's dogs started lunging and growling, trying to get at me.

I shook my head in wonder, then walked the few hundred feet to Yost who stood there nozzling. Water from the hydraulicking unit made an awful roar, and Charlie was hard of hearing. I stood behind him for a long time fearing if I tapped him on the shoulder he would swing the nozzle around and blow me in two.

He finally looked around and saw me. "Hello!" he called, surprised. He didn't see many visitors.

He shut the water off. "How are you, Charlie?" I asked.

"Who are you?" he asked, failing to recognize me.

"Frank Glaser. I used to live at Rapids, when you were still at your roadhouse on the Valdez Trail," I reminded.

"Oh yes. Frank. Yeah. Good to see you Frank," he said. He seemed a little confused as we went to his cabin. He moved his dogs outside, but made no attempt to clean up after them. I think old Charlie was a little deranged, because after a bit he said, accusingly, "You're a scout for a big mining company, aren't you?"

"No, Charlie. I'm a wolf hunter for the government," I reassured.

He didn't believe me, and before we settled down in the cabin he insisted on showing me all his claims. It was still raining hard, and I wanted nothing more than to get out of the rain, dry off and warm up, and have something to eat.

I stayed overnight with Charlie, an experience I'll never forget. I've never seen any other human living like that, and I've been in some pretty primitive situations. Before he started to cook potatoes he reached behind the door to get a towel. I thought it was a black towel, but when he hung it up again I looked closer and saw that it was simply dirty, dried black all over like a piece of boiler plate; I swear I could have cut my finger on it.

A once-enameled plate nailed to the top of his table puzzled me. He dug around and found another old metal plate for me to use, and blew dirt and dust off of it before serving me. It looked to me as if the boiled caribou meat he served had about as much hair as caribou.

He dished boiled spuds and caribou for himself into the nailed-down plate, grinning at my stare. "The dogs lick it clean," he said, "so I don't ever have to wash dishes." After his meals, he always tied one of his dogs close enough so it could put its front feet on the table and lick the nailed-down plate.

As we walked about the cabin we had to watch our step because of the plentiful dog droppings.

Looking more closely, I could see under the nailed-down plate edges dried food the chained dog couldn't quite reach; that plate looked as if it had been nailed to Charlie's table for years.

Charlie told me he wanted to sell his mining ground because people in Eagle had tried to stop him from coming up there that spring, figuring he was too old and feeble. They were afraid something would happen to him since he was all alone. He thought that was a trick to get his mining ground,

At the end of the 1937 mining season Charlie moved into Fairbanks to stay. A year or so later I was walking down Second Avenue in Fairbanks, then deep in mud after a week of rain. I saw Charlie start to weave across the street. He was drunk and feeble. Half way across he sat down in the mud and stayed there.

Several other old-timers saw him, but they knew better than to go near him, because Charlie had a terribly filthy tongue. As I watched from a distance, a very nice white-haired Christian lady, wife of a prominent Fairbanks businessman, saw Charlie sitting in the mud and bravely waded out to help the poor old man. She got behind him and lifted, and had him almost to his feet when he turned his head and roared, "You let go of me you . . . ." and he let out a stream of foul oaths.

The poor lady dropped him like a hotcake. Mud spattered her coat and shoes as he flopped back down. She walked off with a red face. He crawled around and finally got to his feet and staggered off, cursing. That was the last time I ever saw Charlie, who died soon afterward.

At Eagle I had been given mail for Ed Brathord and his wife, who mined at Alder Creek, 64 miles by trail from Eagle. They had been there since April, and I arrived in early September. We spent a pleasant evening visiting after enjoying Mrs. Brathord's fine meal.

"You really spent a night in Charlie Yost's cabin?" they repeatedly asked, amused and, I think, horrified.

Brathord had four or five big malemute dogs. About once a week Ed killed a caribou and Mrs. Brathord would load some of the meat on the dogs and take it down to Yost. She never stayed. She had once tried washing dishes and cleaning the cabin for him, she told me, but old Charlie cursed her out for it.

The Brathords were very nice people, and they seemed reluctant to see me leave the next morning. They were the last people I saw until September 25. I didn't find any cabins in the high mountains where I traveled; it was almost as if no man had ever been there.

September 6, 1937: Found the main migration of caribou. They are coming from the north, going east.

Soon the September nights were dark and snow whitened the high ridges. I was now traveling days. For a few nights I lit two fires to sleep between, with Queenie and Buster on each side of me for additional warmth. Then I had to stop to prepare for cold weather. I shot three yearling caribou, skinned them and rubbed their brains into the hides, continually working the skins until they were soft. With a buckskin needle and sinew from the back of the caribou, I made a sleeping bag from the skins, sewing it hair inside. It only weighed about eight pounds, and was very warm. How wonderful it was to sleep warm for a change. I used that sleeping bag for many years.

Some of the caribou I fed to the dogs, the rest I cut into tiny pieces and dried on a rack near a big fire. Until then we had lived mostly on grayling I caught at every stream we crossed. I boiled mine, and the two wolf-dogs downed theirs raw, often while the fish were still flopping.

I tried to kill porcupines to feed the dogs so I wouldn't have to kill caribou for them. Generally I succeeded. They ate the meat raw. One day Buster's pack leaked as he swam a stream, and the salt he was carrying dissolved, leaving me without salt. I used an old trapper's trick to make up for it; a pinch of ashes from a birchwood campfire sprinkled on meat made a fair substitute.

For two days I traveled through fog, following the top of a high ridge before reaching 5,600-foot-high Mount Sorenson. I had to wait two days for the fog to lift so I could see the country ahead. According to my map, Charley River lay directly below. Sure enough, when the fog lifted, there it was. I studied it with binoculars to find the best place to cross, then picked an easy route down the mountain.

From Mount Sorenson it took about half a day to reach the large, swift, and deep Charley River. With my axe I cut several dry spruce logs, and lashed the logs together into a raft with the 60-foot length of quarter-inch line I carried.

September 7, 1937. Built a raft and crossed opposite the west fork of Charley River.

With my rifle and the three packs, mine and the two dogs' tied to the raft, I shoved off. The dogs followed, swimming strongly for the opposite bank. I misjudged the swiftness and depth of the river. In mid-stream I couldn't reach bottom with my pole, and was swept downstream. It was a mile or more before I reached shore. Pulling the raft up and wedging it so it would stay, I walked back upstream expecting to meet my dogs.

In the meantime the dogs had run up and down the stream looking for me. When I didn't show up they re-crossed the river and took our backtrail.

I found the dogs' tracks where they had left the river and where they had searched for me. I figured they would show up soon, so I camped on the river bank. After a day and no dogs, I realized something was wrong. I returned to my raft and re-crossed the Charley, tied the raft, and followed the dogs' tracks toward Mount Sorenson. I walked for nearly two days, worried about losing Queenie and Buster. Then I saw them in the distance, trotting down the trail toward me, headed back toward Charley River. Were those mutts happy to see me! They had followed our backtrail to where I had dried meat and made the sleeping bag. They had waited, looking for me, until they decided to return to Charley River.

Back at Charley River, I put Queenie on the raft with me, for I didn't want any more lost dogs. I knew Buster wouldn't go anywhere without Queenie. As Buster swam the river, he kept the raft in sight while Queenie and I took a swift downriver trip until I could reach bottom with my pole and push us ashore.

September 8, 1937: My dogs are almost wore out.

September 10, 1937: To Alder Creek over some high ridges. See bands of caribou all day. They seem to be traveling south toward the north fork of the Fortymile River. This was my hardest day. Miserable weather rain and snow all day. I must have traveled over 35 miles of rough country.

September 11, 1937: My dogs are just about all in. This trip is too much for them.

Mid-September found me high in the mountains, about 20 miles as the raven flies south of Woodchopper, a village on the Yukon River. The snow was getting deep and I needed snowshoes. To make them, I killed a big bull caribou, bent some willow sticks over a fire to make frames, whittled cross-pieces, and webbed the shoes with strips from the bull's hide. I spent another day or so drying the meat. By this time all three packs—mine and the dogs'— were fairly light; most of the weight now was dried meat.

Caribou continued to travel northwest. Some days I didn't need to wear snowshoes because thousands of caribou had packed the snow solid.

All the caribou now had shed their scraggly summer coats and were dressed in their beautiful thick winter pelage. Breeding season wasn't far off. When I had started, the caribou antlers were dark and knobby, covered with velvet. Now they were clean and bright yellow. Occasionally I heard and saw bulls challenge one another and rattle each others' antlers. In the distance, white necks of old bulls looked like snow.

The dogs and I broke off from the migrating caribou herd when we reached Harrison Creek, about 15 miles from the Steese Highway. We walked into Circle Hot Springs on September 25, travelworn, but still strong. Both of the 11-year-old wolf-dogs had lost weight, and so had I. Straight-line distance from Eagle to Circle Hot Springs is about 120 miles. In the 28 days of our trek the dogs and I walked at least 450 miles following the sometimes-erratic route of the migrating caribou.

I learned the exact caribou migration route used by the animals that year. I later learned they commonly migrated all the way to the White Mountains, spent time there, and returned to Canada during late winter and early spring on almost the same route, except that on the return trip they traveled at lower altitudes.

From Circle Hot Springs the dogs and I rode a freight truck on its last trip of the season down the Steese Highway to Fairbanks. Snow was deep on Eagle Summit and as the big rig plunged through the drifts, caribou from the herd I had followed for over a month were crossing the highway, still headed northwest toward the White Mountains.

To the White Mountains

In October, 1937, after my trek from Eagle to Circle Hot Springs following the Fortymile caribou herd, and after I reported to my Fairbanks office, I roamed the high country around the Steese Highway north of Fairbanks, witnessing the end of the fall Fortymile caribou migration and, as ever, hunting wolves. One day, from a high ridge at the head of Twelvemile Creek I saw 14 bands of caribou totalling about 2,500 animals migrating northwest.

Near dark, I watched two black and one gray wolf try to make a caribou kill. The next day, hunting in a snowstorm I found three caribou killed by wolves. For a week, I prowled the high ridges walking up to 25 miles a day, watching caribou migrate to the north and seeking the wolves harassing them. On October 11 I found a caribou fawn the wolves had killed. They hadn't eaten any of it.

October 12, 1937: Had a little excitement today. Almost stepped on a good-sized grizzly. He was dug in alongside of a caribou carcass. Did not have to shoot him. Saw three gray wolves just at dark. Too far to shoot.

I failed to see that grizzly when I walked up to examine the kill and I was almost within arm's length when he leaped up and loped a short way, turned, stood up and looked at me, then went on his way. I was lucky he didn't attack. If he'd attacked, he'd probably have caught me by surprise.

From November 1937 until March 1938 I traveled around the Anchorage area and on the Kenai Peninsula teaching trappers how to make sets for wolves and coyotes.

March 24, 1938: Left Fairbanks by auto truck, paid $22.50 on 1034 voucher. Drove to four miles north of Olness. Could not get any farther as snow was deep and drifted on road. Traveled with dog team two trips to Washington Creek—eight miles each way by dog team, 24 miles total. 22 below zero.

The dog team was leased (not my wolf-dogs), and I was bound for the White Mountains, 80 miles north of Fairbanks where the Fortymile caribou herd often milled. If wolves were there as I expected, reducing their numbers could benefit the herd.

I had 500 plus pounds that included dog food, grub for myself, a tent, harness, ammunition, winter clothing, traps, and snares. The light sugary snow was three feet deep, and I had to break trail all the way. The four dogs could pull about 250 pounds on the level and about 150 pounds uphill, so I had to relay. By the time I made a second trip, trail was broken, which helped. Night temperatures dropped to 40 below, but during most days it warmed to near zero.

March 28, 1938: Hauled about 200 pounds today, round trip distance 30 miles, to Snowshoe Cabin. Have a little over 500 pounds to move and four very good dogs, but no trail. One more trip over that hill and I'll have the entire outfit on the Beaver watershed.

On April 1 while I was breaking trail and the dogs were pulling the sled, the best dog in the team fell over. In less than two minutes he was dead. I don't know what killed him, for he was a young dog and wasn't working any harder than usual.

By April 11 I had moved everything to a cabin on Fossil Creek at the foot of the White Mountains. I had worked long hard days for nearly three weeks to get there. I started hunting wolves in and around the White Mountains on April 12 and soon found the remains of several Dall sheep and caribou killed by wolves not far from my cabin headquarters. The caribou that had wintered in the region were gone. It was lonesome country, lacking animals of any kind; I saw no grouse or ptarmigan, few snowshoe hares, only an occasional raven, and a few old moose tracks. A few white sheep high on the distant, sharp-toothed White Mountains was the only sign of life in this vast region.

April 14, 1938: Started at 5 a. m. Found a fresh wolf track and followed it all day, thinking it would lead me to a den. It didn't. This is a hard country to travel in. The mountains are steep with thick timber almost up to where the sheep are. This is lonesome country when the caribou are gone.

On one of my long scouting hikes I found where a big band of caribou had wintered in heavy timber on a steep mountainside. The caribou were gone, but broken and cracked bones and hair were widely-scattered on the mountain, evidence of a heavy wolf kill.

April 28, 1938: The wolf business is looking better. I saw three bands of caribou today, about 125 all told. If they stay, wolves will soon show up.

May 2, 1938: Traveled all day between Fossil Creek and Beaver River. See no sign of caribou or wolves. A bad day to be in the hills, for a snowstorm came roaring out of the north. I found shelter in a cave. Traveled on foot 21 miles.

By May 9 the snow was mostly gone. I had roamed in every direction from my Fossil Creek cabin, often hiking 25 or more miles a day without seeing much of anything. A few small bands of caribou came through, heading southeast. Occasionally fox or wolverine tracks appeared in the snow, but I saw no wolves.

May, 9, 1938: Was up Fossil Creek about 15 miles. While rounding a rock slide I heard a snort, looked, and straight up the hill about 50 feet was a big grizzly. I had to shoot it.

My snowshoes were under one arm, my rifle slung across my shoulder. Footing was tricky on the loose, slick shale, and my moccasins were smooth-bottomed. Watching my step, I was almost in the middle of the slide when I heard a snort and looked uphill to see the grizzly sitting on its haunches and looking at me like a big dog sitting up and begging. I let out a war whoop, figuring the bear would leave. I've encountered literally hundreds of grizzlies, and normally a yell or two will send the biggest bear high-tailing. This one just sat.

I let out another whoop and continued walking. I didn't put my snowshoes down, or even get my rifle ready. Then the bear let out a growl or two and started toward me. The slope was steep and rocks started rolling as the bear half-slid half-jumped toward me. Suddenly he was only 60 feet away. I was taken by surprise, depending too much on what bears are supposed to do.

I jumped back so the rocks wouldn't hit me, and dropped the snowshoes. The grizzly was practically on top of me when I threw the rifle up and fired without aiming. His momentum carried him past and not more than six feet in front of me.

He reached the bottom of the slide, picked himself up, and started back toward me. That puzzled me. He was hit in the chest, and he would have died in a few minutes. Most bears would have kept going, even more likely, most bears would never have charged in the first place.

As this one struggled uphill toward me growling and grunting, I took my time and shot him in the neck. He stopped then; he was dead.

This bear was a mouse-colored, thin, old male with a yellowish-white head and hump. Since the area was not hunted by man, the bear probably had never before encountered a human. Until he met me, probably everything he met had fled from him.

May 11, 1938: Saw an old ram down in the woods. When I was close he stood and looked at me. I sat down 40 yards from him. After a time he laid down. Sheep here don't have any fear of man. Traveled on foot 24 miles.

On May 16 while hunting above timberline on the ridge between Fossil and Brigham Creeks I saw a black wolf. When I tried to cut him off, a gale came up and a snowstorm cut off all visibility. I had to get down into the timber for shelter. That day I traveled 25 miles, arriving back at the cabin soaking wet from snow and rain showers.

May 19, 1938: My food is down to three pounds of beans, two pounds rice, three pounds dried fruit and a small piece of bacon. I have five pounds of dried meat and I can travel a long time on that. It is well over 100 miles of walking to the Steese Highway.

On May 21, I built a long ladder and climbed high to lash a pole between two trees. I put my sled on the pole then put my dog harness, winter clothes, caribou-skin sleeping bag, tent, a bit of coffee and rice, traps and a few other things in the sled and covered it with a tarpaulin. Then I made packs for the three dogs, readying for the hike across country to the Steese Highway. With the snow gone, I had to leave my sled, winter clothing, dog harnesses, tent, and other stuff before hiking to the Steese Highway to get back to Fairbanks.

May 22, 1938: Traveled from midnight until 4:30 a. m. Three dogs with packs and I am carrying 50 pounds. These ridges are sure steep in places. I have to lead the dogs as it is not safe to let them follow. These dogs would chase game.

I had no bedding, but carried two light pieces of canvas I used for a shelter when it rained, and a bed when the weather was dry. I hunted all one day to get something for the dogs to eat. There were no rabbits and all the hunt brought me was three tree squirrels, one for each dog.

The ridges I climbed were steep, but traveling was good when I got above timberline. I had to lead the dogs for it wasn't safe to allow them to run loose and follow. They would tackle a grizzly if they saw one or they'd chase caribou. I made about 24 miles to Brigham Creek before camping.

May 24, 1938: Found a place on O'Brien Creek where it was about 25 feet wide from the bank to where there was ice fast to a bar. Put four trees across, made a good bridge. Traveled 22 miles last night and today.

I couldn't understand why O'Brien Creek was shown on the map as a creek: it was from 25 to 100 feet wide, and from four to six feet deep. I had to walk upstream several miles before I found a place where I could cross on the ice. Next day I had to ford Beaver Creek where it was about 500 feet wide and two to four feet deep. That was a tough crossing in swift water and I was soaked almost to the shoulders when I reached the far side.

I reached the Steese Highway on May 28, and caught a truck headed for Fairbanks.

❧

Six months later, in October, bush pilot Frank Pollack landed me with a ski plane on a bar of Beaver Creek near the cabin I had used the previous winter. He was to pick me up in January. Shortly after I arrived, huge numbers of caribou migrated through the area and I heard wolves howling every night.

Over the next few days about a foot of snow fell. Wolves were killing stragglers from the caribou migration. I got out in the hills and set some traps and snares for them. One day after setting some traps in a little patch of brush I walked into the open and happened to look across to another ridge about half a mile away. There in the deep snow I saw a bunch of animals strung out. At first I thought they were caribou. Before I could look at them with binoculars some of the animals started to howl. I could hardly believe my eyes when, through binoculars, I counted 34 wolves, the largest number of wolves I've ever seen in one pack. They were strung out single-file on the snow, and had spotted me the instant I left the brush patch.

What I was seeing seemed all wrong. It was late October and wolves don't run in huge bunches at that time of year.

Another odd feature: 32 of the wolves were black and only two were gray. The wolf in the lead was by far the biggest wolf I've ever seen. I'd have given anything for a shot at him.

I howled back, and they answered. To have 34 wolves howl in response to my howl raised the hackles on the back of my neck. Their eerie wails made the canyon ring.

Every time the huge lead wolf came to a spur coming up from the Beaver he walked out and looked down while the other wolves waited.

I was so excited I was shaking. I realized I was seeing something extraordinary. In the half hour or so that I watched that bunch of wolves none went near the leader, probably fearing him. He was simply enormous, twice the size of the other wolves. He looked as big as a black bear.

As soon as they filed out of sight over the ridge I hurried to where they had disappeared. As I topped the ridge they howled from a mile and a half away on the far side of Beaver Creek where I picked them up with my glasses again. They were all lined up watching for me. I lost track of them at dark.

About ten days later the weather turned cold. At midday I decided to snowshoe ten miles up Fossil Creek to where I had cached my sled and other gear the previous May. I wanted some traps and my caribou sleeping bag, the one I had made on my trek from Eagle to Circle Hot Springs in 1937. On the way it got dark, but I found the cache, knocked snow off the ladder, and retrieved the traps, my sleeping bag, and some coffee and rice. I started a fire and cooked rice and coffee, then crawled into my sleeping bag and slept for five or six hours.

When I awoke the moon was out. With the fresh, clean snow reflecting light, it was a fine night for traveling, although the temperature was about 40 below zero. I rolled my sleeping bag, put it on my pack, and started back down Fossil Creek. On my way up the creek I had cut the bends of the creek; I tried to cut them a little more on the return.

I had been walking for half an hour when many wolves started howling along the creek ahead of me. I was carrying my .220 Swift and started looking for wolves to shoot. My parka hood was up because of the cold, but I tossed it back to hear and see better. Now, wolves howled both ahead and behind me.

"I'm going to get some shooting here," I told myself. I had heard of wolves following people. Many times when I was at Savage River wolves followed me and my wolf-dogs. But never before had wolves followed me when I was alone.

That night was strange, unearthly. The air was still. The only sounds were the creaking and scuffing of my snowshoes and the wailing of the wolves. Snow sparkled in the bright moonlight. Occasionally, the northern lights flung greenish flames across the sky. Several times I thought I saw a wolf and raised my rifle to shoot, only to realize the shape was a shadow.

As I moved among the moon-shadowed spruces, the wolves seemed to come closer. Once, I whirled around, rifle ready, feeling as if half a dozen of them were about to leap on my back. But there was nothing there. Later, howls came from four or five directions, and I felt certain I'd stumbled onto the band of 34 I had seen.

Those ghostlike wolves followed me all the way to my cabin, but at no time did I see a single animal. When I lit a lamp, the howling stopped.

Next morning I went back up Fossil Creek to where the wolves had started to follow me. As near as I could figure it from tracks and beds scattered around, it had been the band of 34 I had previously seen. They had killed seven moose, two young bulls and five cows, calves, and yearlings. They had fed on the moose for several days leaving only skulls, bits of hide and cracked bones.

I don't know why so many wolves were gathered in a pack in late October. It's the only time I ever saw more than about ten wolves in a group, except during the February-March wolf breeding season. I've puzzled over it for many years.

In January Frank Pollack arrived on schedule and flew me back to Fairbanks.

At Mount Hayes

IN 1926, when I lived at Savage River, I seriously thought of getting into guiding in a big way. To find top game country to take trophy hunters into, one spring I walked with two pack dogs from Healy east along the north slope of the Alaska Range, searching for areas with abundant big game.

I left Healy on May 30, explored the Wood River country, continuing to explore as I walked east until I reached the Delta River. I returned to Healy June 24 after walking about 300 miles through some of the most beautiful, game-filled country in the world. The straight-line distance from Healy to the Delta River where I turned back is 110 miles.

Some diary entries from that trip:

May 30, 1926: At Cody Fork of Wood River. Plenty sheep and caribou. 20 miles afoot.

June 3, 1926: Come from Cody Fork to Kansas Creek. Two cabins. See two moose and 70 sheep. Big bear tracks, fresh. 11 miles afoot.

June 5, 1926: Kansas Creek to Day Creek. Pass is 5,600 feet. See 300 or more sheep around lick at Kansas [Creek]. 10 miles up. 23 miles afoot.

June 10, 1926: East Fork to Dry Delta at Ptarmigan Creek Pass, 4,000 feet. Fine for horses. Hundreds of sheep and caribou. Close to Mount Hayes. 11 miles afoot.

In 1939, two years after I went to work for the U.S. Biological Survey, a trapper who had recently spent a winter near Mount Hayes told me wolves had decimated the big game there. He seemed a reliable observer so I made plans to go see for myself. If his report was accurate, I'd do my best to reduce wolf numbers. The region around Mount Hayes had been filled with moose, bears, and caribou when I was there in 1926.

Bush pilots occasionally landed on a big bar of the Dry Delta River, which has its headwaters near 13,832-foot Mount Hayes. I asked the three Fairbanks air services for bids to land me there. Bill Lavery bid $149.50, Frank Pollack $130, and Noel Wien $90. Following federal policy, I planned to fly with Wien, the lowest bidder. However on August 13, a Wien pilot flew over the bar and pronounced it too short and too rough for a safe landing.

On August 16, 1939, pilot Dick Hawley of Pollack Air Service, made two trips and landed me and Buster, one of my wolf-dogs, and a 1,005-pound outfit on a bar of the Dry Delta about eight miles from the base of Mount Hayes. From Fairbanks the bar was 85 miles straight-line or about 150 miles by foot or dog team.

I pitched a tent and started exploring.

Fair numbers of caribou were running back and forth across the river bars, for it was the time of year the botflies were pestering them. On a 12-mile hike, I saw two moose and the several-day-old tracks of a wolf. Mosquitoes, gnats, no-see-ums and whitesocks—the latter a tiny biting insect—were abundant despite a heavy frost the previous night.

A vacant cabin on Ptarmigan Creek about two and a half miles from the Dry Delta bar where I landed proved ideal for my headquarters, and I moved in. I saw a black bear's track, which meant I had to build a bear-proof cache. Next day I started packing my outfit to the cabin, carrying about 50 pounds each load.

On August 20, I had a strange experience with a large grizzly. I saw him eating blueberries about 400 yards away across a small gulch. When I hollered at him he stood on his hind legs and looked in my direction then galloped toward me. Buster bristled and growled at the sight of the approaching bear. Not wanting any trouble, I fired a shot into the ground in front of old Griz. Most bears will turn and run from a shot. This one didn't. He stood on hind legs, sniffing and looking at us. He appeared to be a large male. The wind was in his favor, so he must have gotten a snootfull of the wolf-dog and me.

He then walked to a high knoll 50 yards away and lay down facing me. I sat and watched him for half an hour and he, in turn, watched me. I concluded that he had probably never encountered a man. The trapper who worked the area generally arrived after the river froze, a time when bears are in their dens.

A torrent of rain washed the land and I left, watching the prone bear over my shoulder as I headed for the cabin. He lay there as long as we were in sight.

By August 25, I had all my supplies at the cabin and safely in the bear-proof cache I built. Next day I climbed to the top of a mountain into fresh snow to look the country over. I spotted ten caribou, of which six were full grown cows. Significantly, none of the cows had calves, a good indication of the work of wolves. I also saw four cream-colored grizzly bears feeding on the plentiful blueberries. I watched a black bear swim across one of the many nearby lakes, then run off as if being pursued.

On September 2 bands of caribou arrived from the east. I counted 121 traveling along the ridges, heading west. On September 7 I counted 11 large bulls in one band of 26, and shot one of the bulls for my own use. He was fat and a fine piece of meat.

By mid-September I had made five wolf sets with #114 traps. I allowed Buster to urinate next to several of them, a surefire way to pull a wolf in. On September 15 I was very close to a large, dark grizzly that got my wind. He left at a fast lope.

Grizzlies had made trails all along the river bars where they were digging pea vine roots. A week later, while in the mountains setting traps, I watched a grizzly with two cubs digging out ground squirrels.

I wired the head of the caribou I had killed in early September to a spruce tree on a knoll, then set several traps at nearby clumps of grass. Scent on a piece of caribou hide dropped near the trap completed the set.

A couple of days later I returned to find that a big grizzly had torn the wired head off the tree. He had also sprung all my traps, and had broken one. Several other baited traps had also been sprung by grizzly bears. I wished that the bears would den up.

On September 23 I returned to where I had set some traps at the entrance of a ground squirrel's hole high in a saddle in the sheep hills northwest of my cabin. One of my wolf traps was gone with its log toggle, which had been buried. I thought I had caught a wolf. The nearest willows were about a mile away, and I thought the wolf had gone down there with the trap and toggle. I expected to find him tangled among the willows.

I lit out down the hill. Here and there I saw where the toggle had struck the moss. I reached the edge of the willows, and ahead I could see where the wolf had gone into the willows, and I started that way.

I had the surprise of my life when a big sow grizzly burst out of the willows about 15 feet away. She was shaking her head, growling and bounding toward me. I quickly fired my .220 Swift, hitting her in the body. The 46-grain bullet slowed her but she kept coming. I backed up and shot again. She kept coming. The bear slowed with each shot as I continued to shoot, but she kept moving and kept absorbing bullets. After dodging the bear several times and doing a lot of leaping and shooting, I finally dropped the animal with my eleventh shot. It fell scarcely a rifle's length away. I hated to shoot the old girl, but had no choice.

The Swift is a good wolf rifle and I was hunting wolves, not bears. I had been trying to avoid grizzlies. I had previously killed a couple of grizzlies with it but picked my shots carefully. Moose and caribou I killed with the Swift dropped quickly and a lung shot, especially, was lethal.

The big sow's yearling cub had been caught in the trap and it had run into the willows. Fortunately, it had yanked free and run off while I was shooting the old sow. It was old enough to survive on its own.

I sat on the bear and took a pinch of Copenhagen snuff to steady my nerves. After a time, when my heart had quit racing, I skinned the bear, then set some wolf traps around the carcass. Wolves love grizzly meat.

Cold weather was near and I needed warmer clothing, so I

took the grizzly hide home. A prospector who had used the cabin during World War I when there was interest in nearby molybdenum deposits had left some sulphuric acid in the cabin. I mixed salt in hot water until it wouldn't accept any more, added an ounce of the acid to five gallons of the brine, and swabbed this on the hide. It tanned nicely.

Using the buckskin needles I always carried, and sinew from along the backbone of the bull caribou I had shot, I made a pair of big fur mittens. Then I sewed fur around my cloth cap so it covered my ears. Last, I made a pair of grizzly fur mukluks, using moosehide I found at the cabin for the soles.

A few days later I returned to find that another grizzly had dragged the old sow's carcass a few hundred feet and covered it with moss and brush. It seemed that almost every trap I set was being sprung by grizzlies.

Next day, I found where a bull caribou had fought two wolves for about two miles along the Hayes River. The wolves finally killed it in the river, and after they ate their fill they left the carcass. Two grizzlies dragged it out of the river and took it 400 yards across a gravel bar and into the woods. I found them lying close to the remains. They ran off when I approached. There wasn't much left of the caribou but bones.

September 24, 1939, Sunday: Saw seven bull caribou, two sheep, and four grizzly bears today. Miles on foot 12.

After six weeks of prowling the region I concluded that the moose so abundant in the area in 1926 were largely gone. Wolves must have cleaned them out, for there was almost no hunting by man in the region.

October 8, 1939, Sunday: Made a long hike down the Dry Delta. Six inches of snow on the ground—good for seeing tracks. Saw four caribou and several fox tracks. Eight above zero all day, and frost falling. When I was here in 1926 moose were plentiful. Now I have just seen one in the last month. Traveled 16 miles today.

By October 10, most of the Alaska Range grizzly bears were in their dens. Snow had fallen, temperatures hovered near zero, and the rivers were freezing over. Caribou were widely scattered, feeding; I counted 200 of them, all in small bands. In the afternoon, a small plane flew over, the first sign of man I had seen since September 3, when another plane had passed over.

I had difficulty keeping my traps working, for snow often covered them. The temperature would climb, it would rain, and ice would form on the traps, preventing them from springing. I had to keep resetting them.

I set snares along the Dry Delta River, and on October 18 I found tracks in the snow where a lone wolf had circled them. He had followed beside my tracks for more than a mile, never once stepping on them, then jumping across them. He must have been a wise old fellow.

On the morning of October 20 while climbing in the hills above Ptarmigan Creek, I came across a big Dall ram with a broken front leg. He was thin and sick, hardly able to hobble. It looked as if he had broken the leg a month or more earlier. I put him out of his misery then rolled him into the canyon of Ptarmigan Creek. I cut the carcass up and dragged the bloody pieces through a patch of willows, then hung them on large willows. I had high hopes for the snares I set along the bloody trails.

No sooner had I set the snares than several small bands of caribou wandered by. Soon, a heavy fog rolled in from the southeast, and I had a tough time finding my way back to camp. The temperature was six below zero at 6 a.m. and 10 above at 6 p.m.

As I was starting up Hayes River a couple of days later, I heard wolves howling on a mountain at the head of Ptarmigan Creek. With binoculars I located three wolves and set out after them. When I reached the top of the peak where they had been, I spotted three wolves chasing Dall sheep on a distant mountain. About then I heard wolves howling in Ptarmigan Creek canyon.

I headed into the canyon and I was on a steep slope stepping carefully on snow-covered rocks when a Dall ewe clattered past me, running as fast as she could. A black wolf was about 40 feet behind her, hot on her tail. He saw me, whirled, and leaped out of sight. I didn't have time to set my feet and lift my rifle.

I reclimbed the mountain and saw the black wolf chasing sheep on a three-mile-distant mountain. I went after him, but had to give up the hunt and head home when it got dark. I think there were five wolves, three grays and two blacks. I hiked about 18 miles in the mountains that day. The temperature was zero when I went to bed that night.

On October 23, I climbed the mountain above Ptarmigan Creek. Two fresh wolf tracks appeared in the canyon, so I followed them to where I had set the snares around the sheep meat. When I neared the place I found wolf tracks everywhere. A big black dog wolf was in one of the snares. Three of the other snares had been pushed aside.

The dog wolf weighed at least 135 pounds and measured 69 inches from tip of nose to tip of tail, and 38 inches high at the shoulders—a big wolf. I had to skin him right there, for he was too heavy to pack out of that steep, snowy canyon.

The next day, when I checked a trap I had set on Hayes River, I found that a wolf had stepped into it and dragged it and the toggle off through the eight inches of snow. I followed the trail into spruce timber for about a mile and found it was a dog wolf weighing about 125 pounds. He was full of fight. He measured 69 inches in length and 37 inches at the shoulder.

By October 25 I was running low on grub and thinking of returning to Fairbanks. Pilot Dick Hawley was scheduled to pick me up November first, provided there was no snow. The foot of snow on the Dry Delta bar where he had landed clearly made it impossible for him to come for me. I had no choice, I had to walk out.

On October 26 I found two young wolves in snares I had set along the Dry Delta River. One was a 50-pound black female, the other a gray male weighing about 75 pounds. The male especially was very fat. It must have taken a lot of moose, sheep and caribou to fatten him like that.

On October 30 I was high in the mountains at the head of Ptarmigan Creek when a south wind suddenly came up, blowing so hard I could hardly stand. The air was full of blinding snow and I had a hard time getting back to my cabin.

By November 6 it was time for me to leave. I had expected to be flown back to Fairbanks, so had brought only summer weight clothes—a suit of wool Filsons, and a Filson mackinaw cruiser coat. My footwear was rubber-bottom leather-top shoepacks.

I left the Ptarmigan Creek cabin at daylight that morning, and snowshoed northeast toward the 30-mile-distant (straight-line) Valdez Trail. At dark, I stopped and lit a fire in a patch of timber. I was without bedding, so had to keep a fire going to stay warm. I had hoped for a moon with enough light to travel, but it was cloudy and I had to stay put for the night.

Next morning I started out at 7 o'clock. By early afternoon I reached the old Sullivan Roadhouse which hadn't been used since about 1919. It was still habitable with a good wood stove.

I had hoped to find a broken trail from this abandoned roadhouse to the Valdez Trail, but no one had been there. I hadn't seen a track of man except my own for more than two months. I rested at Sullivan's for a day, cutting firewood for myself and replacing what I had found there.

On November 9th I left Sullivan's at daylight, heading northeast toward Big Delta. The temperature was 25 below. Travel was exceedingly difficult across a huge tussock flat covered with deep snow. I camped when it got dark and had to work hard all night cutting firewood, but still I couldn't keep warm. The icy north wind continued.

On November 10th I battled my way across snow-covered hummocks three and four feet high, the hardest type of ground to cover. When dark arrived I camped in a patch of timber. Here, I put in another night without sleep. I was bitterly cold. As the icy north wind continued, I sat with Buster lying at my back providing some warmth, constantly feeding a big fire at my front.

Next morning, November 11, I noticed I had frozen my fingertips. Later I found my lips had also been frostbitten. I headed for the round-topped mountain lying across the Tanana River from Big Delta. There were no trails or signs of man in the deep snow. At noon, I waded the Delta River and at last reached the Valdez Trail, which was still open for auto traffic. I sent a wire to Fairbanks from Big Delta and Roy Lund drove out to pick me up. It took him eight and a half hours to drive us back to Fairbanks from Big Delta.

ON DECEMBER 6, 1939 I left Fairbanks headed back to the Mount Hayes area to continue my wolf hunt there, traveling on the Lund Stage for the 72 miles to the town of Richardson. (The *Fairbanks News Miner* carried an advertisement, "Lund's autostage and express goes every other day to Richardson. Leave orders at U.S. Grill.) From there, I planned to walk back to my Ptarmigan Creek cabin. It was a lonely trip, for I was accustomed to having one of my wolf-dogs with me. But Queenie, my favorite, had died the previous January, and Buster died shortly after he and I had returned from Mount Hayes in November. They were the last of my wolf-dogs.

I arranged for trapper Hans Seppala from Richardson to use his three dogs to haul my outfit to Ptarmigan Creek for $10 a day. The temperature was 20 below, with two feet of dry, loose snow when we left Richardson. We put in a long, hard day breaking trail ahead of the small dog team, and camped at dark. Next day we reached the old Sullivan Roadhouse after traveling eight miles.

Seppala turned back about four miles above Sullivan's because one of his dogs was about ready to have pups. I went on carrying a heavy load on my packboard until within 15 miles of my Ptarmigan Creek cabin.

On December 11 I left camp at 7:30, although it wasn't light until 9:30. Travel was easy, for there was lots of overflow ice to walk on in the canyon of the Dry Delta. I arrived at the Ptarmigan Creek cabin at 2:30 that afternoon.

Next day I found the remains of a gray wolf and two red foxes in snares I had left along the Dry Delta in November. Wolves had eaten all three, leaving only hair and bones.

On December 18, one of Pollack's planes dropped the grub I had packaged up before leaving Fairbanks. As I watched, the plane swooped to within 40 feet of the ground. Parachutes I had made opened, gently dropping the boxed groceries. The plane also dropped several well-padded bundles without parachutes. They landed without damage in the deep snow, the long colored streamers I had attached clearly marking where they fell.

December 19, 1939, Tuesday: Worked hard from seven a. m. until way after dark hauling my supplies to the cabin. It is about one mile and mostly uphill. I finished moving about 700 pounds with a small sled. Temperature zero. Cloudy.

A few days later I climbed Ptarmigan Creek canyon and found where two black wolves, and a red and a cross fox had been caught in my snares. Wolves had eaten all four. Again, only hair and bones remained.

Through the rest of December and until January 25 I fought snow, gales, and short daylight hours. My traps froze and wouldn't work. Deep snow hindered the efficiency of snares I set. In all that time I caught two cross foxes and not one wolf. I later took the beautiful fox furs to Fairbanks for the government to auction off. One pack of at least 15 wolves crossed through the area, passing within a few feet of my traps and snares, but none blundered into them.

By January 11, my cabin was almost entirely covered by snow. I heard an occasional wolf howl, and kept snares and traps working the best I could. On Jan 19 I found tracks left by a band of eight wolves. They were afraid to cross my snowshoe tracks, and avoided my traps and snares.

On January 25, I decided to return to Fairbanks, and left the Ptarmigan Creek cabin at 7 a. m., and headed down the Dry Delta, figuring I could cross the Tanana River on the ice when I reached it.

Again, as in November, I had no bedding, and only a couple of day's grub. I was dressed warmly, of course, prepared for the winter cold. I habitually carried a stick when I traveled on river ice. Any place I was in doubt of I'd punch with the stick. When I left the mouth of the canyon where the Dry Delta widens out with great broad bars and plenty of overflow ice, I figured I had it made. I was on dry ice and could see what appeared to be fresh snow on the ice ahead, so I threw my stick away. That was an awful mistake.

I was in the middle of the river, cutting from bend to bend, where the river ice was a full mile wide. When I came to the fresh snow, I put on my snowshoes, in a hurry to get to a good camping spot I knew about where there was lots of firewood; it's easier to siwash overnight with a good fire.

As I walked out on the new snow I thought was supported by

ice, tips of my snowshoes slowly broke through. I could do nothing; I simply had to stand there as the snowshoes kept sinking into the water until I was up to my shoulders in icy water and slush.

Deep chill clamped my chest and I could hardly breathe. I reached down with my left arm and grabbed the tail of my left snowshoe, wriggled my foot out of the siwash hitch, and pulled the shoe to the surface. With my right hand I did the same with the right snowshoe.

I started for the bank, breaking ice and fighting my way for a hundred feet or so in water that was from waist to shoulder deep. I managed to climb out of the slush and water and stand on dry ice.

About then I did some fast thinking. I knew I had to get a fire going quickly or I was dead. The temperature was right at zero— not really cold if you're properly dressed, but when one is freezing and soaked to the skin, extremely hazardous to one's health.

I headed at a lope for the dead spruce trees I'd spotted sticking out of the overflow ice, where, apparently, it formed every winter, killing the trees. My Winchester .220 Swift had gone into the water with me and was frozen into a solid sheet of ice clear above the scope. I was not wearing mittens when I went under, and my hands had gotten wet and cold. The big pair of grizzly skin mittens I made in November hung on a cord around my neck. When I went through the ice, they rested atop the snow and ice and remained dry. I stuck my hands into them, and my hands got warm, even though icy water was running down my soaked sleeves into the mittens. By the time I had run a hundred yards my clothes started to freeze; forming ice crackled as I ran.

I had a Hudson Bay axe on my Trapper Nelson packboard, and in my packsack was a pair of caribou skin socks and a pair of extra moccasins. Luckily the packboard remained on top of the snow when I submerged.

I whacked dry wood with the axe, piled up a bunch of dry spruce boughs, and got dry matches out of the packboard. The wood caught immediately. After the fire was blazing high, I cut a small green spruce tree to stand on, then stripped and put on my caribou skin socks and moccasins. My grizzly fur cap was dry.

Thus I stood near the fire, in moccasins, mittens, and fur cap and nothing else. I must have been a sight.

Luckily, there were many small dead spruces handy. I'd get warm by the fire, dash to a nearby tree, cut some dry branches and run back to feed the fire. I dragged branches close to the fire to hang my wet clothing on. I was sure busy getting wood, snatching up my clothes to keep them from burning, and all the while trying to stay warm. My Filson wool pants warned me with their smell when they were about to burn, and I kept moving them. From time to time I'd grab my wool underwear and dunk it swiftly through the flames.

My wool longjohns were soon warm, so I put them on. They were still wet, but I was warmer in them than without. I kept turning around and around to catch every bit of fire-warmth. After I put the underwear on, the cold really bit me, setting me to chattering and shivering.

Instead of going on to where I had planned to camp, I stayed right there for the night. It required several long hours to dry my clothes. After they were dry and I had them back on, I made a pot of tea and boiled a little sheep meat. Then I built up a good spruce bough bed. By dark I had two fires going and lay down on the bough bed between them.

I hung my ice-encased rifle on a dead spruce that night. Next day I hadn't gone a mile when I saw a big gray wolf approaching. He spotted me, sheared away, then returned to the river ice within 300 yards. I looked back and saw him sitting on the ice looking at me. As I went out of sight he howled a couple of times. That was unusual behavior for a wolf. I believe he sensed that something was amiss. It was frustrating not to be able to even open the bolt on the ice-encased rifle.

I spent a night in an old trapper's cabin on the Dry Delta River, about 14 miles from the town of Richardson. I reached Richardson on January 27 and found the Valdez Trail closed to travel to Fairbanks. I had to telephone Pollack Air Service to retrieve me from Richardson with an airplane.

AUTHOR'S NOTE: The entry in Frank Glaser's FWS diary for Tuesday, November 14, 1939, reads: "At Fairbanks today and decided to marry."

The "decided to marry," written in ink, is crossed out with pencil, but it is still legible.

It was at this time, when Glaser was 52, that he married Nellie Osborne.

Nellie, born in Fulda, Minnesota, in 1889 (she was the same age as Frank) was the fifth child of James Edward and Ellen Moon Gage. Her given name was Ellen, but she was known as Nellie. Her mother died about 1894, and her father moved the family to Webb City, Missouri, and later in 1909, to Portland, Oregon. There Nellie married Charles Osborne, who operated a movie house.

The Osbornes had three children, Roland, Adah, and Calvin. The movie house failed, and the Osbornes moved to Centralia, Washington, where Charles became a railroad worker.

In the mid-1920s the Osbornes moved to Alaska, settling in the Matanuska Valley where Nellie's half-brother Ralph joined them and helped them to build their cabin.

Charles worked for the Alaska Railroad as a section foreman. After their children finished school, Nellie left Charles and moved to Fairbanks, where she met and married Frank Glaser.

Nellie and Frank remained together for the remainder of their lives. She made a home for Frank, and patiently waited for him while he was on field trips. In the early 1940s she accompanied him to the Seward Peninsula where the pair lived in many remote Eskimo villages while Frank hunted and trapped wolves around Eskimo-owned reindeer herds.

Frank Glaser kept his personal and his official lives apart. The only mention of Nellie in any of his FWS diaries is in that crossed-out statement "decided to marry," thus in this recounting Nellie Glaser is a somewhat ghostly figure in Book Three (1937-1955) of the Glaser story. Frank mentioned her only in passing during our tape-recorded interviews because I concentrated almost entirely on his professional work, not realizing that more than four decades later I would be piecing his life together for the book *Alaska's Wolf Man*. I regret being unable to include more about Nellie who I knew casually during the time I tape-recorded Frank's recollections. She was a gracious and courageous lady.

To the Arctic

"FRANK, HOW WOULD YOU LIKE to go to the Arctic to clean up wolves around reindeer herds?" asked Alaska Game Commission director, Frank Dufresne. It was February, 1940, and I was attending an Alaska Game Commission meeting in Juneau.

"Fine," I responded.

That response led me to adventurous years of hunting and trapping wolves that preyed on Eskimo-owned reindeer herds in far northwestern Alaska, both above and below the Arctic Circle. I continued as an employee of the U.S. Fish and Wildlife Service (formerly the U.S. Biological Survey), on loan to the Alaska Native Service.

That fall I hired a carpenter to build two large boxes to pack personal items, plus government equipment, I would need at my new station at Nome. There were also a couple dozen smaller boxes.

On September 17, 1940 my wife Nellie and I were aboard the government steamer *Nenana* as it tooted a few times and pulled away from the beach at the Tanana River town of Nenana and headed downstream toward the Yukon River on its last trip of the season. The *Nenana* and the *Alice* were the only big river steamers that now plied the Yukon and Tanana Rivers. During the previous ten years, airplanes had increasingly assumed the freight and passenger business once owned solely by a huge fleet of paddle wheel steamers.

The *Nenana* pushed three barges. One was loaded with the

last fresh fruits, vegetables and meats that the villages along the Yukon River would see until the following spring. We stopped at every village on the thousand mile voyage downstream.

When we reached the coast we transferred from the *Nenana* to the small diesel-powered *N.C.*, which chugged past pilings marking the channel of the shallow northern mouth of the Yukon River where it extends into the Bering Sea. We reached St. Michael after cruising 60 miles across Norton Sound.

From St. Michael we rode the freighter *Oduna* to Nome. The sea was too rough for the lighter to take passengers or freight off at Nome, and the *Oduna* had to seek shelter behind Sledge Island, 20 miles from Nome. Even there winds of more than 60 knots broke the *Oduna's* anchor chain twice. Each time we drifted until the engine could be started to run behind the island again.

We reached Nome on October 3.

I rented a house on Second Avenue, and readied it for winter. *October 4, 1940. Receipt #797 from Nome post office. 10-4-40. Rent for p. o. box 494 for quarter ending December 3, 1940. Cost .75.*

Cost of shipment of the 1109 pounds of personal and government items Fairbanks to Nome on government bill of lading—$98.89.

I had scarcely arrived in Nome when Sidney Rood of the Reindeer Service, an arm of the Alaska Native Service, hustled me into a chartered Wien Airways bush plane to fly for about an hour searching for a band of wolves that had often been seen near Nome. We saw no wolves.

October 17, 1940: Spent the day looking through Mr. Sidney Rood's files. He was very helpful. Reports have come to Mr. Rood from the main reindeer herders. All tell of large losses from wolves in the last few years. At Unalakleet wolves seem to be very plentiful, from the reports sent in by the herders.

The idea of bringing reindeer to Alaska originated with Captain M. A. Healy of the famous U.S. Revenue cutter *Bear* that long patrolled Alaska waters. In the 1880s he noticed that Siberian Eskimos who had reindeer were fairly prosperous. A few miles away across Bering Straits, Alaskan Eskimos sometimes starved.

Dr. Sheldon Jackson, General Agent of Education for the Territory of Alaska, acted on Healy's idea, and with government and private money, bought reindeer in Siberia and brought them to

Alaska. Jackson, who came to Alaska as a missionary, told Congress that giving Alaska's Eskimos reindeer would ". . . advance them in the scale of civilization...change them from hunters to herders . . . utilize hundreds of thousands of square miles of moss-covered tundra . . . and make these useless and barren wastes conducive to wealth and prosperity...to take a barbarian people on the verge of starvation and lift them up to comfortable self-support and civilization . . . "

He meant well, but ignored or wasn't aware of the rich eons-old, Eskimo culture. He judged the Eskimos against his own background. Eskimos of northwestern Alaska have always been hunters. It was asking a great deal of a hunting people to abandon their traditional way of life to become herders. Why should a skilled hunter, proud of his ability to feed his family and his village, spend his time in the boring occupation of driving reindeer? The rewards of reindeer herding, while they might be substantial, are always in the future, while the rewards of hunting are visible and edible daily.

Alaska's northwestern Eskimos were not acquisitive. If a man had a satisfactory home, a good rifle, a boat, a dog team, and could get enough food by hunting, what else could he want? When seals are plentiful, or when the cries of migrating walrus float on the soft air of an arctic spring, how can a man whose deepest instincts urge him to rifle and harpoon turn his back on the excitement of the chase in favor of the dreariness of following reindeer?

Reindeer, closely related to Alaska's wild caribou, were domesticated from the wild reindeer of Europe and Asia. Shorter-legged than caribou, they may be white or spotted, and have other minor differences. When continuously herded they become tame, but quickly grow wild when left alone. They will breed with caribou, and the offspring are fertile.

Between 1891 and 1902, 1,208 reindeer were brought to Alaska. Lapp, Siberian and Finnish herders came with the animals to instruct Alaska's Eskimos in reindeer care. Many of these herders remained permanently in Alaska. By 1914, Alaska had 65 reindeer herds totalling nearly 60,000 animals. Two thirds were Eskimo-owned, while the remainder belonged to the U.S. government, various missions, and Lapp herders.

By 1926 there were 350,000 reindeer in 110 herds, mostly in northwest Alaska. It was boom time, with fantastic proliferation of reindeer, commonly one fourth to one third increase a year. This produced an abundance of meat and hides in a land that historically had produced little wealth other than gold.

Annual reindeer fairs were held in Eskimo villages, usually in January and February. There were reindeer races, shooting matches, butchering contests and other activities. There was usually a grand parade in which participants dressed in their finest furs and drove their best sleds and reindeer.

Reindeer numbers peaked in 1932, with 641,000 of the valuable deer roaming in controlled herds mostly in northwest Alaska. All were descended from the original 1,280 animals. Natives owned 459,638; the Lomen brothers, white businessmen from Nome, owned 78,905; Lapps 63,930; other whites 28,240; and the U.S. government 10,387.

The crash was abrupt. By 1939, the year before I was called in to control wolves around the herds, Alaska's reindeer numbers had declined by more than half. In October 1940, when I arrived on the scene, there were about 250,000 left. A major change that had virtually exploded the reindeer business came when quantities of high quality reindeer meat started reaching U.S. markets in the mid-1930s. The western U.S. cattle industry panicked and pressured Congress to pass the Reindeer Act of 1937, a racist law limiting ownership of reindeer to Alaska's Natives.

For several years after passage of the Reindeer Act, deer owned by non-Natives were purchased by the U.S. government (the Bureau of Indian Affairs (BIA)) in order to transfer them to Eskimos. Chaos reigned as herds once owned by whites were bought by the government, and the BIA tried to interest Eskimos in accepting them.

Before I left Fairbanks I was told that wolf predation was the biggest problem of the reindeer industry. Now I began to get intimations of other complications.

In Nome that October of 1940 I learned that the Reindeer Service had bought a herd of 3, 000 deer from Frank Williams at St. Michael and driven them 75 miles north where they were combined with a herd of 4,000 they had purchased from some Lapps. Unalakleet Eskimos were hired to herd them. Deer from the mixed herd wanted to return to their home ranges.

October 20, 1940, Sunday: Leave Nome at 9:30 by plane Mirow Air Service, pay with GTR, value $50. Arrive at Unalakleet at 11:45 a.m.

On that Sunday (I worked seven days a week when afield, although as a federal employee I was expected to work five days), about 75 of the residents of Unalakleet, an Eskimo village on the shores of Norton Sound, gathered and I explained to them how to use snares, traps, and scents to catch wolves.

The herd was supposed to be at the head of the Golsovia River, about 35 miles from Unalakleet. Two of the herders had come to the village to get another dog team and supplies. I hired Henry Nasholik, a young Eskimo, with his fine dog team, to take me to the distant herd. With the two herders we traveled to where the herd had been.

October 25, 1940: Leave Unalakleet with dog team at 10 a. m. Traveled up the river until dark. It was dangerous traveling on the river ice. Had to go ahead of the team to test the ice.

About ten o'clock that night we were close to where the herd had been when the two herders left to get supplies. They had been gone from the herd for at least ten days. We kept climbing in the pitch dark. It started to blow from the southwest, and a wet snow started to fall.

We finally reached a willow patch in the mountains. It appeared as a black streak against the snow.

"Here's the camp," one of the herders said.

I could see nothing. The four of us stumbled about looking for the tent, and eventually one of the herders found it. The wind had blown it down and it was buried in the snow. We lifted it and got it set using guy lines still tied to the willows.

We all crawled into the tent. There wasn't a stick of firewood to burn in the little wood stove. The herders had been hauling driftwood ten miles from the beach and had used it all. The herd was gone, drifting away in the absence of the herders.

We lit a couple of candles and started a primus stove. It was bitterly cold, and we all kept our fur clothing on. I started to make tea. Several pieces of frozen reindeer meat looking like they had been chopped with an axe were lying on the floor of the tent. Even before the snow melted for tea water, the three Eskimos were chipping pieces from the frozen meat and eating it. I had eaten raw caribou, and I was hungry, so I chipped off and ate some too. By then we had boiling water and I made tea.

I drank a little tea, ate a piece of hardtack, and chewed down about half a pound of the frozen reindeer. It had an odd, unpleasant taste. Then we crawled into our sleeping bags.

Within a couple of hours I awoke with a terrible stomach ache, really sick. The three Eskimos were also sick. The two young herders thought they were going to die. We all made trips outside to vomit. Then diarrhea struck.

"Maybe we won't die," I kidded the Eskimos. "But if you're going to die, I guess I'll die with you."

"But Mr. Glaser, I've never been so sick," one of the herders moaned.

All of us spent a miserable night. We learned later that the meat was from a dead deer hauled in for dog food. Careful inspection at daylight revealed that shrews had tunneled into the meat, and as they ate they had sprinkled the meat with their droppings and urine, which gave it that awful taste. For days afterward just looking at reindeer meat made me sick.

We found the scattered herd that afternoon. Some of the animals from the St. Michael herd were gone, probably headed home. For a couple of weeks I searched all around the herd for wolves, but I saw no wolf sign and heard no wolves howl.

November 6, 1940, Wed: Could not travel. Gale. Wind blew out of the east. Five of us in a small tent with just willows for fuel.

November 7, 1940, Thurs: Storm bound. Blowing a gale from the east, with light snow falling. Way below freezing, and we are busy cutting green alders for fuel.

November 8, 1940, Friday: Henry, one of the Esquimox [Author's note: Glaser's spelling] *and myself start back to Unalakleet at 7 a.m. We travel all day in thick fog. At dark we camp in willow patch close to the beach. A hard days' travel. At least 20 miles.*

I next checked on a herd that had belonged to the Lomen

brothers, reportedly "back in the mountains" from Golovin, a coastal Eskimo village on the south side of the Seward Peninsula. It had numbered about 5,000 when the government purchased it and 19 herding cabins, paying $50 each for the cabins. The herd apparently had been without attention for nearly a year.

Nellie accompanied me to Golovin, and we found a cabin to live in. She spent much time alone while I was in the field during our stay at Golovin.

December 1, 1940: At Golovin. Made a trip on foot to the mountains east of here. See no sign of life. No wolf tracks or reindeer. Miles on foot 10. Wind blows almost day and night in this locality. It was below zero all day.

Folger, the Lomen company storekeeper in the village, told me that the Golovin reindeer herd had numbered more than 12,000 in 1938. By February, 1940 only 4,600 remained. Folger thought the loss was due to starvation. "The range here has been overused," he said.

I located the head herder who had handled the Lomen deer, a big Eskimo of about 45. "Would you be willing to take over the herd?" I asked.

"I'll never look another reindeer in the face," he told me. "I don't want anything to do with reindeer ever again." Like most coastal Alaskan Eskimos he was a traditional hunter and proud of it. Herding deer was not a way of life he could accept.

I asked many Golovin Eskimos where the herd was, but nobody knew. The only answer I got was, "I dunno where they are."

Then I got lucky and found Ole Olson, a Laplander who had sold 2,000 of his deer to the government. "Go to Battleship Mountain and you'll find them," Olson said. "That's over in the Ichipuk River country. They always winter there." He drew me a map.

I located Mischa Charles, who had once had the contract to haul mail between Nome and Golovin by dog team. Now the mail went by airplane, but he still had a fine dog team, including two Portuguese shepherd dogs. These woolly, black and white, lop-eared dogs looked odd among the wolf-like sled dogs. But they were big, heavy dogs and Mischa said they could hold their own in fights with the other dogs.

Mischa agreed to take me to Battleship Mountain to look for

the reindeer herd and look for wolf sign. Mischa, with his dog team, was to receive $7 a day; I was to buy food for the dogs. Most of the Golovin Eskimos worked all summer at placer mines for a wage of $6 to $10 a day. The federal reindeer service paid Eskimo herders a dollar a day, which was not enough to attract many.

Under a bright early morning moon, on December 19 Mischa and I with his ten-dog team left Golovin for the 50-mile trip to Battleship Mountain. On snowshoes, breaking trail, I walked ahead of the dogs all day. One of the Portuguese dogs, leader of the team, growled threateningly whenever he got close to me. This went on for some time, and I figured he was going to bite me if I didn't do something. I cut a willow cane and deliberately waited for the dog to catch up with me, then I cracked him a good one across the nose. He then kept his distance and quit growling.

It was about 2:30 p. m. and pitch dark when we reached the old, rotten relief cabin. All the galvanized roofing had blown off, and there were four and five inch cracks between some of the logs. We went out in the dark and dug frozen moss, thawed it next to the stove and chinked logs for several hours.

Next day near noon as we reached a high divide, I saw whirl-winds in the snow, a storm warning I knew well. In less than half an hour we were facing an icy northerly gale. We were too far to turn back, so went on. For the last four or five hours of that day we moved at about a mile an hour.

The dogs refused to face that bone-chilling, below-zero wind and kept turning to one side or the other. I tied a rope around my waist, lashed it to the lead dog, and walked ahead. We arrived at the Big Four cabin near dark.

Again, the chinking had mostly fallen out from between the logs, and the back end of the cabin was buried in snow. Even in the moonlight I could see that the front of the cabin leaned out about four feet from the vertical. Hoping it would keep the cabin from collapsing while we were inside, I cut a stout dead spruce tree and propped it against the front. Then we dug moss and chinked so we could have a reasonably tight cabin for the night.

That night wolves howled from the hills around the cabin. Next day we searched for the reindeer herd and located a bunch on top of Battleship Mountain. With binoculars I studied eight or nine of the surrounding bald mountaintops and discovered reindeer on most of them. Wolves had driven them there and they were afraid to come down. It had rained, for the rocks were covered with ice. The only feed available to the deer were a few spots where lichens were free of ice, and black rock lichens. The deer I saw were terribly thin.

In the distance I saw eight wolves chasing a small bunch of reindeer. They were too far away for me to help them. As Mischa and I returned toward the cabin, a lone wolf howled about a mile and a half to the north. I could tell it was a pup because its deep wolf howl ended with "bow-wow-wow." An adult wolf doesn't end his howl with that dog-like sound.

"Let's get out of sight, Mischa," I suggested. "I'll call that wolf and shoot him."

Mischa gave me a strange look, but ducked with me into a low depression. I started howling. The wolf answered and ran toward us, then stopped. I called again. He answered, and ran closer. When he ran into some low rolling hills, I lost track of him, but I had my .220 Swift ready. Then we saw the back of a wolf and the tips of his ears and suddenly he was standing on a snowdrift about 50 yards away. He was looking around trying to find the wolf he'd been talking to.

He dropped dead at my shot.

Mischa left the next morning to return to Golovin to get more grub. "I'll be back in a couple of days," he promised.

He seemed awfully anxious to leave. I learned later that he told the people at Golovin that I was a nice man but that I could talk like a wolf. He told Joe Dexter, the storekeeper, "That's the first time ever a straight trail has been broken from Golovin to Battleship Mountain. And Mr. Glaser was never there before." He didn't know about my sketch map.

He wanted to get away from me so he could think for a few days. Eventually he accepted me, but for a while his superstitious nature made him uneasy in my company. There were some things about me he didn't understand.

December 24, 1940: It is cold and clear, no wind, but about 20 below zero. I had to stay in camp to cut wood. Dry trees are very scarce. Carried wood over half a mile. Have to wear snowshoes.

The snow is over five feet deep here in this little patch of timber. I banked the cabin on the outside with snow, but the heat goes out through the roof. This is an old rotten cabin just about ready to fall down. It is hard to make repairs on it.

I counted 280 dead deer lying around Battleship Mountain. Many had starved. Their deaths could be attributed to the wolves that had driven them onto the mountains where there was no food.

Wolves killed many of the reindeer, but ate very little from them. With all the dead reindeer lying around and the easy availability of live ones, the wolves weren't hungry.

A few days after Christmas I put out a few traps near reindeer carcasses. One day I hid near a bunch of carcasses and started howling. In about an hour I brought a pack of eight wolves within rifle range. I'm not very proud of my shooting that day. Using the Swift and its 48 grain bullets is o.k. when there isn't any wind, but the strong wind that blew that day really tossed those light bullets around. I saw some of them hit as much as 20 feet away from running wolves. I killed two out of that pack of eight but I should have killed four or five.

In late December I found Sigfried, an Eskimo who had herded reindeer since he was a boy, and talked him into taking over the herd scattered around Battleship Mountain. I accompanied him and several other Eskimos and we drove 4,500 deer off of the barren, icy mountaintops to within ten miles of Golovin.

Sigfried made a success of reindeer herding. He stuck with it, and during the early 1950s each winter he trained 45 or 50 sled deer to sell as Santa Claus deer. Plus, of course, he had an excellent market for reindeer meat. During World War II, many Eskimo deer herders abandoned and lost their reindeer, but not Sigfried.

Nellie and I flew from Golovin to Nome aboard a Pan American Airways Pilgrim on January 27, 1941. Golovin had no airplane runway, but during winter ski planes landed on a smooth patch of ice on the bay six or seven miles from the village. The runway was marked by oil drums. There was no shelter at the landing area. Radio communications were poor and all we knew was that the big single-engine Pilgrim was due sometime that morning.

The Eskimo who drove us to the landing place with his dog team waited with us for three hours until the plane arrived, and mushed back to Golovin with the mail the plane dropped off. The temperature was 35 below zero with a brisk wind. Despite our good fur clothing, we were thoroughly chilled when the plane landed to sit with its engine idling while a few mail sacks and some freight was unloaded, and we climbed aboard.

The Pilgrim landed on the sea ice in front of Nome, and we walked to our little house on Second Avenue. Snow had entirely drifted over the back door, and there was a huge slanting drift clear to the roof. Another ten-foot-deep drift had piled against the front of the house, also covering the door. After I had shoveled my way through the snowdrifts and into the house, the oil wouldn't flow into the stoves, understandably, because the temperature was 40 degrees below zero.

Nellie tried to help, but there wasn't much she could do. I persuaded her to go to the hotel where she could sit in the warm lobby until I got fires started.

Diesel oil, all that was available in Nome, flowed about like molasses in the cold. I removed a bung from a barrel and got some of the stiff stuff out and dropped it into the pots of the two stoves. I lit candles and dropped them on the oil, gradually warming the oil enough to get it to flow a little and then catch fire. With a blowtorch, I heated the oil lines to get the oil to flow from the outside barrel. Many hours later the house was warm enough for me to retrieve Nellie from the hotel lobby.

Amaguq Frank

HENRY NASHOLIK WROTE ME a letter early in February, 1941. "Our herd has been moved into the mountains about ten miles from Unalakleet. Wolves are after them. Come and get the wolves," he said. Henry was the Eskimo I had hired with his dog team to take me to the Unalakleet reindeer herd.

On February 7, Nellie and I flew back to Unalakleet and moved into the schoolhouse. With his dog team Henry drove me to the reindeer herd of 2,000 animals. The animals were grazing high on a big mountain where the wind had nothing to break its sweep, and it cleaned snow off of the ankle-deep caribou moss (lichen) the reindeer preferred. The herders' camp was on the edge of timber and I pitched a tent nearby. Every two or three weeks Henry came out with his dog team and took me into Unalakleet for a break.

February 19, 1941: I climbed a high divide and saw three black wolves about half a mile away eating a reindeer. They soon had my wind and ran. Temperature today 20 to 30 below zero.

February 20, 1941: I made a trip to the divide and stayed on the highest ridge. Found a deer that wolves killed last night, and another 12 that had been killed in the last month. The recent gale also uncovered several old kills. The dead deer I found today are very thin. 40 below zero today. Miles on foot 15.

The herders told me a few deer had been killed by wolves, but due to the good herding, losses had been light. I watched the herders rope about 26 deer one day and burn the hair on their hind-quarters; they believed this kept wolves from attacking the deer.

February 21: Last night wolves were around the herd. This morning I found one deer that four wolves had killed. They were hungry, for they ate all of the hindquarters. I stayed on the high ridges all day trying to locate these wolves, without results. Miles on foot 15.

February 22: Saw tracks of four wolves close to the herd. It was a terrible day to be out as the wind was so strong that in places I had to crawl. The temperature is way below zero. It is hard to keep warm in a tent in such weather. Miles on foot 12.

February 23. Today the wind is still blowing hard and it is more than 30 below zero. The herd has been gone two nights. I went with the herders to look for them. We found them about six miles from our tents. Wolves killed one animal last night and they ate most of it. This is a tough life living in tents in this kind of weather. The wind has blown every day since I have been with the herd. That's what makes it a fine range. There is lots of feed, and the wind keeps the snow blown off. Butchered a deer for camp meat. Miles on foot 14.

Henry came for me on February 27. "Your wife bought a ten dollar ham and she wants you to come and help her eat it," he said.

I had been with the herd for three weeks and I knew my wife was lonely. I also knew that she had told Henry about the ham in a joking way, but he had taken it seriously.

It was a fine, calm moonlight night at the reindeer camp. "Let's leave now," I suggested. "It's good traveling weather."

Henry harnessed the dogs and we were off. We moved swiftly, and were traveling down the Unlakleet River about six miles from the village when we ran into a solid wall of clouds, fog, and strong wind. It turned pitch dark and we could barely see the dogs. Then it began to snow, cutting visibility even more. I trotted beside the sled, constantly stumbling because I couldn't see the ground.

"Wait," Henry called. "I turn Almosholik loose."

He stopped the team. To my amazement he unharnessed a small female malemute. She disappeared into the howling snow-storm and I figured she was gone for good. The team waited, and Henry calmly stood at the rear of the sled, also waiting.

In about ten minutes I saw a blur through the snow as Almosholik reappeared. The leaders turned and followed as she headed back into the storm. I had heard of mushers using a loose leader, but I had never seen one until that night. From time to time the team stopped and waited as that little dog disappeared into the storm. She'd be back in a few minutes and again the team would follow her. Time after time she ran ahead, scouted the route, and returned to lead the team. Henry and I were just passengers. Almosholik did it all.

We had no idea where we were. We traveled in the blinding snowstorm on that blackest of nights for what seemed hours, guided only by Almosholik.

"Maybe we pass the village and go out to sea," Henry finally said, clearly worried. "Some people have done that."

Then the sled ran into something solid. I groped along the sled and discovered it was the corner of a log building. We had reached Unalakleet.

Without the guidance of Almosholik we couldn't possibly have found the village in that storm.

During March and April wolves killed more than 20 reindeer in the Unalakleet herd. I stalked the wolves with a rifle, set traps on carcasses, and did everything I could to get the four wolves responsible. I walked up to 25 miles some days patrolling around the herd, but the killers were clever and managed to avoid me and the traps. They made all their kills at night, repeatedly stampeding the herd. The head herder, Reuben Paniptchuk, and his two or three helpers had to walk miles to round them up again. I often helped.

March 8, 1941: It must be 50 below. A stiff breeze is blowing, and one cannot stay long on the ridges before one starts to freeze. I was out for about six hours, stayed up on the highest points. See no sign of wolves. At this temperature a cloud of steam hangs over the deer herd when they bunch close. 12 miles on foot.

A church convention was held in Unalakleet starting March 27. More than 200 Eskimos arrived from villages around Norton Sound and from the Seward Peninsula. I counted 55 dog teams, with a total of 609 sled dogs. Dogs howled and barked day and night during the week long meeting.

The herders cut about a thousand reindeer from the herd, drove them near the village and held them on a big open flat. Visitors were told to help themselves to whatever animals they wanted. A constant stream of dog teams kept going to and from the herd. Each driver would shoot two or three deer, load them on his sled, and return to the village. The deer meat fed the visitors as well as their sled dogs.

Eight or nine big wash tubs were placed over outdoor driftwood fires and shoveled full of snow. The reindeer were skinned, the carcasses chopped up with an axe, and the meat tossed into the tubs. All parts of the deer were included except for the intestines. Anyone who wanted to speared a big chunk of meat with a hunting knife and ate it right there.

A particularly sought-after delicacy was the paunch or stomach of the smaller reindeer that had been feeding on white lichens. I watched one Eskimo collect nearly a dozen of these. He tied the lower end of the full paunches shut, and poured sugar into the upper opening. With a stick he stirred it, being careful not to tear the paunch, then tied the top end tightly. He hung all of the sugar-treated paunches close to the stove in his cabin for a couple of days.

The fermentation that took place with the sugar and partly digested lichens cooked the stomach lining, or tripe. When the paunches were ready to eat, the Eskimo poked a knife into the stomach to allow the gas to escape. The stomachs and their contents were then eagerly devoured.

The women also made Eskimo ice cream, or *akutuq* in one of the warm cabins. Reindeer gut fat, which is soft and easily worked, was put into a tub and mashed with a wooden pestle. Seal oil was added. As the seal oil and fat mixed it became easier to work and a big wooden beater was used. After being beaten for some time, the mixture became a light froth, at which time wild cranberries or blueberries were added (bushels of these berries are picked by Eskimo villagers every fall). Sometimes sugar was added to the mix. That's it—Eskimo ice cream, a favorite with Eskimos throughout Alaska.

I counted 220 reindeer slaughtered from the Unalakleet reindeer herd during March to feed people and their sled dogs who attended the church conference. All the conferees appeared well fed and happy when they harnessed their dog teams and left to return to their home villages.

April 14, 1941: Wolves have killed quite a few fawns, so I decided to stay with the herd all night. I left my tent at 6 p. m. for the herd, which was 12 miles away in the hills. I stayed with the animals until 6 a. m. Nothing disturbed the herd while I was there. It was fairly dark from 10:30 p.m. until 1 a.m. At 2 a.m. it was light enough to shoot. The herd is very restless and nervous. It snowed and rained from 2 a. m. until 6 a.m. I arrived back at camp wet to the skin. Miles on foot 25.

Caribou fawns started to arrive about April 12. Wolves killed a few from cows that strayed from the herd, and other, unexpected (by me) predators started killing fawns. One day, watching with binoculars from the top of a hill, I saw two Eskimo women walking about in the herd and I wondered what they were doing. Then a cow dropped a calf, and the women rushed over, clubbed the calf, and immediately skinned it.

A newborn fawn skin was worth a dollar in trade at the Native store. In July, the dark-colored skin of a two-month-old fawn was worth $4; a spotted skin from a two-month-old fawn was worth $7. The skins were favored for making parkas.

I followed the two women to their camp and found 18 fawn skins from animals they had killed. The drying skins were all stuffed full of grass and hanging from the bushes. I told the two ladies that they must stop killing fawns. They pretended that they didn't understand English.

The herders told me that ravens killed many fawns and I didn't believe them. How could a raven kill a reindeer fawn? I had never seen ravens kill caribou fawns in the Alaska Range.

Then one day I watched a cow slip away from the herd to have her calf. The fawn was no sooner born than three ravens arrived. The cow walked ten feet away from the fawn. One of the ravens landed in front of the fawn even before it got to its feet, and picked an eye out. The cow chased the raven away but the moment she turned her back, another raven picked out the fawn's other eye. Soon the three ravens were perched on the fawn, eating its brains.

That spring Reuben and his four herders found 400 raven-killed fawns and salvaged the skins.

I could have quickly rid the area of ravens if I had been allowed to use poison but my orders were to not use poison under any circumstance. I knocked off a few of them with my .220 Swift, but the survivors soon became very wary and I had difficulty in getting within range. The raven is Alaska's most intelligent bird.

I left the Unalakleet herd that June a little better educated than when I arrived. Four years later, the Unalakleet herd was down to about 200 animals. Wolves had killed a few, but losses from other causes had a lot more to do with the decline.

Later that summer at the Eskimo village of Selawik, 70 miles southeast of the coastal village of Kotzebue, and almost on the Arctic Circle, McClellum, an agent of the Reindeer Service, and I helped count the village herd of more than 5,000 reindeer. We hid nearby as the villagers drove the deer toward a new corral located about ten miles from the village. Through a miscue, the deer were herded toward a nearby 50-foot-wide slough of the Selawik River. As they crowded and pushed, the deer started to leap off a 15-foot-high bank into the slough. Then a solid mass of reindeer followed. As deer splashed into the water, other deer leaped on top of them and more deer on top of them until that 50-foot-wide slough was a mass of injured and dead reindeer. It was a horrible scene. Women from the village fished more than 90 dead reindeer out of the slough, skinned them, and used most of the meat for dog food.

To make a count and to select animals for butchering, after the herd was in the corral they were driven one at a time through a V-shaped chute. An older Eskimo stood at the chute where he could lean over and run his hand over the backs of the animals as they went through. It was July, and the bulls were nice and fat. At about every fortieth bull the old man called loudly, "Butcher."

As each designated animal left the chute five or six husky young Eskimos grabbed it and threw it down. While the others held the struggling animal, one of the men cut its throat. They then allowed the terrified animal to get up and, with blood spurting everywhere, tear off across the tundra for a ways before it dropped dead. This always brought a roar of laughter from the handlers.

Women from the village then skinned, gutted and butchered the animal. The white schoolteacher and his wife fled, horrified. McClellum looked at me and grimaced, but said nothing.

I watched them treat about three big fat bulls in this manner and then quietly walked up and told the big fellow doing the throat cutting, "The next deer you kill, instead of throwing it down, you just hit it as hard as you can on the head with that axe," pointing to a 4½-pound pole axe that stood nearby, "and *then* you cut its throat to bleed it."

He followed my suggestion and hit the deer as hard as he could right between the antlers. The velvet antlers flew into pieces going all directions, and blood spattered the young workers. But the animal was instantly dead, its skull crushed. That brought more laughter from the men, and everyone wanted a turn with the axe. It was a far more humane way to slaughter.

The death of reindeer, sled dogs, caribou, any animal, was taken as a matter of course by Eskimo villagers. They aren't deliberately cruel. As hunters, they live by killing, which is very much a part of their lives.

The following February (1942) a report came to me from Selawik that wolves were killing their reindeer. Would I come and kill the wolves?

I flew to Kotzebue and by dog team traveled to Selawik to learn that the herd was in the Zane Hills, 120 miles east of the village. I fought blizzards and deep cold all the way to the herd and discovered there were only 1,000 animals left.

"You had 5,000 deer last summer. What happened to the other 4,000?" I asked Charlie, the head herder.

"I went to the village for a visit at first snow, and stayed for two weeks," he explained. "When I got back, 4,000 deer were gone. I didn't lose them, Mr. Glaser. They did," he said, pointing to the other herders.

I learned then that the other four or five herders had also gone visiting while Charlie, the head herder was absent. The animals had been alone for at least two weeks. When herding recommenced, 4,000 were missing. They seemed satisfied to find a thousand animals and no one seemed to worry about the missing deer. At the time the average reindeer was worth about $20. Eighty thousand dollars worth of reindeer were lost, and no one seemed upset.

Two wolves had been killing animals from the herd. I put out traps, and soon caught one of them. I stayed with the herd eight days, and when I returned to Kotzebue I left traps set with instructions to the herders on how to reset them if necessary.

At Kotzebue, before going to Selawik I met the Noatak school teacher, Calhoun and his wife, who told me about the Noatak herd of 3,000 or 4,000 reindeer. "Wolves killed a lot of the deer last year. The people there could use your help," he told me. "What are the chances of your getting to Noatak?"

Casually, I said, "If you'll get the villagers to build a new log cabin at Noatak village this summer, and have it done by September, send me a wire and my wife and I will come and I'll spend the winter getting rid of the wolves there."

I promptly forgot my promise. I didn't dream the Noatak people would actually build a new cabin for me. But in mid-September I received a wire from Calhoun. "Cabin ready for your use. Expect you here soon. Wolves still after reindeer herd."

About then Eskimo Lester Gallahorn left Kotzebue with two boats loaded with trade goods for the store he planned to open in Noatak. I paid him $35 to take Nellie and me and our baggage. "We'll be there in three or four days," he promised.

The river was dropping, and the *Swan*, the largest of his two boats, drew about four feet. We putted ten miles across Kotzebue Sound to the mouth of the Noatak River. Fall colors had painted the hills, and new snow had powdered some of the highest ridges.

At dark the two boats were pulled up to the bank for the night. Nellie and I made our beds atop 100-pound sacks of cornmeal. Lester spread his sleeping bag out in the stern, near the engine. Lester's uncle, an old man, positioned himself atop the cabin with a .30-30 rifle across his lap.

"Why?" I asked Lester.

"Oh, Uncle will watch and keep the Indians away," he answered, quite seriously.

I laughed and went to bed. I thought he was joking, but he wasn't. The long-standing enmity between Alaska's coastal Eskimos and Interior Indians was a serious consideration. (AUTHOR'S COMMENT: The hostility between these two peoples has essentially disappeared in the last half century]. I heard Uncle snoring long before I fell asleep, and every time I awoke in the night he was still sound asleep.

We had to start portaging the next day. When the boat couldn't cross a shallow riffle, Lester ran it ashore, put a plank over, and we unloaded all the freight and packed it upstream to deeper water. Then he ran the empty boat through the shallow riffle, put the plank over and we'd reload. Most of the goods in the two boats was hundred-pound sacks of flour, cornmeal, oatmeal, sugar, and I don't know what all. Tons of stuff.

We spent three full days portaging across seven places. On the third day we were only seven miles from Noatak village by land, but we spent all day handling freight. I was intimately acquainted with every bag on those boats before it was all done with and we finally pulled up to the bank at the village of Noatak.

Nellie and I and the school teachers, Mr. and Mrs. Calhoun, were the only whites in this village of 400 Eskimos and 1,200 sled dogs. The new log cabin built for us stood within 20 feet of the clear, gravel-bottomed Noatak River and within about 30 feet of the cabins of some of the Eskimo residents.

Our cabin was well built, except that it hadn't been chinked with moss until after it was built. Much of the chinking was loose and I could push it out wherever I touched it. To remedy this, I found some old burlap used around the reindeer corral, cut it into strips, and caulked the logs by driving the burlap in firmly with a big hammer.

Calhoun loaned us a wood stove and a bed from the school, and Nellie made furniture out of wooden gas cases in which two five-gallon cans of gasoline were shipped.

Snow fell shortly after we arrived, and the ponds started freezing about September 20. I was anxious to assess wolf numbers. Large caribou herds were reported near the Kugururok River about 95 river miles upstream. On the day we arrived at Noatak village, three good-sized cabin boats arrived from upriver with many bales of caribou fawn skins. The hunters had been gone since early July, hunting caribou fawns for their skins, which make wonderfully warm parks. They sold the skins in Kotzebue. Both the hunting and the sale of skins was illegal, but Noatak was so remote that such activities by Eskimos were largely overlooked. I said nothing about it.

"Where did you get them?" I asked.

"Way up the Noatak," one of the hunters replied.

Where there are caribou, there are wolves. Were the caribou herds close enough to bring wolves to the Noatak reindeer? How abundant were wolves around the caribou herd?

Of all things, it warmed up and rained in early October, melting the ice on the river which rose about six inches. For $50 I hired Gordon Mitchell, a Noatak Eskimo, to take me 100 miles upstream on the Noatak in his outboard-powered, 40-foot-long Umiak, a walrus skin boat. As we traveled up that icy, clear river for three days I peered into the water and saw huge schools of whitefish and grayling in almost incredible numbers. In places lingcod (burbot) lay on the bottom in such numbers that I could scarcely see the gravel. I saw vast schools of two kinds of char, running from three or four pounds up to at least twelve pounds. One kind was round, long and slim; the other kind was heavy and deep, salmon-like, and tinted with the most gorgeous colors I've ever seen on fish—red, orange, purple, green, pink. Char spawn in the fall, and these fish were in full spawning color. There were chum salmon, too, but they had mostly spawned and were dying, their bodies drifting downriver and piling up on the bars. The water was incredibly clear, so clear I could see fish ten feet down as if they were floating on air.

We found three parties of Eskimos where the Kugururok River flows into the Noatak. They had traveled there in 40-foot umiaks. The big eddy formed where the two rivers joined was a traditional spot where these villagers annually seined. Gordon and I camped overnight and watched them at their fishing.

Two men would hold one end of the huge seine on the beach while one of the umiaks pulled the seine in a big semi-circle. Then the big net was hauled ashore, invariably full of char, ling cod, whitefish, grayling and a few salmon.

I was surprised that the men weren't taking the fish back downriver to the village. Instead they made a cache for each man in the form of a trench about three feet deep, and about twelve feet long. Fish, still flopping, were tossed into the trench as fast as the Eskimos could throw. When the pit was nearly full, layers of willows were laid over the fish. A distinctive pole was put up at each pit, marking its location, and identifying its owner.

Fish so treated ferment before freezing. In winter the owner would drive his dog team to the spot and dig into the pit with an axe or pick and chop out a supply, toss it in his sled, and take it home for use.

These fish were eaten raw. Skin from a chunk of fish chopped from the frozen block would be peeled back, and little pieces of the frozen fish shaved off with a sharp knife. The piece would be dipped in seal oil, and eaten like potato chips. I don't care for seal oil, so when I ate this fish—I call it pre-cooked because of the fermentation—I dipped it in olive oil or Wesson oil. It has a nice sweet taste and, surprisingly, doesn't taste spoiled. When thawed, it turns soft, but it doesn't have a bad smell.

By the time Gordon and I were about ten miles above the Kugururok River, the Noatak was shallowing and the water level was dropping fast. It had turned cold, and four inches of slush ice was running on the river and ice was coming out of the riverbank. It was October 8. Cold had settled on the land. It was time for Gordon to hustle back downriver with his umiak before the river froze over.

I piled my tent and supplies on the beach. As I unloaded the umiak I saw in the frozen wet sand tracks where a wolf had chased a caribou. Ten feet from that was the frozen track of a huge grizzly bear.

"You will kill lots of caribou, Mr. Glaser," Gordon said, after seeing the caribou track.

"I just want one, for meat," I told him.

I had arranged with Noatak villager Saul Shield to pick me up with his dog team some time in November or December. That gave me a month, maybe two, to scout out the region and trap or shoot wolves.

I built a square foundation three spruce logs high the exact size of my tent. On that I erected a spruce pole frame on which to hang my 8×10 tent. With the tent pitched atop my square of logs, I could stand up straight against the side walls. I sodded up around the logs and the tent for additional insulation. .

Before leaving Noatak, Eskimo Austin Stalker had made me a wood stove. Starting with a new 50-gallon oil drum, he worked for three days, cutting it to size with a cold chisel. He built a fine door and damper, with a good stovepipe hole. It burned 2½-foot-long wood, and was about 15 inches high, with a flat top for cooking. When he delivered it I asked, "How much, Austin?"

"Do you think $5 is too much?" he wanted to know.

I paid him $10, and got a bargain. That little stove beautifully heated my 8×10 sod-insulated tent.

A couple of days after I got my tent set up and a good pile of wood cut, the temperature dropped to 26 below zero, with a strong east wind blowing down the river. The Noatak froze up overnight.

About October 20th I walked 25 feet out on the ice of the river and peered into deep water and saw a school of arctic char swim by. For the only time ever, I was in the wilderness alone without any fishing tackle; I didn't have hook, line, or lure. I thought it would be nice to have a cache of fish on hand.

Next day, lying on a bar below my camp, I found a 60-pound chunk of ivory mammoth tusk. With a wedge-shaped rock I split off a piece and filed a small lure out of it. I bent an eight penny nail, and sharpened it to make a good hook and lashed it to the ivory lure. For line, I used a six-foot piece of reindeer back sinew my wife had given me for patching mukluks.

I cut a good strong willow pole, attached the sinew-line to it, walked to the edge of the ice, and dragged the plug through the water. A big char came up and sucked it in. I lifted his head up and slid him out onto the ice. He didn't know what was happening, and didn't even struggle until he was out of the water.

I caught several hundred pounds of fish that day. That evening, using my packboard, I carried a few to my tent. Next morning after breakfast I saw four otters on the river busily carrying fish I had caught into the water. They had taken only a few by the time I rushed down and stopped them. I packed the rest home. They froze, and I ate off of them for the rest of my time there.

I searched the country for about 15 miles in all directions, but never saw a caribou. The herd had passed through; all their tracks led northwest.

October 16, 1941: Late this afternoon while returning from downriver, when I came out of the timber near my tent I saw a gray wolf on the far side of the river. It was eating on a salmon. I shot at him with the .220 Swift and missed; blew a geyser of sand up right under him. It was 300 yards, and I had thought it was 200 yards. The wolf looked around, and went back to eating. I corrected my aim and killed him with my next shot.

With binoculars I saw three more wolves downstream. They saw me and ran before I could shoot when I came out of the timber across from them.

From my tent I could see the dead wolf with binoculars. Just at dark another wolf started to eat the dead one. I shot at him, he dropped, but got up and ran off. Saw a total of five wolves today—four grays and one black.

I crossed the river the next morning and found where wolves had returned and eaten most of the wolf I shot. I found a few drops of blood where I had hit the other wolf, but there was no snow, so I couldn't trail it far. Wolves had been eating old, spawned-out salmon all along the river. The ice went out while I was on the far side of the river and I had to go a couple of miles upstream to find a riffle I could ford. I had to wade through swift waist-deep water with slush ice running.

A few days later I was at the mouth of the Kugururok River. Spawned out chum salmon had washed up on the bar and two wolves were feeding on them. They saw me and went into the brush and I sat down on a bar trying to figure a way I could get close to them. As I sat there a red fox ran out of nearby willows, looking back. Its tongue was hanging out, and it looked tired. I sat perfectly still and it loped on by me, still looking back.

Moments later a gray wolf came out of the same place in the willows and trotted down a dry slough toward me. Clearly, it was trailing the fox. The wolf trotted along, head and tail down. Occasionally she stopped and looked back. When she was about 20 yards away I had her in my rifle scope and said, "Just a minute."

She threw up her head and jumped, but it was too late. My bullet was already in her chest.

She was trying to catch that red fox for food. I sent that wolf's skin and skull to a museum that had requested a wolf specimen.

On October 27, I found two Eskimos, Enoch S. Sherman and Henry Harris, with two dog teams camped on the far side of the river. I showed them a safe place to cross on the ice. The Noatak is swift, and ice often forms, is washed away, and reforms, so crossings are always hazardous. That night I cooked up a big feed for them, for they had virtually no food. They had been hunting but had found no caribou. They agreed to haul me and my gear back to Noatak for $50. I had decided that the few local wolves where I had been hunting were no threat to the Noatak reindeer herd. It was time to go home.

When we pulled into the village a crowd gathered around, as they always did when travelers arrived. Enoch reached into his sled and one at a time pulled out the three wolf hides I had collected. "Oh, big!" everyone exclaimed as he flourished each hide. They weren't big and it embarrassed me.

I was in for even more embarrassment. Next morning as I left the cabin to go see Calhoun, six old Eskimos who made up the village council were laying for me. When I first saw them they were huddled close together almost like a football team, talking.

As I neared, one called, "Stop, Mr. Glaser." I didn't know what was going on. As I stood there they surrounded me, holding hands. One said, "You're just like an Eskimo, Mr. Glaser. You go out in the hills and you stay. You're not afraid of Indians or anything. And you kill wolves. Now we give you Eskimo name. You are now *Amaguq* Frank—man who hunts wolves."

It was a high honor, and I'm afraid I was so embarrassed that I didn't really express my appreciation the way I should have.

On Sunday, December 7, 1941, my 52nd birthday, we invited Mr. and Mrs. Calhoun for dinner. We started to sit down to eat and turned the radio on to get some music and were suddenly shocked with the news of the bombing of Pearl Harbor. I quickly shifted stations to JOK, Tokyo. Reception was perfect. The Japanese announcer, in English, read off the names of the American battleships Japanese planes had sunk. We could hear Japanese laughing in the studio, and could even hear the crinkling of paper as script pages were turned. Next day we heard all about the bombing of Clark Field in the Philippines.

My salary for 1941 was $2,512.40. In 1942 it was $2,533.33.

For three more years I continued to kill wolves around reindeer herds at Eskimo villages—I spent time at Kivalina, Candle, Noatak, Selawik, Unalakleet, Teller, Golovin, and elsewhere. Then I was assigned to Anchorage and Fairbanks.

In January 1944 I was reassigned to Walden, Colorado, where I was taught the use of poison for controlling predators. This included the use of the cyanide-loaded "getter" gun. The getter, or gas gun, is a foot-long metal pipe-like device driven into the ground or hard snow. An attractive scent is placed on a tuft of fur or wool and left protruding from the ground. When a wolf picks up the scented wool, it triggers a firing pin, which explodes a .38 caliber blank cartridge loaded with a powder which on contact with moisture in the animals' mouth turns into cyanide gas. Death is almost instantaneous. The device is effective in killing both coyotes and wolves.

After a year of controlling mostly Norway rats and coyotes in Colorado, I was reassigned in February 1945 to Alaska and I was again loaned to the Bureau of Indian Affairs. I was sent to Nome where I was again to control wolves killing reindeer.

The Teller Wolf

MOST WOLVES CAN BE TRAPPED, shot or killed in one way or another if a hunter knows his business. Once in a great while though, a wolf becomes wise to the ways of man and somehow manages to evade capture. At the same time it might kill many head of valuable livestock or game animals.

There was the famous Custer Wolf which for about six years lived near Custer, South Dakota. It killed $25,000 worth of livestock. Despite a $500 bounty, it evaded hunters and trappers for at least six years. A government hunter finally killed this wolf in 1920 after hunting it full-time for six months.

Another famous wolf was the 150-pound Lobo, King of Currumpaw, made famous by the writings of Ernest Thompson Seton. This wolf ranged the Currumpaw region of New Mexico for about five years, killing many cattle and sheep.

Three Toes of Harding County, South Dakota, was a livestock killer for 13 years, destroying $50,000 worth of livestock. At least 150 hunters sought Three Toes before a government hunter caught him in the summer of 1925.

There have been others: the Aguila Wolf of Arizona, which for years killed a calf about every fourth night; Old Lefty of Burns Hole, Colorado, accused of killing 384 head of livestock in eight years; and Old Whitey, of Bear Springs Mesa, also in Colorado,

Frank and Nellie Glaser in Eskimo-made parkas sometime in the 1940s. Nellie's parka is made of reindeer skin, Frank's of seal skin.

FRANK GLASER

known as a livestock killer for 15 years. His track could barely be covered by a large man's hand.

Because of their depredations and because they had identifying color, marks, or defects, or unique habits, these wolves earned their nicknames and became famous.

During Alaska's Territorial days, the goal of the federal government was to reduce wolf numbers because of their inroads on moose, caribou, deer, wild sheep, and, of course reindeer. In my years as a private and government trapper I encountered only one wolf I thought was especially clever and on a par with some of the famous livestock killers of the Old West. I came to call that animal "The Teller Wolf," after the area in which it lived and hunted.

For nearly six years I had been hunting, trapping, and finally, poisoning wolves around reindeer herds. More times than I can remember I helped Eskimos gather scattered reindeer herds which had been stampeded by wolves. I couldn't eliminate all wolves around reindeer herds, but in the years that I spent trying to protect these deer I had made an impact. I had removed many wolves, and I had taught Eskimos how to take wolves themselves. Wolf problems around reindeer herds had decreased.

In early 1945 I went to Teller, on the Seward Peninsula, where the Native Service told me wolves were raising hell with reindeer. Teller, on the treeless windswept tundra, was then a tiny Eskimo village of sod and log igloos (houses), some frame buildings, and a trading post.

I hired John Komak, an Eskimo who had a dog team and we started off looking for the reindeer herd. We drove across the wind-packed snow for 25 or 30 miles and found both live and dead reindeer scattered everywhere. In one day I counted more than 400 reindeer wolves had killed. They were lying atop the snow, some partially eaten, some killed and left without anything being eaten. There was no telling how many reindeer carcasses were covered by drifting snow. Whenever deer saw us coming with the dog team they lit out running, spooky from being chased by wolves.

I returned to Teller, angry at being asked by the Native Service to go to this herd to kill wolves and finding that the herders weren't taking care of the deer. What I learned at Teller didn't help. Local Eskimos were helping themselves to the deer, both

*Glaser and a wolverine killed at one of his bait stations on Mount
Fairplay, 1954.*

AUTHOR

by killing them themselves, and by using those the wolves had killed. They were feeding reindeer to their sled dogs, and eating the meat themselves.

I went into the trading post and asked Mrs. Marks, the owner's wife, "Where are the herders?"

"Aren't they out with the herd?" she asked.

"No."

"They must be playing cards," she said, pointing to a cabin.

I found five young Eskimo men sitting on the floor in the cabin playing poker.

"Are you fellows the reindeer herders?" I asked.

No answer. They looked at one another and started talking in Eskimo.

"Let's talk English," I said, getting more angry by the minute. No answer.

Soon in came Maggie Topkok, an Eskimo girl who worked for Mrs. Marks at the trading post. Her father owned an interest in the reindeer herd.

I told Maggie what my trouble was, and she spoke sharply to the boys in Eskimo. Then they started to answer my questions.

"Why aren't you with the herd?" I wanted to know.

"Oh, Mr. Glaser, the wolves keep the herd scattered. No one can keep them together."

"All right," I told them, "I can kill the wolves but not with the deer scattered all over the country. You fellows round them up and get them within ten miles of town, and I'll go to work on the wolves."

They agreed to that, but I could see they were reluctant. I didn't realize why.

Next day they hooked four or five dog teams to a little plywood house on runners and dragged it ten miles or so from town. Then they started to round up the deer. Two or three days later I went out and found the animals bunched at Dese Creek, a willow-fringed stream in a shallow basin.

I pitched my tent near the herder's cabin, planning to stay close to the herd. That night I learned that the young Eskimos were half-afraid of the wolves, and I soon understood their reluctance to go back to herding. As I lay in my tent trying to sleep that night, wolves moved in close to the herd and howled and howled. I had spent 25 years living among Alaska's wolves, and I had never heard anything like it. A wolf song is beautiful, and I've always enjoyed hearing it. But I confess that night, after a few hours, the continuous howling began to get on my nerves. Those wolves were unusually bold. They were perfectly aware that we were there, near the herd, but that didn't dissuade them. The continual howling also got on the Eskimos' nerves; the deer, also frightened by the howling, scattered into the black night.

That night wolves killed half a dozen reindeer, and drove I don't know how many others off into the hills.

The herders had to start all over again.

Wolves can't be trapped in that open windy country, because traps are soon covered by drifting snow. Snares can't be used because there are no trees to hang the snares on. I had walked literally thousands of miles around reindeer herds with a rifle, trying to shoot wolves, with scant results. Strychnine baits and cyanide gas guns, commonly called "getters" were the only practical control methods, and I had started using them.

I picked my spots and put out bait stations and getters. I instructed the Eskimos to travel to and from the herd by a certain creek where I made no sets, for I didn't want them to lose any sled dogs.

I worked around the Teller herd all winter of 1945-46, keeping getters and poison baits out and I pretty cleaned out the wolves. Very few deer were killed by wolves after that first night, and the herders kept the deer pretty well under control.

That summer passed without any wolf trouble at the Teller herd. In the fall (1946) before snow came, whenever the Eskimos butchered reindeer I hauled the entrails and heads out to knolls all around where the herd was kept. When winter came I asked the herders to keep the herd in an area where I could surround it with bait stations. By November I had about 25 bait stations, reindeer guts and heads piled on windswept knolls with poisoned lard baits and getters around them.

November 29, 1946: Trip via dog team, Tony Bernhardt owner and driver. Put out two bait stations on high ridge east of the herd. This makes a string of stations all around the herd.

Frank Glaser at his Fairbanks log cabin, in 1952. The two frozen sheefish he holds were caught by Eskimos at Kotzebue, and flown to Fairbanks. The largest fish weighed 35 pounds.

Whenever a pack of wolves moved in, they would hit one of these knolls and I had them. In December, a group of Eskimos traveled across the sea ice from Wales, a village on a peninsula 60 miles to the northwest. They told me of seeing nine black wolves heading toward Teller on the ice about ten miles offshore. I paid little attention, thinking that the wolves had found some dead walrus on Point Spencer and it was unlikely that they would ever get to the Teller reindeer herd.

But ten days later I found nine black wolves dead at one of my bait stations.

It went that way until January 1947. Every bunch of wolves that arrived hit one of my stations before they reached the herd. No deer were killed, and the herders were pleased.

To add to their joy, my helper that winter, Tony Bernhardt, a part-Eskimo with a lot of savvy, and I found around 500 stray deer and drove them back to the herd, bringing the herd up to about 1,200 animals.

One day in January I went with Tony Bernhardt and his dog team to the herd on a routine check and was met by three long-faced herders. "Six deer were killed by wolves last night, Mr. Glaser," one of them reported.

I looked at the carcasses and found by the tracks that a lone wolf had killed them all. The wolf's tracks showed on the hard snow where it had dug in its toes. It had used the technique common to wolves in killing caribou; it ran beside a fleeing reindeer and slashed its flank. The stomach of the reindeer fell out, pulling the entrails with it. The deer traveled maybe 50 or 60 yards, pulling itself along with its front feet, with the hind quarters dragging, until it died. I found the six reindeer scattered over a stretch of perhaps half a mile, each with its stomach and entrails strung out behind.

While I was looking at the dead reindeer, I saw ravens rising and falling in the wind at a nearby knoll where I had a bait station. When I got there I found seven dead wolves, some black, some gray. As I stood looking at them a gray wolf howled forlornly about a mile away on a nearby mountainside. I looked at it through my rifle scope, and watched it run east toward the Sawtooth Mountains.

At the time I had no idea of the trouble that wolf would bring. To me it was just another wolf. I'm sure that it had been a member of the pack of seven that had been killed at my bait station. I think it saw the others die from the poison and it learned from that. I can't think of any other explanation for the behavior of that wolf that followed.

This was the Alaska of the mid-1940s, when wolves didn't have much of a chance to learn the ways of man. The region was sparsely settled, with only about 80,000 residents in the entire Territory. The Seward Peninsula, except for Nome, didn't have many people. Some of the famous wolves of the west learned about man where there were far more people.

I learned a lot about that lone gray wolf during the next six or seven weeks.

A few days later, during a blizzard, six deer in the Teller herd were killed by a lone wolf. Each had been slashed in the flank, allowing the stomach and entrails to fall out. The right front foot of the killing wolf didn't spread out normally—the killer wolf was crippled.

I put poison baits around several of the deer, using methods I had learned in Colorado. I also put poison in the ears of the slain reindeer, and cut some pieces of hide off and scattered them around with poison baits under them. The Eskimos hauled three or four of the deer home for dog food.

A few days later I found the crippled wolf's tracks all around the dead animals where it had circled and walked up to them. There hadn't been much wind for several days and my poisoned lard baits were lying on top of the snow. The wolf had cracked two or three of the frozen baits open.

I was sure it had eaten some of them, so I circled and found its tracks and followed it for about a mile. It never faltered. It hadn't eaten any of the baits. I began to wonder what kind of wolf I had come up against.

I set a bunch of getters around the dead reindeer. Day after day they remained untouched.

During a howling blizzard a few days later, seven more reindeer were killed by the same wolf. It ate a little out of one hind quarter, pulled a few tongues out, and cut a few throats to lap up the blood. Again I put out my lard baits and getters. I was worried.

It blew all the next night, and I returned to find that the wolf had returned after the storm and had circled my baits, but this time it hadn't cracked any open. It had pawed some out from under pieces of hide, and had rolled them around on the snow, but it hadn't eaten any.

That happened several more times over the next two weeks. I finally realized I was up against a wolf far more clever than any I had ever seen. The Eskimos too, soon realized the wolf was different. One day when I arrived at the herd I found the four herders in their little shack, with the deer scattered. The Teller Wolf, as I had come to call it by then, had made a kill the previous night and the herders didn't want to go into the hills to round up the deer.

January 8, 1947: Leave Teller via Bernhardt dog team at 9 a.m., return at 4 p.m. to visit all bait stations. I put out fresh baits and scent and saw one wolf track. About noon we got into a blizzard. Within minutes the air was a mass of flying snow and all landmarks disappeared. The dogs didn't want to face the wind. When we arrived back at Teller we learned the wind was blowing at 40 miles an hour. Temperature was 12 below.

Loss came not only from the reindeer the lone wolf killed, but from those that it scattered and were lost. The reindeer were now difficult to herd, for they were jittery from the wolf's depredations.

I had orders to leave Teller February 2 to go to Nunivak Island in order to count musk oxen, and I simply had to get that wolf before I left or it would wreck two winters' work. That lone wolf was capable of wiping out the Teller herd through killing and scattering the reindeer, and by intimidating the herders.

The lone wolf with the crippled paw continued to kill reindeer. It preferred to work in a blizzard and at night, and we had plenty of blizzards that winter. Day after day the wind blew, with temperatures ranging from 0 down to 40 below.

From the wolf's tracks I learned that most of the time it stayed in the Sawtooth Range, otherwise known as the Kigluaik Mountains. It would leave the mountains to make a kill of reindeer, then it would high-tail it back into the mountains. It didn't howl much, at least the herders didn't hear it often, nor did I.

One day I found where the wolf had crawled up to several of my getters, put a paw on each side, and then very carefully licked the scent off. The least pull and the shell would have detonated, resulting in a dead wolf.

I could understand how a wolf might have learned of the danger from lard baits. Perhaps when it opened one it got a taste of strychnine, or it saw the others in its pack die from eating the baits. But licking the scent off of the getters was hard for me to believe, and harder to understand. I was using the two most efficient meth-

A team of reindeer driven (and held here) by Frank Glaser on the Noatak River, 1941, when he was hunting wolves around Eskimo-owned reindeer herds.

ods I knew for controlling wolves, and the animal apparently wasn't going to be taken with either. I didn't know what to try next.

I kept putting out my standard scents with the baits, and putting out the getters, and the lone wolf continued to terrorize the herd. The herders were ready to quit and go back to the village and their cards, and I had to keep after them to stay with what deer were left. Secretly, I didn't blame them.

One day as I was making rounds of my sets I suddenly remembered that many years earlier I had experienced some unusual successes when I had used the scent of skunk to lure wolves. That night I wrote to the government bait station at Pocatello,

Idaho, requesting that they airmail me some skunk musk. Nine days later a box containing the musk arrived.

January 27, 1947: Made trip around bait stations with Bernhardt and his dog team. See no sign of wolves. Found the reindeer scattered miles from the herder's camp. Made a trip to herder's camp and told them where the deer were. The herders said a wolf had killed three deer the night before. It was 18 below with drifting snow all day. My skunk scent came from Nome today.

The scent was in a foot-square carton. Inside was a wide-mouth quart jar packed in shredded paper. Inside the closed quart jar was a little jar, also packed in shredded paper. There wasn't a trace of skunk odor when I opened the box.

I was in my warm cabin, and I wasn't thinking; I unscrewed the lid on the inside jar, and the odor of skunk poured out, smelling up the cabin. It started me coughing. I immediately screwed the lid back on, but it was too late. I had to live with that smell for days.

I added a few drops of the skunk musk to one of my regular scents, and put the rest in an outside cache.

Next morning Tony Bernhardt, driving his dog team, picked me up just before daylight. The dog team was lively, it was crisp and cold, and we banged up and down over hard snow drifts along the trail at a dead run. Tony began to cough.

"Mr. Glaser," he said, "what kind of scent have you made up now?" he asked, with a wry look.

I had spilled a drop or two of the skunk odor on my gloves, and that scent in the cold heavy air was strong. With the sled moving up and down, it hit Tony in waves, and I guess it almost knocked him off the back end of the sled.

There are no skunks in Alaska so the strong smell was foreign to Tony. I knew it would also be foreign to the Teller Wolf.

When we arrived at the herd we found that the crippled lone wolf had hit again. Two freshly-killed, blood-spattered reindeer lay stretched in the snow. The distinctive wolf tracks were all around. As usual, it had come from the Sawtooth Range and had returned the same way after having its fun. That animal had taken only a bite here and there from the two deer. It had killed for the sport of it.

By then the kill of that lone wolf was 52 reindeer from the

Teller herd. It had driven at least that many away from the herd, so I figured a loss of anyway 100 deer to that one animal.

January 31, 1947: Find two more wolf-killed deer. Just one wolf doing all this killing. Hauled a dead deer up on a high hill and made a bait station set—a getter with skunk scent.

I also put lard baits on top of the snow with a little of my regular scent (made from rotten brains) on it. I peeled a piece of hide back from the brisket and cut three holes in the frozen fat. Into each of the holes I put a poisoned skunk musk-treated lard bait, then pushed the fat over each bait, covering them.

Then I went back to Teller to wait. Several of the Eskimos in the village spoke to me about the crippled wolf.

"You've got to get that wolf, Mr. Glaser. There won't be any reindeer left if you don't get him."

I had to leave in two days.

The next night a wind came up, and the temperature was 20 below zero. Snow filled the air, streaking parallel to the ground. It was impossible weather.

I stayed in the herder's cabin near the reindeer herd and didn't sleep well but lay awake off and on most of the night as the wind rocked the little hut. I suspected the lone wolf would kill again during the blizzard.

The wind let up somewhat toward morning, the sky partially cleared, and there was fair light from the moon. Well before dawn I decided to slip out to the herd to see if the wolf had been there, so I put on my reindeer parka and sealskin pants, got on my snowshoes and started off, my rifle over my shoulder.

The wind was still gusting. Sometimes wind-blown snow blotted out everything; other times it would die and the moon gave enough light so I could see pretty well. As I neared the herd the wind picked up a bit. Through the blowing snow I saw a dark blob. It was just coming light, and as I got to the blob I saw it was a dead reindeer, still warm, its bloody stomach and entrails strung out behind it. Wolf tracks, still visible in the swirling snow, told me all I needed to know. The crippled wolf had killed again and it was somewhere near.

The wolf's tracks went upwind and I figured it was hunting for another reindeer. I unslung my .220 Swift and followed. The tracks were clear and fresh. I could see about 20 feet ahead through the flying storm. After a hundred yards of cautious walking I found another dead reindeer, also still warm. The wolf had killed it moments earlier.

From that dead deer I followed the wolf tracks up a knoll, not even able to hear my snowshoes creak in the gusting wind and swirling snow. When I reached the top of the knoll, ahead of me perhaps 30 yards I saw a moving, dim shape. It stopped, apparently to stare at me, and then it moved again. It was too small to be a reindeer, but in the blowing snow I couldn't see what it was.

As it started to disappear into the storm I suddenly realized it had to be the lone wolf I was seeking. I pushed the safety off my rifle as I lifted it to my shoulder, then centered the scope on the vague, moving blur. I snapped a Hail Mary shot at the blur, knowing my chance of connecting was small.

The movement stopped, and the blur remained in one place as I ran toward it, working the bolt, hoping for another shot.

It wasn't needed. My first shot had connected, and the wolf lay dead before me.

It was a gray female weighing about 80 pounds. One front foot was crippled; two toes and about half of the foot was missing—perhaps from a trap.

I had killed the Teller Wolf through pure luck. I hadn't outsmarted her at all.

Aerial Wolf Hunting

ALASKA HAD MORE THAN A MILLION CARIBOU during the 1920s. Three decades later, during the early 1950s, caribou numbers were at an all-time low of only 140,000. Wolf predation was probably the primary cause for the decline; human hunting didn't cause the reduction.

For years I was the only full-time predator agent in Alaska, but gradually through the 1940s others were hired and put to work controlling predators. One of the early success stories for the FWS predator control division in Alaska was with the Nelchina caribou herd, which ranges in the vast Nelchina basin between the Wrangell and Alaska Ranges. In the 1940s, because these caribou were accessible by highway, about 65 percent of the caribou legally killed by hunters in the Territory were taken from the Nelchina herd. But the herd was hard hit by wolf predation. For a time there were only seven calves per hundred adults in the fall counts.

Then Bob Burkholder, a federal predator agent from Palmer, and his cohort, Buck Harris, from Anchorage, started trapping and aerial hunting wolves in the Nelchina country. Over a three year period they killed more than 300 wolves there. The number of calves per hundred caribou jumped to 15—more than double the previous figure. As caribou increased in response to wolf reduction, the kill by human hunters doubled. With good num-

*Frank Glaser (under X) in 1948 at the Eskimo village of Hooper Bay
with wolves he killed at a reindeer herd. These two wolves killed
more than 350 reindeer in two months.*

bers of caribou in the herd, wolf hunting was stopped, and wolves
also gradually increased in the area.

A large wolf can eat 20 to 30 or more pounds of meat at one
feeding; in winter every adult wolf needs eight to ten pounds of
meat a day to survive. A wolf cannot live on mice and rabbits as
some writers have claimed; it needs big animals like moose, caribou, deer, or sheep. For a pack of eight or ten wolves, that trans-
lates into a lot of caribou or moose in a year.

Another area that suggested itself for reducing wolf numbers
to benefit caribou was the treeless arctic slope north of Alaska's
Brooks Range. Wolves existed there in large numbers, and caribou had decreased alarmingly. In March, 1952, the Fish and Wildlife Service organized an aerial wolf hunt there. Umiat, on the
Colville River, was our main base.

All seven predator agents in the Territory gathered at Umiat, on the Colville River, with three airplanes. Two of the planes were new 125-hp two-passenger (tandem) Piper Super Cubs; the third was a World War II three-seat Piper J-5 that we called the "Gray Ghost."

Maurice Kelly, director of the division, from Juneau, oversaw the operation, and worked as a gunner. Bob Burkholder, from Palmer, and Buck Harris, from Anchorage, often flew together. Jay Hammond, an ex-marine pilot with a lot of flying time was stationed at Dillingham (Author's note: Hammond became Alaska's fifth elected governor, serving from 1974 through 1982). Joe Miner, with whom I worked for several years out of Fairbanks, was at the time stationed at Kotzebue. Doyle Cisney was an agent from Petersburg. With me, by far the oldest at 63, that made seven predator agents wolf-hunting at Umiat.

We killed 161 wolves in the first three weeks. By May wolf numbers had thinned and we were killing only three or four a day.

The arctic slope is a land of strong winds and constantly drifting snow. In March, when we started the aerial wolf hunt, most of the willow patches were covered by hard snowdrifts, and there were few places for a wolf to hide. Wolves of arctic Alaska are found in a variety of colors—coal black, light gray, white, dark gray and, rarely, bluish.

In most packs there are generally one or two black wolves, which can be seen for miles on the snow. Often we saw a black spot on the snow, flew to it and found a black wolf with several grays.

In the ski-equipped planes we searched for wolves at an altitude of about 400 feet. When we found a wolf or a pack of wolves (generally from five to ten animals) we circled a mile or so away, dropped to within 40 or 50 feet of the ground, and flew directly toward them. The wolves usually ran straight away in single file. We'd fly on their left, and the gunner, using a shotgun loaded with buckshot, shot the wolves out the right side of the plane, often at ranges of 20 or 30 feet.

The wolf is Alaska's brainiest wild animal. He learns well, and learns fast. Usually the first pass at a bunch of wolves was easy, and shooting was simple. But the second pass was often another

Glaser as a bison hunt guide at Delta, Alaska, October 1952.

CHARLES GRAY

story. By then the surviving wolves would have learned a lesson, and some would weave back and forth on a dead run away from the plane.

Occasionally an unusually intelligent wolf learned to dodge sharply left when the plane neared, putting him under the plane and out of the gunner's sight. The wolf didn't know this, of course; he usually learned by accidentally dodging left and discovering that he wasn't shot at.

One quick-learning wolf I shot at was on the edge of a high mountain rim. The terrain forced my pilot, Joe Miner, to fly at him from above, but each time we neared, he leaped from the rim and out of sight. When we were directly above him he was hard to see, and even harder to hit. I fired eight or nine shots at that wolf as we made pass after pass over him for at least half an hour. Finally, Joe made a dangerous approach from below and pushed the animal into the open, where I finally dropped him.

Weather was our biggest obstacle. Temperatures were still hitting 40 and 50 degrees below zero at night. We spent several hours each morning pre-heating the airplane engines. Each night engine oil was drained, and kept warm overnight. Mornings, after the engines were heated, the hot oil was poured back in, and the engines started.

While flying, I wore a heavy sealskin parka, fur pants, and fur socks inside fur mukluks. Heavy wool gloves were essential to keep fingers from freezing. This made it awkward to handle a shotgun when it was thrust into the 60 or 70 mile-an-hour slipstream.

April 12, 1952, was a typical day of aerial hunting for me. Daylight hours were now up to about 18, and it was light at seven a. m. when my pilot, Joe Miner, and I put two firepots under the engine of our Super Cub. The wing thermometer said it was 28 degrees below zero, and there was no wind. We poured in the heated oil we had drained the previous evening, removed wing covers, and the plane was ready to fly.

We had been following the movements of a caribou herd now about 50 miles south of Umiat. Wolves had been killing its members. We headed that way, and within 15 minutes Joe pointed ahead to a lone gray wolf he had spotted. He circled and flew about 40 feet above the ground. As we neared the wolf, Joe unlatched the upper half of the door on the right side of the plane and I opened the lower half.

I released my safety belt and knelt with my right knee on the seat and poked the shotgun out the open door. The below zero air swirled into the airplane, and I could feel its bite on my fingers despite the heavy wool gloves. The wolf was now running from the airplane, and I snapped the shotgun safety off.

Suddenly the wolf bolted to the left; he had probably been shot at previously from an airplane. I couldn't shoot; if I had I'd have hit the propeller.

Joe swung the plane around and made another run at the wolf, this time flying within 20 feet of the ground. The plane was mov-

Frank Glaser at his Fairbanks log cabin, 1954.

AUTHOR

ing faster than the wolf, so I had to hold *behind* the wolf in a reverse lead. At my shot the wolf rolled end over end in the snow.

We circled, looking for a place to land. We recovered the hides where we could, and examined stomach contents to see what the wolves were eating. We also checked females to see how many embryos they were carrying.

There was no safe place to land anywhere near this wolf, so we went on, heading up the canyon of the Chandler River.

The valley was more than a mile wide as we approached five-mile-long Chandler Lake, which lies in a 4,148-foot-high pass. Near the lake we found a pack of five wolves feeding on a caribou they had just killed. After five passes and ten shots three dead wolves lay on the snow. The other two escaped to hide among huge boulders on a ridge. I had to remove my gloves to reload, and the slipstream sucked my right glove out of the plane. I continued to shoot without the glove, and consequently I froze three fingers. I knew better, but in the excitement of the hunt, I was determined to continue shooting.

We landed within two miles of the wolves and snowshoed to them and took their skins. Two were blacks. The third was a gray female carrying seven unborn pups.

Next we flew 60 miles west to the Killik River valley. I saw several running caribou high on a steep mountainside and tapped Joe on the back and pointed. He banked the plane and climbed until we saw a black wolf chasing the caribou.

My shot was good on the first pass, and the black wolf rolled over and over, dead. Joe made a hazardous landing; the plane stopped near the edge of a dropoff into a canyon. We skinned the wolf. I held the plane in place to keep it from sliding while Joe started the engine. As the propeller bit into the icy air the skis started to slide and I couldn't hold the plane any longer. I put my left foot in the step, and threw my weight on the top of the strut, holding onto the back of Joe's seat with my left hand. Then, suddenly, the plane was moving swiftly. It became airborne, and I was still outside the cabin, clinging to the lift strut and to Joe's seat. The icy slipstream caused the fur ruff on my parka to whip my face. I tried to yell at Joe, but the slapping fur in my face all but stopped me. Then Joe saw me. He was in a steep climb to avoid a mountain ahead, but he rolled the plane into a left turn and reached around with his right hand and grabbed the wolf ruff of my parka, yanking me into the plane.

We flew down the Killik River valley, a good place to find wolves, for the main caribou migration had passed through this canyon; straggling bands were still moving through. In half an hour we were on the flats of the north slope. Fresh snow made ideal tracking conditions, and soon we crossed a fresh wolf trail. But which way were the wolves traveling?

Joe flew within ten feet of the ground and we carefully examined the tracks. Wolves travel single file, and in several-inch-deep snow, a wolf drags his hind feet making it easy to see which direction he is traveling. In this case we saw where the wolves had left their trail to urinate on a lone clump of grass. It looked like five wolves. We climbed and followed their tracks east. And then there they were, five wolves all curled up on top of a low ridge, tails over faces, asleep.

They scattered, running. After three passes, three more dead wolves lay on the ground. All were males, we found, when we landed and skinned them. One weighed an estimated 120 pounds. All had caribou meat in their stomachs, and all were fat.

We were low on fuel, so we headed for Umiat. Within five miles we located a lone wolf track, determined its direction of travel, followed it, and I killed it with one shot. We made a rough landing and skinned the large female, which carried five unborn pups.

We landed at Umiat late that afternoon. My frozen fingers put me out of action for several weeks. The other agents continued the hunt until 259 wolves had been killed. Of these, 102 were recovered for their skins and biological information.

To my knowledge, it was the largest scale wolf hunt ever conducted in the United States, and with the possible exception of modern Russia, probably in the world.

The results? There were still plenty of wolves on Alaska's arctic slope. Wolves are among the most prolific of Alaska's animals, and those that survived our hunt soon repopulated the area. By the time the wolf population had rebounded, caribou numbers had also dramatically increased.

Will Wolves Attack a Man?

MOOSE JOHN MILLOVICH, 60, left Fairbanks in April 1933 to trap beaver at Beaver River in the White Mountains, 75 miles to the north. Without dogs, he pulled a sled, bucking spring snow through the rolling hills and low tundra to the big bend on the Beaver, the same route I followed on my trek to the White Mountains in 1938. Moose John was an experienced outdoorsman who had previously lived on the Beaver. Neither he nor any of his many friends foresaw any danger for him.

He was expected back in Fairbanks in late May, but July rolled around, and he hadn't returned. Two of his Fairbanks friends, George Bojanich and Sam Hjorta, hiked to the Beaver to look for him.

They found the door to Moose John's cabin open. Dates on a calendar were marked off through May 9. There were burned hotcakes and burned bacon on the wood stove. The table was set with clean dishes and silverware. But there was no Moose John.

The two men searched upstream and down for several miles, thinking their friend might have fallen into the river and drowned. After three or four days of fruitless scouting along the river they were about to give up. About all the sign they'd found was wolf tracks around the cabin. Wolves occasionally howled from the hills as they made their search.

They finally reasoned that the missing man must be somewhere near the cabin, since he obviously wouldn't wander far while cooking breakfast. So they started circling the cabin, covering the ground inch by inch.

One of the men found a human thigh bone under some large spruce trees in a stand of knee-high red-top grass less than 30 feet from the cabin. It had been cracked open by a powerful-jawed animal. Soon they found a human skull with part of the hair and scalp still attached. Other human bones were found near.

George Bojanich told me later that all they found of Moose John just filled a five-gallon can. The ribs and all the small bones were gone. His clothing had been widely scattered through the gloomy spruces, with an occasional bone clinging to the cloth by bits of dried flesh.

Bojanich and Hjorta decided that wolves killed Moose John. There were certainly plenty of wolves in the White Mountains. Bojanich had trapped the region for marten the previous year, and the howling of wolf packs had made him so jittery he was glad to leave in the spring. Wolves get hungry when there are few or no caribou or moose, which was the case in the region at the time, and wolves *do* become bold.

Did wolves kill old Moose John? No one will ever know. Wolves almost certainly ate him, for his bones were cracked open, almost positive evidence that wolves chewed on them. The biggest of grizzly bears could never have broken those bones. Also, wolf sign was all around the cabin a couple of months after the apparent date of Moose John's death.

I thought about that incident for a long time. George Bojanich told me every detail when he and Sam returned after burying Moose John's remains. Also, in 1938, five years after Moose John's death, I lived for many months in the Fossil Creek cabin where he died. Bojanich and Hjorta had buried the can holding the trapper's remains about 20 feet from the door, in front of the only window. I spent hours sitting at that window, eating, writing, and reading and every time I glanced out I saw Moose John's grave and the cross over it.

Although Bojanich, Hjorta, and others believe wolves killed the old trapper, I don't think so. There are many possible explanations of his death. He was in his 60s, and he might have died of a heart attack while throwing out garbage near the cabin. Wolves could have found and eaten his remains.

The unprovoked charge of the thin, mouse-colored old grizzly while I was crossing a rock slide when I was in that region in 1938 suggests an even better explanation. That old bear came jumping down the slope toward me and I fired at him. He passed not more than six feet from me, turned, and started back for me. That's when I shot him in the neck, putting him down for good.

Others have had similar experiences with grizzlies in the White Mountains. The bears there are aggressive, that's all. I don't know why, unless it's because its often hungry country when the caribou are gone, and grizzlies *have* to be aggressive if they're going to eat.

Moose John had trapped eight or nine beavers before he died and he didn't have any dogs to eat the carcasses. He had probably thrown the skinned beaver in the snow in front of the cabin. Bears usually have been out of hibernation for a week or so by May 9, when he stopped marking the calendar, and I suspect that one of those aggressive spring-hungry grizzlies was feeding on beaver carcasses when, for some reason, Moose John walked near and got swatted down. I think that is much more likely than wolves killing him.

I have never known of a healthy wolf to tackle a man except in cases of mistaken identity. When they see their mistake they back off. Most wolves aren't even aggressive when they're in a trap.

One June day, walking in the Alaska Range with a couple of my wolf-dogs carrying packs, I stumbled onto a pair of wolves. I had left Wood River and was plowing through a thick mass of dwarf birch when two gray wolves howled just ahead of me. Then I saw their heads poke out of the brush 20 or 30 yards away.

They'd heard me coming and probably thought I was a caribou. The moment they howled my two dogs lit out after them and the wolves disappeared. They probably had pups, and perhaps I was close to their den. I'm sure that if they had realized what I was they wouldn't have shown themselves.

Another time I was snowshoeing at the edge of some timber when suddenly I heard animals running in the snow behind me. I turned and saw three black wolves coming for me on a dead run. By the time I had flipped my parka hood back, pulled mittens off, and had my rifle ready they had wheeled back into the timber. I went back to see what had happened. Their tracks showed they'd been loping along slowly, and had apparently heard me walking near the timber before they saw or smelled me. They must have thought they were going to cut off a moose or a caribou. The moment they realized their error they whirled in their tracks, running faster to get away than they had to overhaul me.

Wolves are great ones to follow sled dogs. The wolf-dogs I drove at Savage River may have been an even greater attraction than a dog team without wolf blood; all I know is, wolves often followed my dog sled for miles. I rarely saw them, but later saw their tracks.

Prior to about 1940, trappers and other bush residents commonly killed caribou throughout the summer for fresh meat and dog food. I usually waited until the cool of evening to perform this chore, then I'd go a few miles from the cabin and kill a bull caribou, dress it, and haul it home with my dog team with a wooden-runner sled that worked well on grass and gravel. One evening I arrived home about 8 o'clock with the meat of a big bull on the sled. I leaned my rifle against the corner of the cabin, tied my dogs to their houses and started back to the sled to hang the meat. Suddenly, I noticed the dogs looking toward the river, wagging their tails, straining on their chains. I glanced up and saw three black wolves sitting not 20 yards away.

Wolves seem to sense what a man is thinking and doing. I ignored, or pretended to ignore, those three. Slowly and nonchalantly, I walked to the cabin and picked up the rifle. Then I whirled fast, ready to shoot. I think the wolves started moving as I turned my back. By the time I had one centered in the scope he was jumping off the riverbank to a sandbar. I dropped him into the river, dead. The other two sprinted down the bank and I blew geysers of gravel all around them, missing two shots at each before they disappeared.

It was fairly light all night at that time of year and I was curious, so I walked back to where I'd killed the caribou on a river bar. I found tracks in the sand where the wolves had hit my sled trail a few hundred yards from where I had loaded the bull. There were drops of caribou blood along the way, and that probably attracted them. But my tracks were there, and scent too, no doubt.

The wolves had trailed me and the team right to the cabin, and on a dead run. Why, I do not know.

The wolf is the only animal I know that can identify, by sight, a man that is sitting still. Several times I've had them do this when the wind was in my favor and I was absolutely motionless, leaning against a tree or rock. Moose, caribou, and bears — especially bears — can look right at you from 20 or 30 feet without recognizing you for a man, provided you don't move and the wind is in your favor. Not wolves. They'll stare for a moment, identify you as man, and high-tail it.

That's normal behavior for a wolf encountering a man. I know of one instance when a wolf attacked an Eskimo. I investigated it and know that this wolf wasn't fooling. But the facts go beyond that.

Punyuk was the Eskimo's name and he lived at Noorvik in the Kobuk River country of arctic Alaska. I was living at Kotzebue, about 60 miles away, at the time he was attacked. Marge Swenson, teacher-nurse at Noorvik, had a daily radio schedule with Kotzebue. She asked, during one of these schedules, for me to come to Noorvik to investigate the attack.

I hired a dog team and drove to Noorvik, taking two days for the trip. It was January, cold, stormy, and mostly dark, as the north is at that time of year. I arrived four days after Punyuk had been attacked.

The evening I arrived, Marge Swenson went to Punyuk's house to change his bandages and I went along to hear the story from the old Eskimo himself. He lived in a small, crowded, log cabin, which is unusual in that barren country where logs have to be hauled many miles. Punyuk was lying on a low couch when we entered the lamp-lit, smoky cabin.

Punyuk was 63, and he knew only a few words of English. His married daughter, who assisted Marge Swenson at the school, acted as an interpreter. Here's how she translated the story for me:

Punyuk had been living in a stove-heated tent and trapping on a ridge between the Kobuk and Selawik Rivers. He had his sled dogs tied to willows near the tent. Sometime during early evening (that far north it gets dark about 2 o'clock at that time of year) he heard his dogs growling and making a fuss. Stepping outside, Punyuk saw what he took to be one of his dogs running loose. It was dark, but the moon and stars reflecting from the snow gave a fair amount of light. He picked up a chunk of ice from a pile he kept to melt for cooking and drinking and tossed it at the "dog," ordering it to come.

When the ice hit the animal it rushed Punyuk, jumped up with its front feet on his shoulders, and bit at the top of his head. Of course Punyuk realized instantly that it wasn't one of his dogs, both from its behavior and its size. It was twice as big as any of his dogs; he was dealing with a wolf.

The animal knocked him down and started chewing on his head. It ripped three or four places clear to the skull, and tore the whole length of his scalp before Punyuk grasped the animal's throat and managed to get his knees on it and choke it down. He got a small pocket knife out after the animal had relaxed a bit from being choked, and slashed with it a few times. He didn't stab.

He stood up, looked closely, and saw for sure it was a black wolf. He didn't try to finish it off.

Figuring that a trapper normally would have a pile of wood outside his tent, I asked his daughter, "Did he have some stove wood there, or an axe?"

"Yes."

"Then why didn't he hit it with a piece of wood or the axe and kill it?"

She talked with him for a long time then, and he seemed reluctant to tell her. Finally she said, "My father cannot kill a black wolf."

That puzzled me at the time, but I learned later that many of the Eskimo oldsters believed that when some old village grandmother died, her spirit would go into a wolf, preferably a black wolf. To kill one was like killing a respected old woman.

Punyuk stood over the black wolf he had choked into unconsciousness until it revived, making no move to harm it.

"You have hurt me enough, grandmother," he said. "Now go and leave me in peace."

As his daughter translated, I tried to picture simple old Punyuk standing in the arctic moonlight, his scalp torn loose, blood running down his head and face, talking to the wolf.

Marge Swenson dressed his wounds as Punyuk related the story. It made a strange setting in the dim light of the tiny cabin, and the old Eskimo's guttural tones emphasized the bizarre tale he was telling. He didn't wince as Marge pulled the blood-stuck bandages free and probed to drain his wounds.

The wolf got up and grabbed Punyuk's right thigh and sank its teeth in deep. The Eskimo wore a pair of overalls, having just stepped from the heated tent. If he had had his regular outdoor wear of sealskin pants he'd have had better protection.

The wolf lifted him clear of the ground and threw him down, then placed his forepaws on him and pulled, trying to tear a chunk out of his thigh.

I could see bone in the two main holes in his leg where the wolf's upper canines had entered. On the opposite side, where the two lower canines had sunk in, I saw a couple of ligaments or cords the teeth had caught as the animal tried to pull out a chunk of meat. They were terrible wounds.

When the wolf found it couldn't yank that chunk out of Punyuk's leg it let go, and Punyuk struggled to his feet. But the wolf jumped up and grabbed his shoulder, biting twice clear to the bone. Then it tried Punyuk's head again, driving one tusk in just above his ear. If it had been a little lower, it probably would have killed him. Evidently Punyuk passed out then, for his daughter said, "My father didn't know any more."

When Punyuk revived, the wolf was gone and his dogs were barking. He dragged himself into the tent and washed the blood off, bandaged himself crudely, and put on his fur clothes. He crawled around harnessing his dogs, and crawled into his sled and the dogs pulled him to Noorvik.

When Punyuk told the story to his two sons, they immediately harnessed a dog team and left to track down the wolf. The old beliefs didn't mean anything to them.

As they followed the wolf's tracks they found a little blood, and saw where it had staggered and fallen a number of times. Several times it went out of its way to attack a lone spruce tree and to chew limbs from it.

The trail zigzagged to the village of Kiana, about 12 miles from Punyuk's camp. When the boys arrived there they learned that someone in the village had killed the wolf as it was eating some malemute puppies.

The day after Punyuk told me his story I went to Kiana. The wolf had been skinned, but I found the carcass and cut off the head. The animal was an adult, in excellent condition. He'd have weighed more than 100 pounds.

I turned the wolf's head over to Dr. Bauer of the Native Health Service in Kotzebue and he sent it out to a laboratory somewhere. For some reason, the lab report didn't get back to Kotzebue for several months, too late to help Punyuk. In March word reached the reindeer camp I was in that the old Eskimo was dead. He had apparently recovered from the wolf's attack, then had died suddenly while lying on the ice and fishing for sheefish.

The laboratory report confirmed what I suspected; the wolf had rabies. By then, of course, all the excitement had died down and many people, in saying that Punyuk was attacked by a wolf, let it go at that. One account of this incident published in a national magazine said that Punyuk died of his wounds shortly after being attacked by a wolf. Period. Rabies wasn't mentioned.

I don't know of a single proven instance of a healthy, normal wolf attacking a human. And I have tried to learn as much as possible about every reported attack in Alaska since 1915 when I arrived in the Territory. Wolves just don't take to people. Even when captured as pups before their eyes are open, most wolves do not gentle well. The young wolf I caught in a trap and took home for breeding purposes could never be trusted.

In the 1940s, while working as a federal wolf hunter I discovered a wolf den on the Chatanika River, 50 miles north of Fairbanks, and managed to kill several of the half-grown pups. I suggested to Ted LaFon, watchman at a nearby mining operation, that he check the den the following May. The pair might come back and he could get a litter of pups.

He did just that, and acquired 13 lively, squirming, wolf pups, a number of which he sold to people in Fairbanks.

I was in Nome at the time, but the next November I arrived in Fairbanks. As I started to walk into the Nordale Hotel for a room, I was astonished to see a big gray wolf crouched in front of the doorway. A woman was holding it by a leash.

"That's a nice wolf you have there, lady," I said, as I took the leash and skidded the animal aside so I could walk through the door.

"It isn't a wolf, its a dog," she shouted after me as I went up to the desk to register.

I read in the paper that night that the city council had called a special meeting to warn two or three people who had full-grown wolves to get them out of town or they'd order them destroyed. They were a danger to kids and even to adults who might encounter them.

The half-tame wolf I dragged out of the doorway at the Nordale Hotel was scared. I saw fear in its eyes and it was flattened out on the sidewalk, afraid to move. A half-tame wolf is dangerous. There's no telling how it might react if a youngster pulled its tail or tried to pet it. The Fairbanks city council was right.

But a wild wolf is different. I think humans are safe from attack by wolves in the wild.

Epilogue

STATEHOOD CAME TO ALASKA in 1959. On January 1, 1960, the state of Alaska assumed management of its fish and game, taking over after 45 years of federal management. A governor-appointed citizen-member Board of Fish and Game now established policies and established hunting, fishing, and trapping regulations for Alaska.

This board halted all predator control and classified the wolf as a big game animal as well as a furbearer. It made it illegal to use poison on wildlife. Bag limits were set for the hunting of wolves, with appropriate open and closed seasons for each game management unit (Alaska has 26 such units). Seasonal closures were established for trapping wolves. In time aerial wolf hunting for sport was halted. In addition, the payment of bounties was halted, as was authority to hire hunters and trappers to suppress predators The wolf was finally recognized as a valuable member of Alaska's wildlife family.

During the first decade after statehood, Alaska's moose, caribou, sheep and deer reached unheard of population highs. Many Alaskans believe the wolf control program of the FWS during the 1950s brought about the sudden and almost explosive increase.

Did it?

No one knows for sure, for no long term Territory-wide scientific evaluation studies accompanied the federal wolf control program. North Slope caribou increased dramatically after the aerial wolf kill there in 1952 as described in Chapter 29, and it's hard to argue this increase didn't result from wolf control. Caribou also increased dramatically in the Nelchina Basin after the FWS removed most of the wolves there about 1950.

Studies have revealed that overall in Alaska in most years about 85 percent of the annual ungulate mortality is due to predation by wolves and bears; 2 to 7 percent is due to hunting by man; and the rest is from accidents, disease, and weather.

Alaska's wolves increased after statehood, and by the late 1960s and early 1970s they were probably as abundant as they were in the 1930s and 1940s. Now, at the turn of the century, Alaska's wolves are still abundant, and they occupy virtually all of their original range.

❧

Frank Glaser retired from the U.S. Fish and Wildlife Service in June, 1955. He was 68. For his outstanding service Interior Secretary Douglas McKay presented him with the Meritorious Service Award of the Department of Interior. It read, in part: "He spent most of his adult life in the wilderness of Alaska studying and observing wildlife. His primary responsibility was the control of predatory animals. However, his inquisitive mind led to an unequaled store of information as to the previously unexplained causes of behavior of wild animals. Working under almost inconceivable hardships in difficult terrain and severely cold weather, Mr. Glaser, far from communication lines and other methods of assistance and protection, traveled the Arctic by dog sled, teaching the Eskimos how to protect their reindeer from wolves. Through his undaunted courage, physical durability, and spirited concern for the natives, he withstood the extreme physical hardships encountered in his work."

Frank and his wife Nellie left Alaska about 1957 and for the next 15 years they lived in Idaho, California, and Oregon. Frank showed his Alaskan movies to audiences but bookings were difficult to get, and he eventually abandoned the effort.

In their old age the Glasers returned to their beloved Alaska. For a time Frank lived in the Anchorage home of his stepson,

Calvin Osborne. One evening he became upset, insisting he heard wolves howling. "They don't belong in town. They'll kill dogs, and a lot of kids are running around too. I'm worried about them. Those wolves have to be killed." He became so agitated that Dr. Louis Mayer was called. Mayer made a house-call, talked with Frank, gave him a sedative.

The next day Mayer learned that the Fish and Game Department was holding captive wolves nearby. Frank Glaser knew a wolf howl when he heard it, even though his aged mind did wander.

Ray Tremblay, one of Glaser's long-time FWS associates, visited the old wolfer several times at an Anchorage nursing home. Frank would know Ray for a time, then he'd drift off and forget Ray's name. Once when his mind was clear he said when he gained strength he was going back to Savage River to the life he had left 37 years earlier.

Perhaps Frank did go back to Savage River, for that wild and lovely region was his idea of the Happy Hunting Ground. He died May 16, 1974, at the age of 86. Nellie, with him at the nursing home to the last, died 15 days later.

Oscar Vogel, the Talkeetna Mountains guide and trapper told me, "Although it was well attended, there were only two wolf trappers present at Frank Glaser's funeral. I was one of them."

Index

Previously Published Rearden/Glaser Stories

"Boxed With a Bear" *Outdoor Life*, April 1954 (Chapter 7 in *Alaska's Wolf Man*).
"My Lady Judas" *Outdoor Life*, May 1954 (Chapter 19).
"Doctor's Orders" *Outdoor Life*, Sept. 1954 (Chapter 8).
"Will Wolves Attack a Man?" *Outdoor Life*, Oct. 1954 (Chapter 30).
"Too Mean to Kill" *Outdoor Life*, Nov. 1954 (Chapter 22).
"Habits of Death" *Outdoor Life*, Jan. 1955 (Chapters 20, 21).
"My Share of Moose" *Outdoor Life*, June 1955 (Chapter 18).
"The Crazy Deer" *Outdoor Life*, Jan.1956 (Chapter 18).
"The Wolf in a Dog" *True's Hunting Yearbook*, No. 7, 1956 (Chapter 16).
"Kenai,"*Alaska Magazine* (Chapter 16).
"The Ghost Grizzly," *Alaska Magazine* (Chapter 17).

"Boxed with a Bear," "Doctor's Orders," and "The Ghost Grizzly of Savage River" (Chapters 7, 8 and 17 in this volume) appeared in *Tales of Alaska's Big Bears*, a collection of Rearden-written bear stories published in 1989 by Wolfe Publishing Company, 6471 Airpark Drive, Prescott, Arizona 86301.

Upon Glaser's death, my profile, "Adventure Was His Life," appeared in the July, 1975, *Outdoor Life*.

About the Author

Jim Rearden is a World War II veteran who served aboard a U.S. Navy destroyer escort in the Pacific theater of war. He holds wildlife degrees from Oregon State University and the University of Maine; both have honored him as a distinguished alumnus. In 2005 he received an honorary Doctor of Science degree from the University of Alaska Fairbanks for his teaching, conservation work, and writings on Alaskan subjects. He has been a resident of Alaska since 1950 when he organized the department of wildlife management at the University of Alaska Fairbanks, and taught as head of that department for four years. He has worked as a construction laborer, a registered hunting guide, a clerk in a trading post, a state fishery biologist, and a commercial fisherman. He is a licensed private pilot.

He served on the Alaska Board of Fish and Game, and the Board of Game, for twelve years, and was Outdoors Editor for *Alaska Magazine* for twenty years, serving at the same time as a Field Editor for *Outdoor Life*. President Gerald Ford appointed him to the National Advisory Committee on Oceans and Atmosphere where he served for eighteen months. He has written twenty-four books, and more than 500 magazine features, on Alaskan subjects. He lives on the Kenai Peninsula with his wife, Audrey, in a log home he built himself.

Also by Jim Rearden

Sam O. White, Alaskan: Tales of a Legendary Wildlife Agent and Bush Pilot

Forgotten Warriors of the Aleutian Campaign

Castner's Cutthroats, Saga of the Alaska Scouts

The Wolves of Alaska, A Fact-Based Saga

Koga's Zero, The Fighter That Changed World War II

Jim Rearden's Alaska; Fifty Years of Frontier Adventure

Travel Air NC9084; History of a 75-year-old Working Airplane

Slim Moore, Alaska Master Guide; A Sourdough's Hunting Adventures and Wisdom

Hunting Alaska's Wild Places; Half a Century with Rifle and Shotgun

All books in this list can be found in most Alaskan books stores. The above nine books may also be ordered directly from the publisher (406) 598-8488. See copyright page for address, website, E-mail and fax.

Tales of Alaska's Big Bears

Shadows on the Koyukuk; An Alaska Native's Life Along the River

Arctic Bush Pilot; From Navy Combat to Flying Alaska's Northern Wilderness